Language and Ethnicity among the K'ichee' Maya

Language and Ethnicity among the K'ichee' Maya

Sergio Romero

THE UNIVERSITY OF UTAH PRESS

Salt Lake City

The Defiance House Man colophon is a registered trademark
of the University of Utah Press. It is based on a four-foot-tall
Ancient Puebloan pictograph (late PIII) near Glen Canyon, Utah.

CIP data for this book available from the Library of Congress
at https://lccn.loc.gov/2014038541.

Errata and further information on this and other volumes available at UofUpress.com.

Printed and bound in the United States of America.

For Pierre Robert Colas
(1976–2008)

Contents

Figures

Tables

Preface

This book is an ethnographic study of K'ichee', a Mayan language spoken by more than one million people in the western highlands and southern piedmont of the Republic of Guatemala. It seeks to elucidate the complex dialectic between this diverse, widely spoken language and the distinct ethnic identities of its speakers. Rather than restrict it to one locale and time period, as is customary among anthropologists, I chose to examine different incarnations of K'ichee' discourse across the wide geographic, social, and temporal space inhabited by its speakers. Contrary to the received wisdom in Mayanist circles presupposing that mutually intelligible linguistic varieties entail a shared ethnic identification, the K'ichee' are a diverse congeries of ethnic groups with different histories and collective self-representations. K'ichee' identities are multiple, layered, and overlapping, the result of a long and diverse history of subordination and resistance since the Spanish invasion.

Following the seminal intuitions of Friedrich Barth (1969), further developed by Andreas Wimmer (2013), I argue that ethnic "boundary work" among the K'ichee' involves interaction frames—ethnic frames—cued by configurations of signs in diverse media, in which language plays a fundamental role.[1] Above all, ethnicity in the Maya highlands is about communication, a kind of language ideology making interaction with individual interlocutors intelligible in diverse local, regional, and national ethnoscapes.[2] Contact between different language varieties in the Maya highlands is the norm, not the exception, and the discourse roles of linguistic variation reflect it. My interest in linguistic interaction complements the work of other Mesoamericanists who have examined ethnicity as an ideological construct or in terms of its sociopolitical implications, especially in the last thirty years. Power relations grow through microinteractions constrained by language ideologies and pragmatic norms. If power indeed diffuses in a Foucaultian, capillary fashion, then examining the linguistic incarnations of ethnicity is a must if we are to understand the dynamics of power in indigenous communities.

Ethnic stereotypes—linguistic forms iconic of particular ethnic groups—play a host of indexical roles inside and outside the boundaries of K'ichee' communities.[3] For the K'ichee', an iconic relation between ethnic substance and linguistic form holds as crucial semiotic principle. In this book "iconicity" denotes not only a particular type of relation between sign and object but also the quintessential highland Maya representation of the texture of language as cultural artifact. The texture of K'ichee' discourse is inseparable from (ethnic) boundary work. Language is experienced as an ethnically marked object labeled—for example—*qach'ab'aal* "our language," *kastiiy* "Spanish," or *K'ichee' mezclado* "mixed K'ichee.'" The K'ichee' re-create and hybridize in ever more creative ways this complex linguistic repertoire in spite of purist ideologies that construe K'ichee' and Spanish as vulnerable, corruptible substances that should not be "mixed."

The crystallization of ethnic frames of interaction is a historical process, the discursive deposition of hundreds of years of Spanish and *ladino* imposition, community resistance, and individual innovation. Colonialism has left its imprint on K'ichee' discourse practices, which the K'ichee' have in turn co-opted and resignified to carve out and maintain spaces of political and cultural autonomy. Since the Spanish conquest, the state, churches, and corporations have engaged the K'ichee' language, trying to turn it into a vehicle of domination and cultural legitimation. Spanish colonialism and its republican successor indeed speak K'ichee'! Contrary to the widely held but naive notion that native languages are intrinsically subversive of colonialist projects, I show that K'ichee' has been a tense field of struggle between K'ichee' communities and the forces of colonialism in its various incarnations. This tension is manifest today in the ethnic frames that embody ethnicity among the K'ichee'.

Chapter 1 begins with the history and changing denotations of the name "K'ichee'". The concept of ethnic frame is introduced as a heuristic device to theorize the relation between ethnicity, ethnolinguistic stereotypes, and the different indexical roles they play in K'ichee' speech. The chapter also provides a brief sketch of geographic variation in K'ichee' and of the hybrid K'ichee'-Spanish registers performed in K'ichee' communities. Finally, it adumbrates the linguistic consequences of "Mayanization" in the last thirty years.

Chapter 2 focuses on the colonial co-optation of K'ichee' as linguistic vehicle of both secular and religious domination. It begins with the *reducción* of the K'ichee' language by Franciscan and Dominican friars and continues with its co-optation by Liberal brands of authoritarian *indigenismo* in the late nineteenth and early twentieth centuries. The chapter also discusses the translation project of the Wycliffe Bible Translators and the emergence of multiculturalism as state ideology in the mid-1980s.

Chapter 3 examines "local" ethnic frames and the role of linguistic stereotypes in communication. It argues that ethnicity in the Maya highlands is fundamentally a language ideology. Contextually, K'ichee' speech is situated in multiethnic, layered spaces of interaction in which lin-

guistic stereotypes perform a crucial, intelligible role in boundary work. My discussion is based on many years of ethnographic observation in the townships of Santa María Chiquimula and Nahualá in the western highlands of Guatemala. It relates language to other semiotic media such as dress code in the performance of boundary work.

Chapter 4 extends the analysis to language contact phenomena, exploring the pragmatic role of Spanish loanwords and K'ichee'-Spanish code switching. Hybrid speech registers (code switching) embody the tensions intrinsic to the complexity of power and hierarchy in K'ichee' communities. This chapter is perhaps where the interleaving of power relations and semiosis (meaningful symbolic behavior) in the Maya highlands is most evident for the reader.

Chapter 5 examines honorific registers and their articulation with authority in K'ichee' communities. The norms of honorific address vary regionally in K'ichee' and have undergone multiple changes and local recalibrations since the Spanish invasion. Not surprisingly, Mayanization is a form of contemporary "invention of tradition," involving new licensing conditions and indexical roles for honorific forms.

Chapter 6 discusses the successive recreations of K'ichee' ethnic frames in the centuries since the Spanish invasion. It also examines the role of K'ichee' as linguistic template for the pastoral registers used to Christianize other Mayan groups in the highlands. It explores as well the impact of K'ichee' intellectuals as precursors and protagonists of pan-Maya revitalization today. For this purpose, I concentrate on the influential work of the philologist and historian Adrián Inés Chávez and the poet Humberto Akabal.

This book is based on more than two years of ethnographic work, especially nine months of intensive participant observation in Santa María Chiquimula in 2005, as well as during shorter stints in the townships of Nahualá, Santa Cruz del Quiché, Cunén, and Zacualpa in 1995, 2004, 2007, 2008, 2010, and 2013. Methodologically, it is multidisciplinary, combining philological, ethnographic, and sociolinguistic approaches.

First, I relied on philological methods, discourse analysis, and archival work in libraries and archives in Guatemala and the United States for the genealogies of selected colonial texts and twentieth-century publications. Second, my ethnographic work focused on naturally occurring conversations, public events, and rituals. My fluency in K'ichee' allowed me to participate and witness numerous speech events, affording a better understanding of pragmatic context and social meaning. Third, I gathered a corpus of 125 monolingual interviews in K'ichee' with both men and women from both rural and urban areas of Santa María Chiquimula and Nahualá, targeting particular sociolinguistic variables, both phonological and syntactic. Although conceptually my work is fundamentally anthropological, my ethnographic observations were helped by the systematic analysis of sociolinguistic variation in my interview corpus. Only a multidisciplinary approach can begin to penetrate the richness and complexity of linguistic practices and their interweaving with ethnicity among the K'ichee'.

Maya personal names and the Spanish names of Mayan languages are spelled here in the unified alphabet recognized by the Academy of the Mayan Languages of Guatemala (ALMG) unless otherwise stated. However, villages, towns, cities, townships, and departments are spelled in Spanish, as is customary in Guatemala. Texts in K'ichee' are spelled in the unified alphabet recognized by the ALMG, except where additional phonetic detail or orthographic analysis is required. The K'iche' Mayab' Cholchi' (Academy of the K'ichee' Language) recently adopted an orthographic reform that makes it unnecessary to mark vowel length except where minimal pairs are involved. Nevertheless, I duplicate vowels when phonemically long. For example, the *ee* in the word *K'ichee'* marks the vowel as long. In my transcriptions I use 4 to represent the *quartillo*, a grapheme introduced by the Franciscan Francisco de la Parra to write the velar ejective consonant [k'] of Mayan languages.

Acknowledgments

Many friends contributed in small and large ways to make this book a reality. It would be impossible in this brief space to show my appreciation to all. However, I cannot fail to mention a few people whose support and inspiration were critical. First and foremost, I cannot thank enough the residents of Santa María Chiquimula and Nahualá in western Guatemala, whose friendship and patience over the years have been the source of any insight the reader may find in this book. Their generosity, love of life, and hope despite centuries of oppression are lessons in humanity and a permanent reminder of where the loyalties of scholars should ultimately rest. Special thanks are due to the priests and lay activists of the parish of Santa María Chiquimula, especially Fr. Ricardo Falla, Fr. Juan Hernández-Pico, and Fr. Victoriano "Vico" Castillo, whose commitment to social justice, sense of humor, enlightening critique, and warm friendship have always been inspirational. In Nahualá special thanks are due to my good friend Manuel Tahay and his family: their friendship over the years opened many doors and taught me the best of what I know about the K'ichee'.

Without the love and support of my partner, Lilian Márquez, this book would not have been as fun to write. Her valuable comments on the first draft helped me to purge the manuscript of unnecessary technicalities and obscure prose. Khristian Mendez's skill and patience were priceless during figure correction and formatting. Reba Rauch and the competent and patient staff at the University of Utah Press were also indispensable. Special thanks are due to Kim Vivier for her keen eye and editorial skill.

Finally, this book is dedicated to my good friend and colleague Pierre Robert Colas (1976–2008), whose senseless murder left not only a chasm in my soul but also a gap in Mesoamerican studies that will be very hard to fill. Many of the ideas I present here were developed during conversations with him. His keen insight and careful scholarship were a constant inspiration for these pages.

Abbreviations

AHp	Plural honorific addressee	PF	Phrase final marker
AHs	Singular honorific addressee	S	Superlative
AP	Antipassive	TR	Trace
COM	Completive	1pA	1st person plural absolutive
HAp	Plural honorific agreement	1pE	1st person plural ergative
HAs	Singular honorific agreement	1sA	1st person singular absolutive
HON	Honorific	1sE	1st person singular ergative
IN	Incompletive	2pE	2nd person plural ergative
MAR	Santa María Chiquimula K'ichee'	2sA	2nd person singular absolutive marker
N	Nominalizer	2sE	Second person singular ergative
NC	Negative concord	3pE	3rd person plural ergative marker
NEG	Negator	3sA	3rd person singular absolutive
NPI	Negative polarity item	3sE	3rd person singular ergative marker

Notes

1. "Boundary work" references semiotic practices creating and maintaining boundaries between culturally relevant groups (Wimmer 2013).
2. I appropriate the notion of "ethnoscape," first developed by Appadurai (1990), to reference the distinct ethnic groups that share the same territory but whose distinct corporate identities are reciprocally acknowledged and deictically displayed.
3. An index is a sign grounded on a relationship of proximity with its object. Indexical effects are undetachable from their context, as their referent or pragmatic force depend on the precise spatial, temporal, and social coordinates of the exchange.

CHAPTER 1

Accent and Ethnic Identity
in the Maya Highlands

1.1. *Ex pluribus unum*: The Cultural Construction of K'ichee' Maya

K'ichee' is one of the twenty-two officially recognized Mayan languages spoken in Guatemala (see Figure 1.1). It boasts more than one million speakers, the largest number for any Mayan language (Richards 2003). The name "K'ichee'," however, has had a long and troubled history since 1523, when the Spanish invaders and their Mexican allies entered the western highlands of Guatemala. Its current denotation, naming the most emblematic language of the K'iche'an branch of the Mayan stock, is a lexical product of Spanish colonialism. Before the Spanish arrived, "K'ichee'" was the proper name of the expanding polity whose seat was located in the citadel of Q'umarkaaj, near the modern town of Santa Cruz del Quiché in western Guatemala (Fox and Brumfield 1994; Carmack 1981; Fox 1978).[1] Its inhabitants were known as *K'ichee' winaq* "K'ichee' people," as attested, for example, in the first lines of the Popol Vuh, the famous K'ichee' chronicle written sometime after 1530 by scribes affiliated with the ruling lineages of Q'umarkaaj (Tedlock 1996; Van Akkeren 2003):

(1.1)
Are uxe ojeer tziij waraal K'ichee' ub'i'.
Waraal xchiqatz'ib'aj wi, xchiqatikib'a wi ojeer
   tziij,
utikirib'aal, uxenab'aal puch ronojeel xb'an pa
   tinamit K'ichee', ramaaq' K'ichee' winaq.

This is the beginning of the ancient word in this
   place named K'ichee'.
Here we will write down, we will start [the
   telling of] the ancient word,
the beginning, the origin of everything that
   happened in the town of K'ichee', the polity
   of the K'ichee' people.[2]
                              (Popol Vuh, Folio 1 recto)

Text (1.1) deictically anchors the Popol Vuh in the Q'umarkaaj area (see Figure 1.2). It introduces the book as a retelling in writing of the "ancient word" of the K'ichee' people in their polity (*amaq'*) and citadel (*tinamit*).[3] In contrast to its current meaning, in its original denotation "K'ichee'" made no direct reference to any language. In fact, sworn enemies of Q'umarkaaj, such as the Achi, whose seat of power was located in the citadel of Kaqjyub (near the modern town of Rabinal in the department of Baja Verapaz), spoke mutually intelligible linguistic varieties (López Ixcoy 1997; Van Akkeren 2000).[4] Not all speakers of the language we call K'ichee' today identified ethnically as K'ichee' in the Postclassic period (950–1523 CE): the name "K'ichee'" used to be an ethnonym rather than a glottonym.[5]

Responding to the Spanish wish to reorganize, control, and administer their new subjects, however, the denotation of "K'ichee'" shifted, becoming a glottonym for the language of Q'umarkaaj, its speakers as well as those who spoke

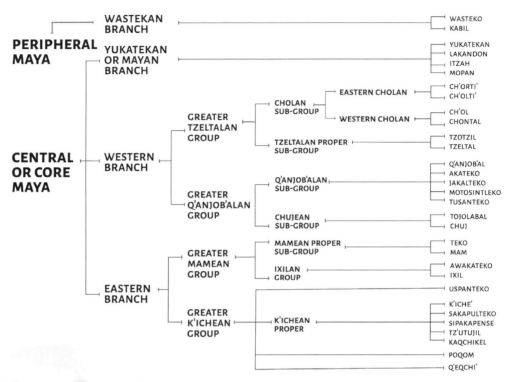

FIGURE 1.1. The Mayan linguistic stock (Campbell 1997).

FIGURE 1.2. Remains of the central plaza at Q'umarkaaj, ancient capital of the K'ichee' (photograph by Sergio Romero).

other mutually intelligible varieties, even if this usage did not respect prehispanic ethnic and political boundaries. Language was an essential criterion used by the Spanish to classify native populations, as attested, for example, in the questionnaires sent to local officials in preparation for the *Relaciones geográficas* in 1579–1586, which required written descriptions of the land and the people and explicit identification of their language or languages (Acuña 1982; Mundy 1996).

Nevertheless, local identities and their linguistic markers did not disappear and started to coexist in tension with Spanish ethnic classifications. The latter were not simply the result of misrecognition between colonizers and colonized but key categories used in the reorganization of the highland Maya. The Spanish strategy was called *reducción*: a political, religious, spatial, and linguistic reorganization of social life in the highlands according to peninsular cultural and political mores (Sáenz de Santamaría 1972; Todorov 1982; Hanks 2010). Spanish colonialism sought to redefine and co-opt ethnic boundaries. It tried to simplify and streamline the multiplicity of corporate units, such as lineages and lineage clusters (*amaq'*), as well as their semiotic manifestations, such as regional dialects. For example, the linguistic materials used to evangelize the K'ichee'—both descriptive (dictionaries and *artes* "pedagogical grammars") as well as pastoral (*doctrinas* "doctrines" and *confesionarios* "confessionals")—were written in a form of K'ichee' standardized by Dominican friars and their collaborators, based on the variety spoken in Q'umarkaaj. Dialectal variation was ignored when the language and ritual of Maya Christianity were crafted.

Colonial ethnic categories eventually became what I call "ethnic frames," after Erwin Goffman's seminal work. Ethnic frames are interactive templates embodying the values and structural inequalities presupposed in Spanish *policía* (Goffman 1974). They are cued by configurations of signs in diverse media in which language is decisive. Methodologically, theorizing ethnicity as frames allows us to focus on visible communicational practices and concrete

material artifacts, including language, rather than ideology or abstract classification systems. The literature on ethnicity in Mesoamerica is copious, but few works have examined its role in structuring linguistic interaction and indexical practice (Hanks 1992; Becker Richards 1998; Kockelman 2003; Flores Farfán 2009; Romero 2009). A focus on interaction frames also affords insights as to the genealogy of the diverse and apparently inconsistent ethnic identities inhabited by the K'ichee'.

The changing denotation of "K'ichee'" illustrates the vicissitudes of ethnic "boundary making" since the Spanish conquest. Old identities persisted in modified guise as new ones emerged. Ancient kin allegiances rooted in prehispanic lineages started to change as prehispanic mores gave way to a hybrid culture in which native forms of semiosis and ritual containing interwoven elements of Mesoamerican and Spanish origin crystallized (Bricker 2009; Gillespie 2010). Ethnic frames multiplied in response to the complexities and contradictory interests of individuals and communities in colonial Maya society. As Andreas Wimmer argues, "boundary making"—the reproduction and maintenance of social boundaries—requires constant "work" and the inevitable transformation of the "content" of ethnicity (Wimmer 2013). The artifacts, rituals, and ideologies embodying ethnic boundaries mark historical and cultural continuity but are also constantly transformed as political hierarchies; economic exchange networks, rebellions, and revolutions perpetually recreate the local spaces where they thrive (Colson 1968; Assad 1970). Social change entails changing forms of boundary work: new emblems,[6] new stereotypes, and constant resignification of foundational events. Ethnicity is embodied in emblematic practices and ideologies ripe with contradictions and inconsistencies. Different representations of the past—of legitimate authority, intelligible communication, and cultural continuity in the midst of radical change—lie behind innovation and conflict.

For the K'ichee', ethnic boundary work involves, first, discourses about the past as the source of legitimate, ancestor-sanctioned authority; second, a series of templates for communicative behavior (see Chapter 3); and third, a number of operative constraints on culturally acceptable innovation. This is transparent, for example, in oral tradition, a variegated group of narrative genres construed as a secular channel for the transmission and reproduction of ethnic identification. Storytelling entextualizes ongoing discussions of the moral dilemmas stemming from the traumatic social changes wrought by modernity in K'ichee' communities. The contradictions between individual self-interest and the collective demands of *communitas* are dramatized in narratives told and retold in the piedmont of Nahualá and Santa Catarina Ixtahuacán, Guatemala, for example (see Figure 1.3). As attested in scores of oral stories recorded by James Mondloch in the early 1970s, myths and fables dramatized the moral dilemmas faced by rural K'ichee' in the changing social landscapes of that era (Mondloch 1971). With the rapid expansion of Catholic Action and the militant, orthodox brand of Catholicism it advocated, traditional Maya religion and the practices of religious specialists such as the *ajq'ijab'* "calendar specialists" were stigmatized by orthodox Catholics and actively condemned by catechists (Warren 1978; Brintnall 1979; Cabarrús 1979; Falla 1980; Rojas Lima 1988; Konefal 2010). In one of those stories, an astute peddler was able to defeat an *aj itz* "witch" who had transformed himself into a goat to push the peddler off a ravine. The peddler held tight to the goat's horns, riding it until daybreak, and was finally able to defeat his enemy, who could not return to human shape before dawn and remained a goat. The goat finally yielded and asked for the peddler's help before parting:

(1.2)
"Chakuyu b'a numaak, oom, chakuyu na numaak. Na xinkowin ta chaweech. Pa nuk'u'x in xaq ab'anik kincha', xa'cha xatink'am loq pues, pero entonse k'o sta'q ana'oj pues komo na kinatzaqopij taj," xcha ri k'isik' che ri achi. "Pues, xewila' kaawaj jasa modo kinab'an joder pues…" xcha ri ajkomersiyante cheri k'isik'. "Entonces pues, la mas k'o jun sekreta aweta'am

om cheri kinutzir chi na. Wa' we maj kinto'wik, maj kayo'w nuna'oj, ay diyos, wa' kinb'an joder wib', kinkamik porke xuujal ora cheech ri nuchaak in. Kamiik ya saq chik. Le' keen na kinutzir ta chik," xcha ri k'isik' che ri achi.

"Forgive me, man, forgive me. I could not beat you. I thought I would easily prevail. That's why I brought you here. But you are cunning: you did not let go of me!" said the goat to the man. "Well, it was you who wanted to screw me like that!" said the peddler to the goat. "Is there maybe a spell you know that I could use to regain human shape? If no one helps me, if no one gives me advice, oh God, I am screwed! I am going to die because the hour is past for me to conclude my job. It is light already. I am surely not going to be able to recover!" said the goat to the man.[7]

(Mondloch 1971)

In Mesoamerican thought, ritual specialists have the power to take animal shape. Taking the physical form of an animal species is believed to be a manifestation of the spiritual powers of especially gifted individuals (Boremanse 1986; Foster 1994; López-Austin 1996; Stanzione 2003; Bocek 2009). Nevertheless, since the beginning of Christianization, animal transformations have been actively persecuted and stigmatized by the Catholic clergy, both Spanish and Guatemalan (Mendelson 1965). In text (1.2) the peddler outsmarts the shaman, who admits his defeat and in a surprising turn of events even begs for help in regaining human form. The story does not simply reflect today's official Catholic discourse, which adamantly denies the existence of human-animal transformations, dismissing them as mere superstition, but warns about the possible destructive consequences of traditional ritual practices in the new social context.[8] Oral traditions are part of a tense, continuous conversation on ritual, tradition, and their normative role in an ever-changing community. The performance of ethnicity and its iconic artifacts undergoes constant innovation and resynthesis to successfully effect "boundary work" in shifting social landscapes.

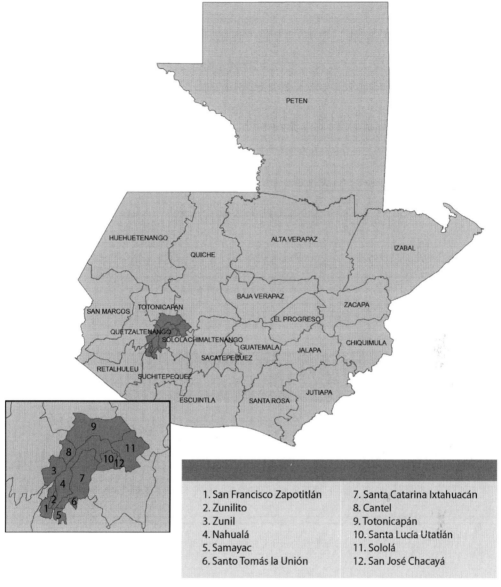

1. San Francisco Zapotitlán	7. Santa Catarina Ixtahuacán
2. Zunilito	8. Cantel
3. Zunil	9. Totonicapán
4. Nahualá	10. Santa Lucía Utatlán
5. Samayac	11. Sololá
6. Santo Tomás la Unión	12. San José Chacayá

FIGURE 1.3. Nahualá and neighboring townships (map by Luís Velásquez).

1.2. Words and Ethnic Boundaries in K'ichee'

Ethnic identities in K'ichee'-speaking communities are multiple. The K'ichee' perform alternative and apparently inconsistent forms of boundary work, inhabiting different ethnic frames. For example, K'ichee' from Santa María Chiquimula in the Department of Totonicapán in Guatemala may identify as "Chiquimula" in rela-

tion to K'ichee' speakers from the neighboring township of Totonicapán (see Figure 1.4).[9] At the same time, they may also identify as "K'ichee'" in relation to the ethnic Sacapultecos who share the territory of the township of Sacapulas with Chiquimula migrants (see Chapter 3).[10] Also, they will definitely consider themselves and their community *naturalib'* "indigenous" in relation to the *moso'ib'* "non-indigenous" Guatemalans.[11]

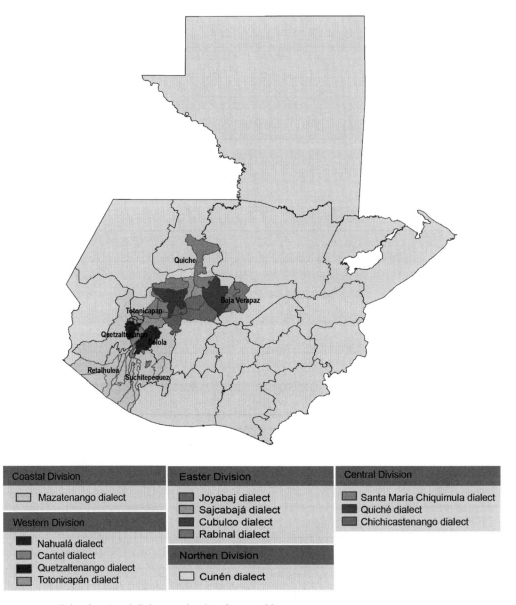

Coastal Division	Easter Division	Central Division
☐ Mazatenango dialect	▨ Joyabaj dialect	▨ Santa María Chiquimula dialect
	☐ Sajcabajá dialect	■ Quiché dialect
Western Division	■ Cubulco dialect	▨ Chichicastenango dialect
■ Nahualá dialect	▨ Rabinal dialect	
▨ Cantel dialect	**Northen Division**	
■ Quetzaltenango dialect		
▨ Totonicapán dialect	☐ Cunén dialect	

FIGURE 1.4. K'ichee' regional dialects today (Kaufman n.d.).

Furthermore, they would enthusiastically root for the Guatemalan national soccer team, especially in matches against the Mexican team, considered Guatemala's soccer archenemy.

Social identification, ethnic or national, is not just an explicitly declared loyalty but also a set of recognizable semiotic performances and communicational stances. Boundary making among the highland Maya is eminently interactive, involving culturally defined roles and emblematic semiotic and linguistic repertoires—in short, ethnic frames. For the K'ichee', ethnic frames bridge *communitas* and *lingua* in their broad socio-cultural sense. The multiple ethnic frames inhabited by the K'ichee' entail contrastive configurations of interactive roles, languages, dialects, styles, registers, and socio-indexical practices. The public role of *principalib'* "elder" in Nahualá, for example, could not be appropriately discharged in Spanish. Even though certain meetings with officials at the city hall may require some Spanish-K'ichee' code switching or Spanish translation when non-K'ichee' visitors are in attendance, a felicitous elder performance needs to be recognized as *puro K'ichee'* "pure K'ichee'" (Ajpacajá 2001; León Chic 2002; Romero 2006).[12] This requires not only the prescribed discourse in K'ichee' but also appropriate demeanor and bodily gestures.

Performing an indigenous ethnic frame, however, does not necessarily exclude the Spanish language. Spanish speech may be accompanied by the iconic display of a Mayan language to index an indigenous identity in the marketplace, for example. Walter Little (2009) describes such nondetachable effects in exchanges between tourists and Kaqchikel vendors in the handicraft market of Antigua Guatemala. Kaqchikel vendors use Spanish to address international tourists but simultaneously display their indigenousness by loudly addressing other vendors in Kaqchikel within hearing distance of possible customers (Little 2009). Note that such iconic linguistic performances are embedded in exchanges occurring fundamentally in Spanish. In globalized tourist markets in Guatemala as elsewhere, authenticity is a crucial component of commoditized indigenous crafts (Little 2004; Comaroff and Comaroff 2009; DeHart 2010). The emblematic valence of Mayan languages does not rule out the use of Spanish in the quotidian performance of indigenous ethnicities.

In summary, among the highland Maya, ethnicity is a kind of language ideology, a set of practices, attitudes, discourses, and patterned affects focusing on language (Irvine and Gal 2000). Boundary work and identity discourse are woven with linguistic threads. Although other media embody ethnic frames as well, the centrality of language in Maya conceptions of ethnicity is paramount (Tedlock and Tedlock 1985; Christenson 2001; Romero 2012). An iconic relation between the imagined texture of language and ethnic "substance" is presupposed in K'ichee' social life, as we see in Chapter 3. Each of the three ethnic frames mentioned above—Chiquimula, K'ichee', and indigenous—entails a particular, contrastive linguistic repertoire: the Chiquimula variety in relation to other K'ichee' regional dialects, the K'ichee' language in relation to other Mayan languages, and Mayan languages in relation to Spanish, respectively.

1.3. Dialectal Variation: A Historical Precipitate of K'ichee' Histories

An extraordinary degree of dialectal variation is one of the most striking sociolinguistic features of highland Mayan languages, especially K'ichee' (see Figure 1.4). Every level of linguistic structure is involved (phonology, morphology, syntax, discourse), turning the highlands into a veritable linguistic kaleidoscope. K'ichee', with its ample geographic extension and more than one million speakers, is perhaps the most diverse (Campbell 1977; Kaufman n.d.; Par Sapón and Can 2000; Richards 2003). Scholars of Mayan languages have sometimes explained this geographic diversification as the structural consequence of migrations followed by long periods of geographic isolation. In this view, areas originally sharing a common vernacular break into isolated pockets in which innovations are constant but spatially contained (Swadesh 1954). Nevertheless, this view ignores much linguistic, historical, and archaeological evidence that among the Maya, communication across languages and regional dialects continues to be the norm, not the exception (Campbell and Kaufman 1976; Justeson et al. 1985; Campbell et al. 1986; Sharer 2005; Van Akkeren 2012). New dialect formation in today's Mayan languages is the cumulative result of changes in social meaning and discourse role that have co-occurred with innovations in lexicon and grammar, as has been documented for Q'eqchi' Maya in the lowlands of Alta Verapaz, for example (Romero 2012). The emergence of Lowland Q'eqchi' as a distinct linguistic variety is inseparable from the congregation of Q'eqchi' settlers of diverse geographic provenience in multiethnic rural settlements. Sociolinguists have suggested that in situations of dialect contact in areas in which no group is culturally or demographically dominant, a universal, structural preference for unmarked forms sets in.

FIGURE 1.5. Traditional dance drama in Cubulco, Baja Verapaz (courtesy of Archivo Frank Lee Mays, Fototeca Guatemala, CIRMA).

New vernaculars, it has been argued, often discard the structurally "marked" features of the dialects spoken by the original settlers (Trudgill 1986, 2004). However, in Lowland Q'eqchi' the diagnostic features are socially motivated: they stem from the avoidance of forms stereotypical of highland townships. The enregisterment of Lowland Q'eqchi' is the linguistic manifestation of a new Q'eqchi' *communitas* defined against the ancestral highland identities of the first lowland settlers (Romero 2012).[13]

As argued by Blommaert (2005), socially motivated variation is layered and cumulative. New lexicons, loanwords, and structural innovations develop indexical roles as stylistic cues or social markers. However, their original illocutionary effects or social meanings change and sometimes disappear. In turn, they may become elements of new indexical configurations. Like the dance dramas performed in highland Maya towns, in which history is telescoped and two or more historical events are merged into one traditional costume or scene (Van Akkeren 2000; Bricker 2009), dialectal variation is a material precipitate of the social history of the highland Maya (see Figure 1.5). Regional varieties are layered deposits of collective experience. Despite mutual intelligibility, differences attest not only to structural innovation but also to idiosyncratic discourse histories. For example, whereas in Achi the noun *kristiyan*, from Spanish *cristiano* "Christian," denotes the abstract category "human being," the equivalent noun in western K'ichee' dialects is *winaq*. The difference may seem to the reader a minor lexical detail; however, it is a sharply defined dialectal isogloss that overlaps with the territorial boundaries between the Verapaz and the rest of Guatemala.[14] In other K'ichee'an languages spoken in the Verapaz, such as Poqomchi' and Q'eqchi', we find *kristiyan* as well, rather than the corresponding cognate of *winaq*. After successfully subduing native resistance in the forests of the Verapaz, formerly dubbed "the land of war," the Dominican Order directly administered the territory for centuries and was solely in charge of the evangelization of its various Maya groups (Bierman 1960; Saint-Lu 1968; Bossu 1990). The isogloss *kristiyan/winaq* was the result of idiosyncratic lexical choices made by the Dominicans in the Verapaz when composing catechetical materials in the languages of their Maya charges. A lexical precipitate of different Christianization histories thus became a dialect marker. Eventually, it became a stereotype, a shibboleth marking an ethnic boundary between the K'ichee' and the Achi (Labov 1994; Sis Iboy 1997).

Even phonetic changes common across the world's languages often follow ethnic boundaries in K'ichee'. The debuccalization of consonants—the loss of their articulatory features, leading to the replacement of a fully articulated consonant with a glottal stop [ʔ]—is a widespread process seen, for example, in colloquial British English, in which glottal stops replace [t] in certain intervocalic environments, as in "water" and "butter" (O'Brien 2012). In Achi the debuccalization of uvular ejectives [q'] is categorical, as in [q'aq'] "fire," which is articulated as [ʔaʔ], or [q'uq'] "quetzal," which is articulated as [ʔuʔ] (Campbell 1977). This is one the most commonly mentioned stereotypes of Achi for K'ichee' speakers. The glottal articulation of [q'] is unknown in central and western K'ichee', with the exception of "intermediate" varieties spoken in Joyabaj, east of Santa Cruz del Quiché, a township with a distinct ethnic identity, neither K'ichee' nor Achi. Commonplace structural innovations are co-opted as ethnic stereotypes in spaces in which mutually intelligible varieties are spoken. Internal changes—those responding to structural factors—add to the layered complexity and idiosyncratic texture of each regional variety.

Regional varieties are evident not only in boundary work but also in social deixis, embodying meaningful social categories and cultural roles (Manning 2001). Ethnic stereotypes are deeply imbricated in the structure of discourse, acting as stylistic cues as well. Thus, eth-

nicity and social deixis for the K'ichee' are two sides of the same coin.

1.4. Accent, Ethnic Boundaries, and Social Deixis in the K'ichee' Highlands

As discussed earlier, dialect stereotypes mark ethnic boundaries for the K'ichee'. They are linguistic hues used to color regional ethnoscapes. In large regional markets and in rural settlements close to disputed municipal boundaries, they cue interlocutors' ethnic provenience and help calibrate style and deictic practice in potentially threatening exchanges. Market days are recurring spaces in which thousands of interactions occur between people speaking different K'ichee' varieties.[15] Often "accent" is the only unambiguous index available as to someone's provenience. As any tourist visiting the highlands of Guatemala will notice, however, the colorful blouses worn by women and to a lesser extent the *traje* "traditional outfit" worn by some men are spectacularly visible markers of particular townships, identified by color and pattern (Asturias de Barrios et al. 1989; Holksbeke and Montoya 2008). Dress code, nevertheless, can be an ambiguous code, as women sometimes wear the emblematic blouses of other townships and most men sport Western apparel. Wearing one's hometown *huipil* is required only on special occasions such as high school graduations, weddings, and city hall functions (Hendrickson 1996). The pragmatic roles of dress and language overlap only in the explicit, theatrical performances of boundary work (see Figure 1.6).

Stylistic markers perform also as dialect stereotypes, sort of second-order indices (Silverstein 2003). As we see in Chapter 5, in Santa María Chiquimula honorific address is licensed in very few situations. In Santa Cruz del Quiché, in contrast, licensing conditions are much broader. Chiquimulas believe Santa Cruz to be more faithful to ancestral styles requiring honorific address than Santa María Chiquimula (Romero 2006). As a result, in addition to marking stylistic shifts to *puro K'ichee'*, Chiquimulas construe honorific address as a stereotype of Santa Cruz del Quiché. Santa María

FIGURE 1.6. Nahualá couple wearing the traditional *traje* during a class graduation (photograph by Sergio Romero).

Chiquimula's ethnoscape—which includes Santa Cruz del Quiché—is the deictic space, the socio-pragmatic background where the indexical effects described above occur.[16] K'ichee' perceptual dialectology is thus part and parcel of the way in which ethnicity and linguistic stereotypes are articulated in oral interaction.[17] The social meaning of "accent" depends on local representations of linguistic variation and ethnic diversity.

1.5. "In Spanish or in Our Language?" Spanish in the Linguistic Economy of the K'ichee'

Ethnic frames involve not only the choice of appropriate K'ichee' registers but also the complex and sometimes hybridized performance of Spanish varieties, as most K'ichee' speakers have at least a rudimentary knowledge of Spanish (see Chapter 4). In fact, in several predominantly K'ichee' areas Spanish is the primary language today. In the city of Quetzaltenango, for example, the cultural and political hub of the K'ichee' in western Guatemala, few speak K'ichee' fluently and many professionals, political leaders, and intellectuals are monolingual Spanish speakers. Important political figures such as Rigoberto Quemé Chay, former mayor of Quetzaltenango, and Otilia Lux de Cotí, former minister of culture in the Alfonso Portillo government, are not known as proficient K'ichee' speakers (Narciso Cojtí, personal communication 2006). Proficiency is unevenly distributed across geography and social class.

Spanish plays a host of discourse roles in K'ichee' speech. It is a cue marking stylistic and situational shifts. Metaphoric code switches into Spanish are frequent in K'ichee' conversation, and speakers frequently code-switch, although balanced bilinguals are rare.[18] It may seem like a paradox, but the ubiquitous presence of Spanish in K'ichee' colloquial styles does not contradict its status as stereotype of the *amu'sab'*, or nonindigenous Guatemalans. The *indígena/ladino* ethnic dichotomy and its emblematic linguistic repertoires are part of the cultural background presupposed in every interaction.[19] As Blommaert (2005) points out, the set of linguistic means and communicative skills available in the speech community are part of the context of every linguistic exchange. In consequence, language choice for bilingual K'ichee' speakers responds to more than audience design. It is decisive in the construction of the speaker's public persona, indexing forceful stances or prestigious roles, such as teacher, policeman, or mayor, in Guatemala's linguistic market,[20] which continues to be profoundly racist (Bourdieu 2001; Cojtí 1995). An unequal proficiency in *español*

culto "standard Spanish" across social classes and ethnic groups is a condition for its role as ethnic, social-class, and education marker. K'ichee' is excluded from central political, educational, and business spaces at the national level, and therefore even militant pan-Maya activists are often compelled to switch to Spanish when addressing legal, scientific, or political issues (see Chapter 6).

Spanish is therefore an ambivalent linguistic code for the K'ichee'. In the essentialist constructions of indigeneity advocated by pan-Maya activists in the last thirty years, Spanish is represented as a sort of corrupting substance that needs to be extirpated from indigenous languages (Cojtí 1995; Warren 1997; French 2010). Code switching is prescriptively avoided in Mayanist discourse. Even the famous K'ichee' poet Humberto Ak'abal had to make lexical adjustments in subsequent editions of his poetry after the presence of Spanish loanwords was noted by some readers (Rusty Barrett, personal communication 2007). The etymology of words was adopted as guiding criterion for linguistic standardization.

1.6. Linguistic Purism and Pan-Mayanism

In the last thirty years pan-Maya activism has changed the way the state and international organizations think about indigenous peoples, their collective rights, and their participation in the Guatemalan state. Although poverty, exclusion from national decision making, and *ladino* racism linger, the state has recognized some collective rights of indigenous communities and created programs devoted to their defense and promotion (Maxwell 1996; Bastos and Camus 2003; French 2010; Konefal 2010). In the struggle for state recognition, cultural and linguistic rights played a crucial mobilizing role, especially during the grim years of the civil war, when any indigenous activism was regarded as a direct threat by the military. The creation in 1986 of the Academy of the Mayan Languages of Guatemala (ALMG) was a turning point for pan-Maya activism. The ALMG became the sole institution officially in charge of the protection and advancement of Mayan languages.

The adoption of a unified orthography, the development of standardized written varieties for all Mayan languages, and the establishment of bilingual education programs in primary schools in predominantly Maya areas were some of the milestones in the struggle for linguistic revitalization (Kaufman 1976; Maxwell 1996; Richards and Richards 1996; England 2003; French 2010).

The strategic decision that pan-Maya activists made in the 1980s to focus their struggle on language rights had important consequences for Mayan languages. Pan-Maya activists advocate an essentialist notion of Maya culture in which language, traditional ritual practices, and the authority of elders and *guías espirituales* "spiritual guides" embody shared cultural principles transcending linguistic, cultural, and political differences between Maya groups. Maya activists imagine the emancipation of Maya peoples as a release from *ladino* colonial socioeconomic, cultural, and political domination (Cojtí 1995; Warren 1997; Nelson 1999; Fischer 2001; Bastos and Camus 2003). From this perspective, the revitalization of Mayan languages demands not only opening the halls of power and academia but a careful effort of prescriptive reordering and purification. The adoption of an orthography that did not simply follow Spanish conventions, the systematic creation of neologisms in semantic domains in which Mayan etyma were lacking, and the proscription of hybrid forms of oral communication such as code switching are the three ways in which this linguistic agenda has been enacted.

Pan-Mayanism changed the socio-cultural context in which Mayan languages were spoken, especially K'ichee'. The latter's public profile, access to print and other media, styles, and indexical practices were touched in subtle and not so subtle ways by these changes, as we see later in this book. The new discursive practices that became normative were contemporary incarnations of enduring language ideologies that construct the relationship between language and ethnicity as iconic, a lasting cultural principle behind the dialectics of cultural change and continuity in highland Maya history.

Because of its adaptability, K'ichee' has shown stunning resilience and vitality. The interleaving of language and social change in K'ichee' society cannot be easily untangled, however. Understanding ethnic frames requires teasing apart a complex articulation of discourse, grammar, colonialism, and resistance. The following chapters are an attempt to penetrate the intimate link between the re-creation of K'ichee' societies and the languages they speak.

Notes

1. The greater area of the site included at least three densely populated highland plateaus and at least six other settlements in the immediate vicinity (Fox 1978).
2. My translation from the original K'ichee'.
3. In K'ichee' *ojeer tziij* "ancient word" refers to diverse genres of orally transmitted historical narratives and myths.
4. To this day the Achi consider their variety a different language despite mutual intelligibility with K'ichee'.
5. Unpublished work by Ruud van Akkeren argues that the term "Achi" was an ancient glottonym used to reference K'iche'an languages such as K'iche', Kaqchikel, and Tz'utujil without precisely distinguishing among them. The specific variety denoted by "Achi" depended on the context and geographic coordinates in which it was used. Colonial titles written by Mam-speaking scribes, for example, used it to refer to the language of the K'ichee' polity of Q'umarkaaj (Van Akkeren n.d.).
6. An emblem is an object to which a social persona is conventionally attached (Agha 2007:235). A dialect emblem is a linguistic form—a word, sound, syntactic construction, intonation contour—conventionally associated with the population of a specific geographic location: a town, region, village, etc.
7. The English translation is mine.
8. In the past, Catholic clergy did not deny the occurrence of such transformations but explained

them as the work of the devil among Native Americans (Cañizares-Esguerra 2006; Ximénez 1965).

9. A "Chiquimula" (Sp.) is a native of Santa María Chiquimula.

10. A Sacapulteco is a native of the township of Sacapulas irrespective of his or her ethnic identification. An ethnic Sacapulteco, in contrast, claims a specific genealogy, language (Sakapulteko), and ethnic identification that distinguish him or her from other ethnic groups in Sacapulas such as the K'ichee' and the Ixil.

11. An alternative K'ichee' term is *amu'sab'*.

12. *Puro K'ichee'* is the emblematic linguistic register of the *principalib'* "elders." It is cued by the avoidance of Spanish and the use of archaic lexicon, honorific address, parallel constructions, and a dignified demeanor.

13. Agha (2007) defines enregisterment as diachronic "processes whereby specific speech forms come to be recognized as indexical of particular speaker attributes" in a given speech community.

14. Isoglosses are map lines marking boundaries between dialect areas; each isogloss focuses on the realization of one linguistic variable. The Verapaz includes the territory of the departments of Baja and Alta Verapaz in north-central Guatemala.

15. Exchanges occur between speakers of different Mayan languages as well. Communication is easier between closely related languages such as K'ichee' and Kaqchikel, though many Maya are bilingual in distantly related languages, as in the townships of Cotzal and Nebaj, where K'ichee' often speak Ixil as well.

16. Deictic spaces are sites of linguistic and semiotic exchange in which social markers are calibrated in mutually intelligible ways despite political or cultural differences.

17. Perceptual dialectology references the cultural construction of dialectal variation. It contrasts with dialect geography, in which dialectologists' observations, rather than speakers' views, are paramount.

18. This is the result of Guatemala's deeply imbalanced linguistic markers and the exclusion of K'ichee' from academia, high government offices, and corporate business (see Chapter 6).

19. *Ladino* is a broad category including all Guatemalans who do not identify as indigenous. Etymologically, it derives from the Spanish *indio ladino* "Indian fluent in Spanish," a colonial category that eventually fell into disuse.

20. Bourdieu's "linguistic market" references the set of personal, class, and institutional relations in which individuals, social classes, and ethnic groups compete for prestige, resources, and power by means of an unequally distributed "cultural capital," whose assets include proficiency in the dominant language, especially its standardized varieties.

CHAPTER 2

Orthographies, Foreigners, and Pure K'ichee'

2.1. The Colonial Appropriation of Writing in K'ichee'

Despite their exclusion from the halls of civil, religious, and academic power, indigenous languages were essential vehicles of Catholic indoctrination and useful instruments for the Spanish civil administration, especially in the first two hundred years after the conquest. Spanish colonialism did not seek to destroy native identities or indigenous languages. On the contrary, it recruited and tried to turn them into technologies to establish Catholicism and the regime of Spanish *policía*, on which the colonial extraction of resources and labor was based.[1] As argued by William Hanks (2010), the *reducción* of Mayan languages—including systematic grammar description, adaptation, and coining of new lexicon, and development of new genres in the pastoral and administrative fields—was part of the Spanish strategy to transform the Maya into loyal Catholic subjects of the Spanish king. Franciscan and Dominican *lenguas* wrote descriptive grammars, compiled dictionaries, and wrote scores of pastoral materials such as confessionals and books of homilies.[2] They also taught a select group of native collaborators the use of the Spanish script to write in Mayan languages.

The adoption of the Spanish alphabet did not simply add a new technology to K'ichee' scriptural practice. It marked a discontinuity between prehispanic and colonial writing traditions and transformed the ways in which texts were written, read, performed, and transmitted. New genres emerged—notarial, doctrinal, ritual, and historical—and new kinds of content were addressed.[3] Writing became an ambivalent space of subordination, contestation, and native resistance. In fact, the secular tension over the form and content of writing in Mayan languages explains the centrality of pan-Maya demands for institutionalized indigenous control over writing norms in pan-Maya struggles in the 1980s and 1990s.

As we see in this chapter, the Spanish empire and the Republic of Guatemala capitalized on writing in K'ichee', first as a strategic vehicle for Christianization, then for capitalist modernization, and finally for multicultural political legitimacy. *Reducción* was the permanent, though not always entirely successful, linguistic strategy used by the state and the church to control and reshape the K'ichee' Maya in response to changing elite needs and native resistance. Successive episodes of lexical readjustment and discourse recalibration have accompanied the production of secular and religious texts since the Spanish conquest. As scholars have found elsewhere, colonialism seldom hesitates to engage native languages as vehicles of proselytism and empire, and the K'ichee' Maya were no exception (Errington 2008; Durston 2007; Burkhart 1989; Rafael 1988; Fabian 1986). A permanent engagement with the K'ichee' language is a crucial historical element of the generative social system

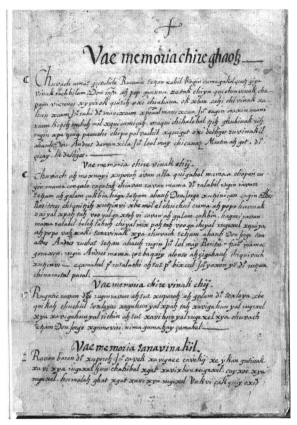

FIGURE 2.1. Folio 1 of the *Memorial de Tecpán-Atitlán* (courtesy of Berendt-Brinton Linguistic Collection, Rare Book and Manuscript Library, University of Pennsylvania).

of creation and transformation of utterances and written statements—what Foucault called the "archive" (Foucault 1969)—that conditions language use in the Maya highlands.

2.2. *Doctrinas* and K'ichee' Writers

The K'ichee' had a rich prehispanic scriptural tradition, according to attestations in Spanish chronicles and references in indigenous annals. The *criollo* Francisco Antonio de Fuentes y Guzmán, for example, briefly describes in his *Recordación Florida* from 1690 the *lienzos* and maps in which the K'ichee' and Kaqchikel recorded their history, migrations, genealogies, and territorial boundaries (Fuentes y Guzmán 1932–33; Sampeck in press).[4] Among the numerous indigenous chronicles, the title of the Popol Vuh—from *popol* "mat" and *wuj* "book"—is itself

a metalinguistic piece of evidence for the use of writing by K'ichee' elites.[5] The sixteenth-century annals known as the *Memorial de Tecpán-Atitlán*, written in Kaqchikel, list writings and paintings among the symbols of rule brought by Kaqchikel and K'ichee' lords from the mythical land of Tulán together with flutes, shields, arrows, and spears (Maxwell and Hill 2006) (see Figure 2.1). Unfortunately, no prehispanic codex from the Maya highlands survived the zeal of the friars and the violent upheavals of the colonial and republican periods.[6]

Although Spanish friars tried, on the one hand, to extirpate native writing as a dangerous relic and lingering reminder of what they regarded as devil worship, on the other hand they taught native collaborators Spanish orthographic conventions to write in K'ichee'. Not only are

FIGURE 2.2. Manuscript copy of the *Theologia indorum* (K'ichee'), held at the American Philosophical Society in Philadelphia (by permission of the American Philosophical Society).

the Spanish and K'ichee' languages structurally incommensurable, but the alphabetic and logosyllabic conventions on which their writing systems were respectively based used dissimilar principles of correspondence between speech and writing.[7] Franciscan linguists such as Francisco de la Parra and Dominicans such as Domingo de Vico, however, soon developed ad hoc orthographies to adapt the Latin script to the phonology of K'ichee' and Kaqchikel.[8] Distinguished works on K'ichee' grammar and lexicon include Domingo de Basseta's *Vocabulario de lengua quiché* and Bartolomé de Anleo's *Arte de la lengua 4iche* (Anleo 2002; Basseta 2005). These early Dominican linguistic and doctrinal works show an excellent knowledge of syntax and morphology as well as an effective and generally accurate adaptation of the Spanish orthography to K'ichee' phonology, as can be seen in Vico's *Theologia Indorum* (see Figure 2.2).

K'ichee' phonemes lacking in Spanish include the bilabial implosive [ɓ], the alveopalatal affricate [c], the velar occlusive [q] and a series

of ejective "glottalized" consonants: [t'], [c'], [ʧ'], [k'] and [q'] (see Table 2.1). The sole phonemic feature of K'ichee' systematically left out of the colonial script was vocalic length, represented in the International Phonetic Alphabet (IPA) as a colon following vowels in Table 2.1. Postvocalic glottal stops were represented inconsistently: after word-final /i/ they appear irregularly as –*ij*, a convention borrowed from Medieval Latin and found in some Nahuatl and Yucatec texts as well, which can be seen in [riʔ], written as *rij* in Table 2.1 (Perry Wong, personal communication 2007). In contrast, postvocalic glottal stops are missing in *4ux* [k'uʔʃ] "heart" and *etamabal* [etaʔamaɓal] "knowledge." For natives, context was usually enough to reconstruct phonological features in cases of ambiguity. K'ichee' writers soon started to compose hundreds of texts, many of which were not meant for the inquisitorial eyes of the Dominicans and Franciscans. In addition to wills, letters, *títulos*, and other notarial documents produced in the field of *reducción*, K'ichee' writers composed *cholq'ij* "260-day

TABLE 2.1. K'ichee' Consonants Lacking in Spanish and Their Respective Orthographic Conventions.

Phoneme (IPA)[1]	Colonial script	Example (IPA)	Example (Colonial Script)[2]	Gloss
ɓ	b	etaʔamaɓal	etamabal	knowledge
c	tz	ucilax	vtzilaj	excellent
q	k	winaq	vinak	person
t'	tt	t'ot'	ttott	snail
c'	ttz	c'ikin	ttziquin	bird
tʃ'	gh	tʃ'a:ɓal	ghabal	language
k'	4	k'uʔʃ	4ux	heart
q'	ɛ	kiʃmiq'	quixmiɛ	you all warm up
iʔ	ij	riʔ	rij	that, which

[1] International Phonetic Alphabet.
[2] These examples were culled from Folia 1–3 of the *Theologia Indorum*.

ritual calendars," dance dramas, compilations of myths, and annals such as the Popol Vuh (Carmack 1973, 1981; Edmonson 1997; Breton 1994).

Nevertheless, in spite of the success of K'ichee' writers in using the Latin script to carve spaces of autonomous discourse, K'ichee' writing was constrained by the cultural and political order of the *república de indios*.[9] As argued by Hanks (2010), even "forbidden genres" such as calendars and annals were heavily influenced by *K'ichee' reducido*, having substantial lexical and discursive influence from pastoral registers (Edmonson 1997; Dürr 2006). Furthermore, *K'ichee' reducido* became a poetic and lexical template that was later applied to other highland Maya languages in the development of doctrinal language (Romero 2011).

After the Council of Trent, despite serious reservations on the part of ecclesiastical authorities regarding the production of Christian literature in indigenous languages, Franciscans and Dominicans continued to write and manually copy books of homilies and confessionals. For clergy in charge of *doctrinas* (indigenous parishes), books of *pláticas* in indigenous languages were essential for effective proselytism and sacramental practice;[10] *artes* and dictionaries were required for clergy to attain the linguistic proficiency needed for the surveillance of K'ichee'

souls and bodies. Furthermore, in times of open rebellion and violent resistance, the clergy doubled as mediators between rebels and Spanish civil and military authorities, as documented by Severo Martínez Peláez (1970), Robert Patch (2002), and Kevin Gosner (1992). Proficiency in indigenous languages enabled them to play the role of brokers in the maintenance of Pax Hispanica in the highlands of Guatemala.

Indigenous languages were present in colonial institutions into the twentieth century, but interest among the clergy had already diminished somewhat by the eighteenth century.[11] This was the result of changes in the ecclesiastical organization of the highlands as well as the expansion of Spanish as official and colloquial language. The third generation of Spanish priests, consisting mostly of *criollos*, was less interested than the pioneers in studying and using indigenous languages in sacramental practice, and the corpus of pastoral and linguistic works is smaller for the eighteenth than for the previous two centuries.[12] Notarial documents continued to be drafted in K'ichee', however, as attested by the large corpus of wills from Rabinal in possession of the Princeton University Library. The Rabinal corpus shows consistent colonial orthographic conventions and notarial formulae, suggesting that writing remained a common practice in Rabinal into the early nineteenth century. Far to the west, Bishop Pedro Cortez y Larraz confiscated a *cholq'ij* during a pastoral visit to Quetzaltenango in 1722, showing that at the time such texts were still in the possession of literate shamans (Cortez y Larraz 1958; Edmonson 1997).

2.3. *El General* Speaks K'ichee'

The second half of the nineteenth century was a time of rupture for K'ichee' writers, both religious and secular. Independence from Spain in 1821 was followed by protracted instability and the rise of Guatemalan Liberalism, which was strongly anticlerical. Religious orders were expelled and their properties confiscated (Woodward 1993). The legal foundations of the *república de indios* were systematically undermined. After a radical reorganization of the linguistic division of labor in Guatemala, indigenous languages were no longer used in notarial and pastoral documents, and Spanish became the sole official language. Very few original texts—linguistic, notarial, and doctrinal—were composed in this century. Linguistic and historical works such as those of Brasseur de Bourbourg, a French friar and antiquarian, were ethnographic rather than pastoral, and the target readership consisted of educated Europeans rather than Guatemalans (Bourbourg 1961). More important, the few manuscripts in K'ichee' composed in this period used the colonial orthography in a haphazard way, with inconsistencies and spelling errors. This can be seen in manuscript transcriptions of colonial *títulos* and other foundational texts such as the *Memorial de Totonicapán* and the *Título de Yax*, which appear to be the work of scribes who were literate in Spanish but no longer familiar with K'ichee' spelling conventions (Mondloch and Carmack 1983, 1989). Spanish eventually replaced K'ichee' as the language of notarial and pastoral texts even in towns that continue to be predominantly K'ichee'-speaking today.

In the 1930s, however, during General Jorge Ubico's long presidential tenure (1931–1944), the Guatemalan state turned again to Mayan languages to refashion indigenous peoples according to the needs of Guatemalan elites and to shore up its political legitimacy.[13] Official

breviaries such as the *Cartilla de civismo* were widely published and translated into the four indigenous languages with the largest number of speakers, including K'ichee' (Teletor 1942b). Despite Jorge Ubico's explicit denial of the existence of ethnic conflict in Guatemala—even refusing to join the Instituto Indigenista Americano (INA), institutional cradle of Latin American *indigenismo*[14]—the *Cartilla* embodied an authoritarian *indigenista* stance, in which the dictator cast himself as protector of indigenous peoples after he abolished indentured labor (Casey 1979; Konefal 2010). The infamous *habilitadores* (labor contractors) would pay advances to indigenous men, who had to pay off the loans by working in sugar and cotton plantations on the southern piedmont. This arrangement led to many abuses by planters, who used all kinds of illegal devices to keep their laborers even after the debts had been paid. Furthermore, the sanitary conditions of the living quarters were atrocious, leading to numerous deaths from easily preventable diseases (Grieb 1979; Bunzel 1981) (see Figure 2.3). Although Ubico did not eliminate all forms of forced labor, the abolition of *habilitación*, the construction of public works, and his surprise motorcycle visits to indigenous communities to check on local officials render him surprisingly popular among many indigenous Guatemalans even today (Carey 2001; Adams 2004). Despite the proscription of *habilitadores*, the *Cartilla* demanded—under threat of punishment—obedience to and a quiet acceptance of the Ley de Vialidad, requiring annual labor on public works, which weighed heavily on indigenous communities.[15]

The *Cartilla* is a complex and fascinating example of official discourse, highlighting the central role of indigenous labor in the modernization and expansion of plantation capitalism in the 1930s (Cambranes 1985; McCreery 1995). The author was Father Celso Narciso Teletor Tecún (1891–1968), a Catholic priest and scholar from Rabinal, Baja Verapaz (Figure 2.4). Teletor was a prolific writer, authoring a monograph about his native township, a catechism in K'ichee', a K'ichee' conversation manual, and Spanish translations of indigenous chronicles in

FIGURE 2.3. Coffee pickers in the Pacific piedmont during harvest season (courtesy of Fototeca Guatemala, CIRMA).

Kaqchikel, among other historical works (Teletor 1942a, 1942b, 1946, 1951, 1955, 1964, 1965; Rojas Lima 2004; Van Akkeren 2013). Published in bilingual Spanish-K'ichee' format, the *Cartilla* places the K'ichee' text opposite the original Spanish, which it paraphrases. It is organized into thirty-one *pláticas*, whose form and hortative lexicon bring to mind the rich homiletic production in K'ichee' in the sixteenth and seventeenth centuries and probably result from Teletor's ecclesiastical background.[16] The preface states that the *Cartilla* was addressed specifically to literate K'ichee' (Teletor 1942b).

Teletor's claim that the target readership was native K'ichee' is surprising given that in the 1930s very few K'ichee' were literate. To the best of my knowledge, there were no bilingual schools at the time, but more research is necessary for an understanding of literacy in K'ichee' during Ubico's tenure. It is likely that many readers were educated priests and *ladinos* living in K'ichee'-speaking towns. In the first decades of the twentieth century it was not uncommon for *ladinos* growing up in indigenous towns to become fluent in the local language. In the 1930s some acted as spokespeople for government discourse and often were handpicked as city hall officials. In fact, priests such as Fr. Teletor,

FIGURE 2.4. Father Celso Narciso Teletor in 1951 (Teletor 1951) (by permission of Academia de Geografía e Historia de Guatemala).

TABLE 2.2. Some Idiosyncratic Spellings in Teletor's *Cartilla de civismo*.

IPA	Colonial Script	Teletor's Spelling	Example (IPA)	Example (Teletor's Spelling)	Gloss
q'	ɛ	Not represented	q'iːx	ij	sun/day
ɓ	b	b and v	ʃuːɓan	xu van	he did it
			uːɓiʔ	ubi	his name
ʧ	ch	ch and x	ʧuːwaʧ	chuhuach	in front of
			ʧiːwilaʔ	xiwila	look at it!

nonreligious foreigners, and *ladinos* fluent in Mayan languages sometimes became knowledgeable scholars of the communities they lived in and published ethnographic or historical works, such as Juan de León's book on the K'ichee' of Santa Cruz del Quiché and Erwin Paul Dieseldorf's publications on the Q'eqchi' (Dieseldorf 1929; de León 1945). Dieseldorf's papers, in possession of the Latin American Library at Tulane University, include sixteenth- and seventeenth-century manuscripts in Q'eqchi' and several published and unpublished articles. The role of cultural broker played by *ladinos*, foreigners, and priests fluent in Mayan languages in the late nineteenth and early twentieth centuries has not been sufficiently studied by scholars, however.

Several aspects of the *Cartilla* will strike the careful reader: first, Teletor's idiosyncratic but inconsistent Spanish-based orthographic conventions. For example, /q/ sometimes appears as "k" and sometimes as "c" (Table 2.2). Second, his spellings are phonetic and do not distinguish homophonous allophones of distinct phonemes such as /ɓ/ and /q'/, which in Rabinal are realized as a glottal stop, the former variably and the latter categorically. By the same token, /ɓ/ is spelled as "v" after [a] but as "b" after [i]. The latter inconsistency probably reflects the phonetic palatalization of [ɓ] caused by the high front vowel [i] (see Table 2.2). Furthermore, [ʧ] is written as "x" rather than "ch" in imperative forms such as *Xiwila!* "Look!"[17] Third, Teletor's parsing of sentences suggests that he used Spanish templates to analyze K'ichee' syntactic categories. For example, he misconstrued K'ichee' verbal ergative and absolutive prefixes, treating them as independent pronouns, which he called *pronombres denominativos* "denominative pro-

nouns," and incorrectly parsed them as free morphemes in *quin chau chiwe* [kinʧʼaw ʧiwe] "I speak to you," which unnecessarily splits the aspectual and absolutive marker *quin* from the verbal root *chau* (Teletor 1942b, 1951:28).[18] Such idiosyncratic usage suggests a rupture between colonial and early twentieth-century spelling practices.

Teletor was an educated historian, a member of the elite Academia de Geografía e Historia de Guatemala, acquainted with colonial texts—both linguistic and doctrinal—and familiar with the philological work of his contemporaries José Villacorta and Adrián Inés Chávez (Teletor 1959: 117–123). Raised as a native speaker of Achi in Rabinal, either he received no training as a scribe or his native variety was no longer used in notarial texts and pastoral documents. His reliance on Spanish syntax and spelling conventions as templates for his K'ichee' prose suggests that the systematic transmission of writing had ceased in Rabinal, where he spent many of his adult years (Rojas Lima 2004).

Teletor and his *Cartilla* evince a complex authorial relationship. He was admittedly the sole author, but the national state was the "principal" on whose behalf the Spanish original and the K'ichee' periphrasis were composed. The K'ichee' text preserves the general content and illocutionary force of the Spanish, recalibrating the latter's polished vocabulary to a more colloquial, forceful, and authoritarian register. Despite the apparent orthographic rupture between the colonial pastoral literature and Teletor's prose, there is continuity in the authoritarian, paternalistic attitude running through Domingo de Vico's sixteenth-century homilies, for example, and Teletor's twentieth-century admonishments

(Teletor 1942b; Sparks 2011). A discrete indexical configuration of lexicon, pronominal forms, and verb inflection mirrors and reproduces the unequal relationship and power differential between author/principal and audience/readership. The politeness conventions of *español culto* "standard Spanish," for example, are ignored. While the Spanish text uses the honorific plural address form *vosotros*, Teletor translates it with the unmarked form *ix* rather than the honorific *alaq*. Furthermore, Teletor ignores the mitigation strategies common in hortative discourse in K'ichee'. For example, he uses the imperative form *Xiwila!* "Look at it!" rather than the polite form *Chiwilampe!* in which the clitic *–ampe* mitigates the imperative force of the utterance.

The text constructs a K'ichee' subject that is male, childlike, unruly, oppressed, frightened, and in permanent need of fatherly protection. The strategies employed include the use of direct imperatives, avoidance of honorific address forms, and the vocative use of *achijab* [*achijab'*] "men" rather than *huinac* [*winaq*] "people," which effectively erases women. For example, in one of the *pláticas*, parents are advised to send their children to school and not to be afraid of what might befall them there: *Qui tac ri hual patac tijonic (escuela). Man ta qui xibij ta i huib*[19] "Send your children to school. Do not be frightened!" The possessed noun *ri hual* [*ri iwaal*] "your children" presupposes a female addressee. K'ichee' has different terms for consanguine kin for male and female egos. Interestingly, *ri hual* is inconsistent with Teletor's use of *achijab* "men" as vocative throughout the text.[20] When Teletor speaks of Ubico, readers are encouraged to "obey" to make sure "nothing bad" happens to them: *Quimolobeg, que cuyubeg ri cu tac chihué, je lá na itzel taj cu van chihué*[21] "Pay attention, bear with what he orders you to do so that nothing bad happens to you." The second half of the sentence is ambiguous between "so that nothing bad happens to you" and "so that he does nothing bad to you," a veiled threat to any potential challenger. At the same time, the president is portrayed as a benevolent and wise "father and grandfather," a standard couplet denoting community elders: *Utz ru cux y sac chi ru jolom ri ca tatá mama ka tal tzij*[22] "Our father

and grandfather president has a good heart and is a wise elder." The text literally describes Ubico as having "white hair" (*saq ujoloom*), a standard metonym denoting the wisdom and status accrued by elders (Ajpacajá 2001). He is said to have made many laws protecting indigenous "men" (*achijab*): *Y u banom quiy chomabal ka tal tzij [leyes] pa ri achijab e ral uleu*[23] "He has made many laws on behalf of indigenous men." The text calls them *ral uleu* "sons of the land," a common phrasing in Achi, rather than *naturalib'*, the usual ethnonym in western K'ichee'. Paradoxically, the *Cartilla* denounces the abuses of foreigners and *ladinos*, both of whom are referenced as *mozoib* [*moso'ib'*] "foreign/*ladino*," an ethnic slur used in K'ichee' and Kaqchikel, as in *Relezaj ri mozoib-habilitadores ro caij huinac patac pinca*[24] "He took out the *ladinos*/foreigners who used to sell people to plantations" (see Table 2.3).

Despite Ubico's hostility to *indigenismo*, the *Cartilla* is clearly influenced by its tenets. In addition to claims that the dictator is protecting indigenous peoples from the abuses of the *mozoib* "foreigners/*ladinos*," the *Cartilla* reproduces in K'ichee' translation the letter addressed to the participants at the 1940 Inter-American Congress at Pátzcuaro, Mexico, by Jasper Hill, a Native Canadian elder. Hill's letter had previously been published in Spanish in the pages of *El Imparcial*, the most important newspaper in Guatemala at the time and a mouthpiece for the dictator.[25] This rare publication suggests that Ubico was paying attention to *indigenismo*. Ubico rejected it as official policy but found its discourse useful as a way to cast himself as a progressive ruler responding to the needs of the indigenous demographic majority in Guatemala. Such a stance was not a threat to the *casta* system on which Guatemala's plantation economy continued to be based (Grieb 1979; Cambranes 1985). On the contrary, it reveals a discursive continuity between the colonial period, in which the king regarded himself as benevolent protector of indigenous peoples, and the Liberal regimes of the twentieth century, embodied in the authoritarian personalities of Justo Rufino Barrios and Jorge Ubico (Ximénez 1965; Cambranes 1985; Handy 1994; Dakin and Lutz 1996;

TABLE 2.3. Fragment from Teletor's *Cartilla de civismo*.

Teletor's Original Spanish	Teletor's Original K'iche'	Unified Alphabet	My Translation from the K'iche'
Breves pláticas con vosotros	Tzij chabalanic ruc achijab	Tzij ch'ab'alanik ruuk' achijab'	Words to be spoken with men
Mas antes os he querido hablar y no lo había podido hacer porque eran pocos los que sabían leer, pero ahora que hay algunos y quienes tienen sus hijos que leen, lo hago. Ved cómo Dios ve desde el cielo a sus hijos los indios. Mandó antes un padre, Fray Bartolomé de las Casas, quien vio todo lo que los españoles os hacían e hizo cuatro viajes a España para decirle al rey y darle cuenta del trato que se os daba; pues se os trataba como a animal irracional, como a coyote o tigre. El rey dió leyes para que se os tratara bien pero no se cumplieron o se cumplieron en poco, por eso insistió en que se os tratara como a gentes.	Aré ojer cahuaj ri in quin chau chihué; majani la nuvanom taj, que je la quiy ri na quix tzun taj, hua kami co i hual catzunic, ri ix co jun caib catzunic. Xi huilá ri ca tatá ko chilá chikaj (Dios) quix huil wi y xu riló ronojel ix ral uleu. Xu tac ojer jun ca tatá ajau (Patré) Fr. Bartolomé de las Casas ubí, ix riló ki van chihué ri mazoib; xu van cajib bey (viaje) pa jun chic tinamit ubí España y xu biij chiré ri ajahuaral uleu (Rey) ronojel ri qui van chihué jun itzelal ri ooib; puch je lá manta cu van ka ban (cumplir). Xe ec tanchic chuhuach ri ajahuaral uleu (Rey) y xu biij ronojel ri itzelel cu van chiré ronojel huinac.	Are ojer kawaj ri in kinch'aw chiwe. Majani la' nub'anom taj, ke je la k'iy ri na kixtzu'un taj. Wakami k'o iwal katzu'unik, ri ix k'o jun ka'ib' katzu'unik. Chiwila ri qatata k'o chila chikaj (Dios) kixril wi y xurilo ronojel ix ral uleew. Xuutaq ojeer jun qatata ajaw (Patre) Fr. Bartolomé de las Casas ub'i' xrilo kakib'an chiwe ri moso'ib'. Xuub'an kajib' b'ey (viaje) pa jun chik tinamit ub''i' España y xuub'ij chiri ri rajawaraal uleew (Rey) ronojeel ri kakib'an chiwe jun itzelal ri moso'ib' puch. Je la man ta kuub'an kaqab'an (cumplir). Xb'ek ta na chik chwach ri rajawaral ulew (Rey) y xuub'ij ronojel ri itzelal kuub'an chire ronojeel winaq.	For a long time I have wanted to speak to you all but I have not done so because so many of you did not know how to see/read. Now, however, your children and some of you know how to see/read too. Look at the way Our Father in heaven watches over you and over all of the "sons of the earth"! A long time ago he sent a father, a lord (priest) whose name was Fray Bartolomé de las Casas. He saw what the foreigners were doing to you. He made four trips to another country called Spain and told the lord of the land, the king, all the evil things that the foreigners were doing to you. And so we did not fulfill them. So he went again to the lord of the land (the king) and told him about the evil things done to all the people.
Hace cinco años mas o menos que entró a la presidencia un General de buen corazón y claro intelecto quien ha creado nuevas leyes a favor de vosotros los indígenas . Y si no, ved y oíd. Quitó los habilitadores y se ha preocupado en la enseñanza militar y mandando instructor para que vinieran como	Goob junab xoc nim re kelem aj chich (general) pa nimá ka tal tzij (Presidente); utz ru cux y sac chi ru jolom ri ca tatá mama ka tal tzij y un vanom quiy chomabal ka tal tzij (leyes) pa ri achijab e ral uleu. Xi huilá, xi tó. Relezaj ri mobzoib-habilitadores ro caij huinac patac pinca; na co ta chic huacamí, quiy. Xu relezal ri cazt ruc ri mozoib. Xu	Oob' junab' xok nim rejqileem aj ch'ich' (general) pa nima q'atal tzij (Presidente). Utz ruk'u'x y saq chi rujoloom ri qata mama q'atal tzij y ub'anom k'iy chomab'aal q'atal tziij (leyes) pa ri achijab' e raal uleew. Xrelesaj ri moso'ib'-habilitadores kakik'ayij winaq pa taq pinka. Na k'o ta chik wakamik. K'iy xrelesaj ri k'as	Five years ago a great man of arms (general) entered the great government office (became president). His heart is good and his hair is white, our father and grandfather. He has made a lot of great laws on behalf of men, of sons of the earth. He took out the *ladino*

han venido el 30 de junio a las maniobras y que los mismos ladinos hombres y mujeres han visto que los mismo tomáis el machete como manejáis las armas. Si algunos leen, o leen sus hijos, es por la creación de escuelas y vigilancia para que asistan vuestros hijos, que es cosa buena para vosotros aprender a leer en las escuelas rurales: id, no tengáis miedo. Muchas cosas ha hecho el señor General Presidente, y cuyo nombre es don Jorge Ubico; obedeced y cumplid todas las leyes que es para vuestro bien y no es cosa mala lo que se os hace.

yá chihuach ko ti jun u ti kel patanic aj chich (servicio militar) u tacom jun achí cut chihué, utz hua kami ix petanac pa juhuinac lajus ic re ri huaquib ic re junab (30 de junio) y ronojel ri mozoib ruc ri rixaquil rilom ri quixvan pa nimá sac abom kó (Campo de Marte) utz chilá, utz que je lá quixchap ri machete y quix chap chich. Quix tzunic ri gug je lá u tacom u biij chiré ajahuab tinamit (Intendente) qui tac ri hual patac tijonic (escuela) manta qui xibij ta i huib. Quiy la, quiy u banom nimá ka tal tzij (Presidente) y huará ca nu coj rubi General Jorge Ubico, quimolobeg, que cuyubeg ri cu tac chihué, je lá na itzel taj cu van chihué.

ruuk' mooso'ib'. Xuuya chiwach k'o ti jun utukeel patanik aj ch'ich' (servicio militar), Utaqom jun achi k'ut chiwe. Utz wakamik ix petenaq pa juwinaq lajuj ik' re junab' (30 de junio) y ronojel ri mooso'ib' ruuk ri rixaqil rilom ri kixb'an pa nima sa ab'om k'o (Campo de Marte). Utz chila', utz ke je la kixchap ri machete y kixchap ch'ich', Kixtzu'unik ri wuj, je la utaqom ub'i chire ajawab' tinamit (Intendente). Kitaq ri iwal pa taq tijonik (escuela). Man ta kixib'ij ta iwib'. K'iy la, k'iy ub'anom nima q'atal tzij (Presidente) y waraal kanukoj rub'i' General Jorge Ubico. Kimolob'ej, kikuyub'ej ri kutaq chiwe. Je la na itzel ta kuub'an chiwe.

labor contractors that sold a lot of people to the plantations. They don't exist anymore today. He released many from debts to the *ladino*. He put before you a small service as soldiers (military service) and has sent you one man. It would be good if you all came on June the 30th[1] when all the *ladino* and their wives will see what you do at the Campo de Marte. It would be good that you hold out your machetes, that you hold out your weapons. Read books! That it what has been ordered to the mayor. Send your children to school. Do not be frightened. The president has made many, many laws. I am putting down his name here: General Jorge Ubico. Obey what he orders you to do. Thus, nothing bad will happen to you.

[1] June 30, Army Day, is a national holiday in Guatemala.

DISCIPLINA Y COLOR.

FIGURE 2.5. Indigenous militias marching on Army Day. The caption reads "DISCIPLINE AND COLOR" (Partido Liberal Progresista 1943) (courtesy of Fototeca Guatemala, CIRMA).

Grieb 1979; Hanks 2010; Matthew 2012). Another interesting example of Ubico's discursive self-construction as "protector of the Indians" is found in the captions to the official pictures in the *Album gráfico*, published in 1943 by the official Partido Liberal Progresista to commemorate thirteen years of *ubiquista* government (Partido Liberal Progresista 1943):

(2.1)
Espiritual y materialmente el general Jorge Ubico ha redimido al indio. Leyes protectoras emitidas por el han libertado de la esclavitud económica al indígena que fué durante centurias un verdadero paria, victima de la brutalidad de los patrones y de los vicios degeneradores. Dentro de su ambiente propio, fiel a sus costumbres, fiel a sus ritos, el indio se ha incorporado al progreso y en su voluntad está, y a su alcance el entrar de lleno a la vida común de todo ciudadano, cualesquiera que sean su clase o condiciones.

Spiritually and materially, General Jorge Ubico has redeemed the Indian. Protective laws that he has decreed have freed the Indigenous from economic slavery. [The Indigenous] was for centuries a true pariah, victim of brutal plant-ers and degenerative vices. In his own space, loyal to his mores and rites, the Indian has been incorporated into progress. In his will and within his reach lies now his full incorporation into the common life of every citizen, no matter what his class or conditions might be.[26]
(Partido Liberal Progresista 1943)

Text (2.1) embodies the ideological continuities between the colonial period and the Liberal dictators of the twentieth century. Indigenous peoples provided the labor with which the planter economy of the 1930s was built and were also the focus of Ubico's self-legitimizing discourse. Ubico's Spanish discourse was patronizing and racist at the same time. It negates indigenous agency and constructs the Maya as a decayed, utterly oppressed, homogeneous group. Notice the explicit preservation of "indigenous mores"—a form of boundary work—claimed by text (2.1) in spite of the "full incorporation" of indigenous peoples. Ubico's regime presupposed an ethnic division of labor in the national economy, and indigenous "mores," languages, and dress were co-opted by the Liberal state for use in boundary work (Figure 2.5).

The collusion between a priest, Teletor and a Liberal dictator, Ubico, in the *Cartilla* shows the mutual ideological dependence of the church and the planter economy of the 1930s despite the official anticlericalism of state Liberalism (Miller 1996). A significant number of Teletor's linguistic and catechetical works were produced during Ubico's tenure. The dictator was famous for micromanaging state affairs and for his tight control of presses and newspapers, especially the national press, the Tipografía Nacional, where most of Teletor's books were published (Grieb 1979). It is unlikely that Teletor would have succeeded in publishing without the explicit sanction of Ubico's government.

One of the most intriguing aspects of the *Cartilla's* K'ichee' vocabulary is its deliberate lexical purism.[27] Teletor avoided Spanish loanwords and did not hesitate to introduce his own neologisms—with their respective Spanish glosses in parentheses—when K'ichee' lexemes were lacking. The iconic relation between language and ethnicity presupposed by such practices is present also in the standardization strategies adopted by the ALMG in the 1980s and 1990s (Maxwell 1996; French 2010). It responds to overlapping European and highland Maya language ideologies in which language and ethnicity are represented as co-substantial, as we saw in Chapter 1. Teletor deliberately avoided Spanish loanwords to such an extent that intelligibility was sometimes compromised. His preference for lexical periphrasis such as *nima ka tal tzij* [*nima q'atal tzij*] "great judge" rather than the commonly used Spanish loanword *presidente*, or *ajau tinamit* [*ajaw tinamit*] "lord of the town" rather than Spanish *intendente* "presidential delegate," did not suffice to identify unambiguously the desired referent for the reader. Teletor was aware of this and provided Spanish glosses in parentheses. This juxtaposition of periphrasis and glosses entextualized ethnic boundaries and indexed the institutionalized division of labor in Ubico's planter economy. *Finqueros* "planters," teachers, army officers, and government officials were foreigners or *ladino*, while field hands, soldiers, and road workers continued to be indigenous (Cambranes 1985; Grandia 2009). This rigid ethnic hierarchy is iconically indexed through the avoidance of hybrid K'ichee'-Spanish discourse.

Lexical purism was a textual strategy to perform boundary work, a sort of co-optation of etymologically pure K'ichee' registers.

As direct heir of the Liberal state founded by Justo Rufino Barrios in 1871, Ubico's authoritarian incarnation of *indigenismo* used indigenous languages to shore up the regime's legitimacy and its racist brand of capitalism. K'ichee'—both oral and written—remained an uneasy but integral part of the thread binding Spanish colonialism and Guatemala's planter capitalism (see Figure 2.6).

2.4. Jesus Comes to Guatemala: Biblical Translation and Pentecostalism in the 1940s

The arrival of Pentecostalism in the Maya highlands in the 1930s marked another inflection in the history of writing in K'ichee'. New linguistic technologies were introduced, new topics were broached, and native speakers became junior partners in an ambitious translation program that included the teaching of literacy skills in K'ichee' communities. The achievements of evangelical translation were soon appropriated by the state, and orthographies and materials developed by the Summer Institute of Linguistics, associated with Wycliffe Bible Translators, became templates for bilingual education programs directed by the Ministry of Education, the Instituto Nacional Indigenista, and the army (French 2010; Piedrasanta 2011). In spite of the Eurocentric, assimilationist agenda inspiring many Pentecostal missionaries, their linguistic work and the successful co-optation of writing as a tool of religious proselytism helped rekindle interest in Mayan languages in the Catholic church and among indigenous intellectuals (Cabarrús 1979, 1998; Warren 1997; French 2010).

Following in the stead of William Cameron Townsend, founder of Wycliffe Bible Translators, missionary linguists working with native speakers developed a Spanish-based orthography, which they applied in a consistent and generally accurate way (Svelmoe 2008). For example, *Ri Gkagk Testament re ri Ka Nim Ajawal Jesucrist* "The New Testament of Our Lord Jesus Christ," published in K'ichee' in 1946, introduced a few digraphs and diacritic marks for K'ichee' sounds

NAHUALA

EL EXCELENTÍSIMO SEÑOR MINISTRO DE LOS ESTADOS UNIDOS EN GUATEMALA, ASISTE A LA VISITA DE INSPECCIÓN OFICIAL DEL SEÑOR PRESIDENTE DE LA REPÚBLICA, A UN PUEBLO DEL PAÍS.

FIGURE 2.6. Jorge Ubico visits the Nahualá city hall in the company of the American ambassador in 1943 (Partido Liberal Progresista 1943) (courtesy of Fototeca Guatemala, CIRMA).

TABLE 2.4. Idiosyncratic Orthographic Conventions Used in the New Testament.

IPA[1]	Colonial Script	New Testament (Anonymous 1946)	Unified Alphabet	Example	Gloss
k'	4	gk	k'	gkagk	new
q'	ɛ	k'	q'	bak'wäch	eye
t'	tt	d'	t'	d'uyulik	sitting
tʃ'	gh	ch'	ch'	ch'utin	little

[1] International Phonetic Alphabet.

lacking in Spanish (see Table 2.4). Pentecostal translators seem to have been cognizant of the colonial script, which they adopted with the exception of the graphemes listed in Table 2.1. As was the case with the Spanish-based colonial orthography, the only phonemic feature not systematically represented was vowel length.

Ri Gkagk Testament re ri Ka Nim Ajawal Jesucrist[28] (Anonymous 1946) marks a transition to a stylistically more complex and orthographically consistent prose. It is a good example of Bakhtinian polyphony outside the novel: different oral genres are woven together to achieve a terse, colorful textual unity (Bakhtin 1981). Lex-

ically, there is a preference for reviving archaic words over the creation of neologisms. Unlike Teletor's *Cartilla*, *Ri Gkagk Testament* abides by the canons of K'ichee' politeness in requests and commands. In poetic structure and lexicon it is a good instantiation of *puro K'ichee'*. The volume itself does not provide any biographic details about the translators, but it was probably done by a team of native K'ichee' translators working under the supervision of Paul Burgess and Doris M. Burgess, long-term missionaries and translators based in Quetzaltenango (Svelmoe 2008). President Juan José Arévalo (1945–1951) and the Instituto Nacional Indigenista took a keen in-

FIGURE 2.7. President Juan José Arévalo (*fourth from left*) receiving copies of the K'ichee' and Mam Bibles from the translators (courtesy of Archivo del ex-presidente Dr. Juan José Arévalo, Fototeca Guatemala, CIRMA).

terest in this translation initiative and saw it as a model for the production of educational materials in K'ichee' and Mam (see Figure 2.7).

The text in Table 2.5—Matthew 20:1–6—illustrates the linguistic continuities and novelties in this new biblical prose (Anonymous 1946). First, we continue to see a preference for archaisms and neologisms over loanwords.[29] In verse 1, for example, the nominal derivation *ajawibal*—derived from *ajaw* "lord, owner"—translates "kingdom." *Ajawibal*, also spelled *ajawbal*, is probably a neologism, as it is not attested in any colonial source. Since then, it has become a standard term in both Catholic and Protestant pastoral materials, as attested, for example, in the sacramental guides and catechisms used in the parish of Santa María Chiquimula today and in K'ichee' materials published by Jehovah's Witnesses in Guatemala (see Figure 2.8). Additionally, quantification and numerical sequence involve etymologically K'ichee' rather than Spanish cardinal and ordinal numbers, as in the heading *ujuwinak k'at* [*ujuwinaaq q'at*] "Chapter 20" in Table 2.5. This was a deliberate archaizing decision because the diffusion of Spanish arithmetic displaced K'ichee' numbers early in the twentieth century, as evidenced in the K'ichee'

narratives from Chichicastenango recorded in the 1920s by Leonhard Schultze-Jena (1933), in which Spanish decimal numerals had already replaced their K'ichee' vigesimal equivalents. K'ichee' etyma were used to index an indigenous ethnic frame (see Chapter 1), effectively placing the translation within K'ichee' discourse patterns. The New Testament in K'ichee' was meant to be an intelligible, emotionally transparent work, aiming to move and persuade the readership. Teletor's authoritarian *Cartilla*, in contrast, seems to have been intended to intimidate and impose. In terms of audience design, the two texts construct very different indigenous readerships. While their illocutionary goals were similar, the locutionary strategies were distinctly different (Austin 1975; Grice 1989).

Second, *Ri Gkagk Testament re ri Ka Nim Ajawal Jesucrist* utilizes larger lexical resources, including affect roots, and a more diverse range of styles. Affect roots include etyma referring to sound, qualia, motion, and gesture (Baronti 2001). In verse 1, for example, the intransitive *cämukukic* [*kamuquqik*] "it was dawning" identifies the time of the day when the farmer was leaving his home. The reduplication of the root vowel [u] and the final root consonant [q] in /-muq-/ is

TABLE 2.5. Matthew 20:1–6.

Original Script (Anonymous 1946)	Unified Alphabet	My Translation
Ujuwinak k'at	Ujuwinaq q'at	Chapter 20
¹Ri ajawibal que ri caj xak junam rugk jun achi rajaw ja, ri cämukukic xel-bic che qui bomaxic ajchaquib che ri u ticbal uv.	¹Ri ajawib'aal ke ri kaj xaq junam ruuk' jun achi rajaaw ja ri kamuquqik xel b'ik che kib'omaxiik ajchakib' che ri utikb'aal uuv.	¹For the kingdom of heaven is like unto a man that is an householder, which went out early in the morning to hire laborers into his vineyard.
²Aretak xugkul u wäch cugk ri ajchaquib che jujun denar ri qui k'ij, xebutak pa ri u ticbal uv.	²Aretaq xuuk'ul uwach kuuk' ri ajchakib' che jujun denar ri kiq'iij, xeb'utaq pa ri utikb'aal uv.	²And when he had agreed with the laborers for a penny a day, he sent them into his vineyard.
³Aretak xel-bic chunakaj ri rox or, xeril chi gku nigkiaj e tagkatoj quesak'orin pa ri gkayibal.	³Aretaq xel b'ik chunaqaaj ri rox oor, xeril chi k'u nik'aj etak'atoj kesaq'orin pa ri k'ayib'aal.	³And he went out about the third hour, and saw others standing idle in the marketplace.
⁴Xubij chque ri': Jix xukuje' ri ix pa ri ticbal uv, quinya-gku-na ri takal chiwe. Xebe gku wa'.	⁴Xuub'ij chike ri': Jix xuquje' ri ix pa ri tikb'aal uuv, kinya k'u na ri taqal chiwe. Xeb'e k'u wa'.	⁴And said unto them: Go ye also into the vineyard, and whatsoever is right I will give you. And they went their way.
⁵Xel-chi-bic jumul chunakaj ri uwak xukuje' ri ubelej or, xak junam xubana.	⁵Xel chi b'ik jumul chunaqaj ri uwaaq xuquje' ri ub'eleej oor, xaq junam xuub'ana.	⁵Again he went out about the sixth and ninth hour, and did likewise.
⁶Xel-gku-bic chunakaj ri ujulajuj or, xeburika chi nigkiaj e tagkatoj quesak'orinic, xubij chque: Jasche ix tagkatoj waral ronojel ri jun k'ij ix sak'orininak?	⁶Xel k'u ub'ik chunaqaaj ri ujulajuuj oor, xeb'uriqa chi nik'aj etak'atoj kesaq'orinik, xuub'ij chike: Jasche ix tak'atoj waraal ronojel ri jun q'iij ix saq'orininaq.	⁶And about the eleventh hour he went out, and found others standing idle, and saith unto them, Why stand ye here all the day idle?

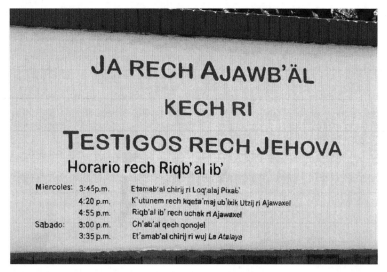

FIGURE 2.8. Sign outside a Jehovah's Witnesses Hall in San Francisco el Alto, Totonicapán: "Jehovah's Witnesses' House of the Kingdom" (photograph by Lilian Márquez).

a diagnostic of affective derivations. Such forms are abundant in poetry, games, and narratives. Another example of the subtle range of stylistic effects triggered by lexical choices is the utilization of two verbal derivations of the noun *sak'or* [*saq'oor*] "lazy": first, *e tagkatoj quesak'orinic*[30] "they were bumming around standing," and second, *ronojel ri jun k'ij ix sak'orininak?*[31] "You have been bumming around all day?" Laziness is a topic for laughter for the K'ichee'. There are scores of jokes and comic stories about lazy men and women (Hostig et al. 1995). In contrast to the solemn style that characterizes biblical registers in English and Spanish, the intrusion of *sak'oril* [*saq'ooril*] "laziness" would provoke amused reactions in the K'ichee' reader. Sacred beings in K'ichee' mythology are often involved in comic episodes, as in the adventures of the Hero Twins in the Popol Vuh. Raucous laughter, euphoric dance, and copious libation are the flesh and marrow of much K'ichee' religious ritual (Rojas Lima 1988; Tedlock 1983, 1996; Cook 2000). Lexically, *Ri Gkagk Testament* was consistent with the complex, ambivalent universe of K'ichee' religious discourse in spite of the constraints imposed by biblical translation.

The literary complexity of the gospel and the participation of native speakers in its translation opened new avenues for K'ichee' prose and revitalized it. We see later in this book that the consequences of this breakthrough resonate in the work of even contemporary K'ichee' writers who have explicitly rejected Christianity. The *Ri Gkagk Testament*'s prose, defined by lexical purism and a style reminiscent of *puro K'ichee'*, embodies an "indigenous" frame and makes the text, first, discursively intelligible and, second, emotionally moving. *Ri Gkagk Testament* exploits the indexical, stylistic resources of the K'ichee' language, successfully constructing a text that is indigenous in form if not in content. It performs ethnic "boundary work" (see Chapter 1), avoiding "Spanish" discourse and foregrounding styles and lexicon emblematic of "tradition."

Recently, the materials published by evangelical missionaries have been severely criticized by linguists and Maya activists. The missionaries'

religious agenda, conservative politics, and collusion with the state have been rightfully denounced (Stoll 1993; Cojtí 1995; England 2003; French 2010; Konefal 2010). However, their seminal influence in the contemporary revival of writing in Maya languages, especially K'ichee', has not been sufficiently recognized. In addition to rekindling interest in indigenous languages among churches and state institutions, missionary linguists and their collaborators alphabetized hundreds of catechists in the highlands. They also introduced the methods of modern linguistics into the standardization debate and opened new avenues for written discourse, which became stylistically more complex as a result of the innovative collaboration between linguists and native speakers, even if the latter played a subordinate role.

2.5. Democracy and Civil Rights in K'ichee': The Mayanization of Writing

The path to democracy in Guatemala after a long series of military rulers began with the drafting of a new constitution in 1985. It signaled a return to the rule of law and was the first step in ending the long civil war (Schirmer 1999; Jonas 2000).[32] Although the army continued to kidnap, torture, and murder opposition activists, the Guatemalan state began to respond to pressure from human rights groups, and civil society and institutional spaces began to open for Maya activists, especially those with a cultural and linguistic bent (Nelson 1999; Bastos and Camus 2003a; Manz 2004; Konefal 2010). Having opponents both left and right of the political spectrum, pan-Maya activists seized the stalemate between the army and revolutionary groups in the 1980s as an opportunity to gain societal recognition and the status of state interlocutors on matters directly affecting indigenous communities (Cojtí 1995; Fischer 1996; Warren 1997; Nelson 1999; Morales 2002; Bastos and Camus 2003).

As a gesture of rekindled interest in indigenous peoples, the new constitution was rapidly translated into the four Mayan languages with the largest numbers of speakers: Mam, K'ichee', Kaqchikel, and Q'eqchi'. Changes in the texture of discourse in indigenous languages have accompanied all major transformations of the colonial and republican orders, as we have seen in this chapter, and the publication of the constitution was no exception. It was a milestone marking the onset of Mayanization as a form of state discourse, the last in a long series of attempts to co-opt indigenous languages for changing state agendas (Asamblea Nacional Constituyente 1986).[33] Mayanization entails not only a particular ethnic perspective on the violence and structural inequalities bedeviling the nation-state of Guatemala but also innovative stylistic configurations of discourse in indigenous languages. Mayanization is about linguistic form, not just content, and accordingly it subtly exploits the indexical and stylistic resources of Mayan languages, especially K'ichee' (see Chapter 6).

When the new constitution was officially promulgated in 1985, the unified alphabet had not yet become official. In fact, the K'ichee' version was one of the last official publications in the old orthography developed by missionary linguists in the 1930s (Asamblea Nacional Constituyente 1986). Mayanization was already an accomplished linguistic project, however. Created by activists working outside the state who were admittedly seeking to transform it, it entered official discourse in the mid-1980s. The K'ichee' version of the constitution displays some of the features that distinguish "Mayanized" discourse from other pro-indigenous state discourses. First, the iconic relation between ethnicity and lexicon continues to constrain lexical choices: it shows a marked preference for periphrasis and neologism rather than borrowing from Spanish (see Table 2.6).

Table 2.6 lists a few items in the glossary at the end of the *Constitución política de la república de Guatemala en idioma quiché* "Political Constitution of the Republic of Guatemala in K'ichee' Translation" (Asamblea Nacional Constituyente 1986). Most are indeed phrasal paraphrases or one-word definitions. For example, the Spanish *Registro de la Propiedad* "Property Registrar" becomes *Ri k'atbal tzij jawi catz'ibax wi ronojel uwujil ulew* "Government office where all land deeds are registered," and *república* "republic" is

glossed as *nim tinimit* "great/large town." K'ichee' did not have a systematic adaptation of Spanish legal terms when the translation went to print. The translators avoided Spanish loanwords, but their paraphrases were not always successful in unambiguously identifying the desired referents. It must be granted to the translators, however, that constitutional discourse is a legal genre that does not allow much leeway for creative rephrasing. An accurate paraphrase of the constitution in terms familiar for a K'ichee' reader unacquainted with the Guatemalan legal system would have required hundreds of additional pages. Furthermore, this publication was meant as a *visible* iconic artifact to be displayed, not only *read*, and had to be woven with etymologically K'ichee' threads, even if they did not always successfully perform their role as referring expressions.[34]

Second, Mayanization is evident in the militant, assertive, and richly evocative language used to translate Spanish legal formulae, as seen in text (2.2):

(2.2)
Ucaj takanic—Ri yatalic ruc' ri xak junam cakil kib. Pa ri nimalaj tinimit Guatemala, conojel ri uwinakil xak e junam quilic xukuje' xa junam ri yatalic ya'om chique. Ri achi ruc' ri ixok wene' c'ulanic wene man e c'ulan taj xak junam quibanic, xukuje' xa junam ri quekle'n. Man yatal che jun winak cuban käx che jun uwinakil chic. Ronojel ri winak rajawaxic cacaj quib. (Asamblea Nacional Constituyente 1986)

Fourth commandment: Rights and equality [before the law]. In the Republic of Guatemala all inhabitants have equal dignity and rights. Men and women whether single or married have the same opportunities and responsibilities. No one has the right to harm someone else. It is necessary that all people love each other.[35]

Text (2.2) reproduces Article 4 of the constitution. Identifying it as a *taqanik* "command," rather than *artículo* "article" as in the original Spanish, enhances its performative force and

TABLE 2.6. Some Neologisms in the K'ichee' Version of the Guatemalan Constitution.

K'ichee' Neologism[1]	Spanish Gloss	English Gloss of the K'ichee'	English Gloss of the Spanish
Aj waral	Guatemalteco	Local	Guatemalan
Comon winak nim queta'mabal	Colegio de profesionales	Association of people with great knowledge	Professional associations
E jupuk winak quituquel wi	Empresa privada	Group of people who are on their own	Private business
Jamaril	Paz	Quiet	Peace
Man je ta wa cubij	Excepción	It does not say that	Exception
Nimaq taq eta'mabal	Ciencia	Great knowledge	Science
Maj jun c'o puwi' ri k'atbal tzij	Soberanía	There is no one over the government	Sovereignty
Nimalaj k'atbal tzij	Estado	Great government	State
Nim tinimit	República	Great town	Republic
Ri k'atbal tzij jawi catz'ibax wi ronojel uwujil ulew	Registro General de la Propiedad	Government office where all land deeds are registered	Property Registrar
Ri nimalaj aj c'amal be	Ministro	Great guide	Minister
Ri ajk'axal tak tzij	Medios de comunicación	Deliverers of information	Media
Ri winak nimak quibanic	Funcionarios	Important people	Government officials
Yatalic	Derecho	Deserving	Right
Yatalic winakil	Derechos humanos	What people intrinsically deserve	Human rights
Usac'ajil kape pa ri chomabal	Iniciativa	Intelligent thought	Initiative
Ch'ich' k'axal tzij	Radio	Device to deliver words	Radio
Ri cuterenej ri tijonic	Fines de la educación	What education aims for	Educational goals
Ri yatalik caquiban ri winak	Derechos	What people have the right to do	Rights

Note: English glosses are by the author.
[1] I am preserving the original spellings of Constituyente (1986).

adds urgency to its subject matter. Referring to the citizens of the republic, it admonishes that they are equal in rights and obligations: *conojel ri uwinakil xak e junam quilic xukuje' xa junam ri yatalic ya'om chique*[36] "All inhabitants have equal dignity and rights." The nominal form *junam* "same, one, together" is dense with cultural associations and evokes principles of K'ichee' *communitas*, extending them to the entire national territory and all its inhabitants.

"Dignity" is translated as *quilik* "their look," which foregrounds physical differences among the citizenry. In Guatemala, even though phenotypic differences are not marked, ethnic boundaries are expressed in a language that is markedly racist (Casáus-Arzú 1998; González-Ponciano 2004; Hale 2006). An abstract noun is thus rendered physically concrete, sharpening its rhetorical force. In this way, as the constitution is translated, the text is recreated for K'ichee' readers. These powerful indexical associations are absent in the original Spanish. The racist foundations of the republic are thus being doubly undermined: first in the original Spanish and again in the K'ichee' version. However, few *ladinos* would be aware of the latter, as very few are literate in K'ichee'.

Pan-Maya activists succeeded in subverting the traditional division of labor between the Spanish and Mayan languages in state discourses. Since the Spanish conquest, neither the Spanish nor the Guatemalan republic abandoned writing in Mayan languages as a vehicle for governance and legitimation; nevertheless, never before was it deemed necessary to translate into a Mayan language the basic law of the republic. The K'ichee' were meant to obey it, not to enforce it, much less to read it in their own language. State-sponsored publications in indigenous languages had been restricted to educational materials, health brochures, and compilations of oral traditions. That the state was forced to expand the fields in which it produced texts in indigenous languages attests to the success of pan-Mayanism. It also shows flexibility and the will to accommodate and absorb new discourses in indigenous languages without necessarily carrying out the socio-political reforms needed to empower Maya peoples. In fact, multiculturalism is arguably hegemonic in today's Guatemalan state.

Mayanization has led to sometimes acrimonious debate among Maya leaders and intellectuals regarding cultural legitimacy, representation, and engagement with the body politic. Reconciling local interests and the plurality of ethnic frames inhabited by the highland Maya within a unified pan-Mayanist discourse and leadership has been a rocky endeavor, to say the least. Language standardization has been a stage on which conflicting agendas and opposing ideologies have played out. As we see in the next section, while the debate is apparently about orthographic conventions, what is at stake is control over discourse in indigenous languages and the co-optation of an ethnic frame that is not just *indígena* but also *Maya*.

2.6. Alphabets, Mayanization, and Resistance

Late in the summer of 2008, after many years of inconclusive discussion, the members of the K'iche' Mayab' Cholchi' (Academy of the K'ichee' Language) finally agreed on a prescriptive norm to represent vowel-length distinctions in the new standard alphabet (see Figure 2.9). In K'ichee', vowel length is a phonemic category, that is, the duration of vocalic articulations can be the sole difference between otherwise homophonous words. A minimal pair such as [tʃax] "pine" and [tʃa:x] "ashes" is perceptibly distinguished by vowel length: the first is short whereas the second is noticeably longer, especially when the two are uttered in sequence.[37] The decision not to represent vowel length was the culmination of more than a decade of fractious disagreement among K'ichee' language activists. The arguments were apparently about the technical convenience of one or another orthographic convention,[38] but the roots of the conflict were deeper, involving K'ichee' conceptions of language, ethnicity, and self-representation. Activists' emotional identification with their own regional varieties made consensual decisions very hard to achieve. Furthermore, K'ichee' communities sometimes questioned the academy's mandate: how could a government institution make decisions about the way K'ichee' communities should speak? Staff turnover at the K'iche' Mayab' Cholchi' also made it hard to maintain a sense of continuity and cumulative progress in decision making (Luis Enrique Sam Colop, personal communication 2006).

K'ichee' language activists were caught in a Saussurean dichotomy in their zeal to construct a unified pan-K'ichee' alphabet. There is a clear

FIGURE 2.9. Headquarters of the K'iche' Mayab' Cholchi' (Academy of the K'ichee' Language) in Santa Cruz del Quiché, Guatemala, in 2008 (photograph by Sergio Romero).

isomorphism between Saussure's *langue*—the ordered system of synchronic rules generating grammatical sentences in the language—and the standardized orthographic conventions established for K'ichee', on the one hand, and between *parole*—the messy realization of *langue* in embodied natural speech—and the phonologies of the regional and stylistic varieties of each local dialect, on the other (Saussure 1968). The construction of local varieties as *parole* and the standard as *langue* was perceived as the imposition of an artificial norm that many activists felt did not reflect their hometown's speech. The debate became so bitter that some dissidents were accused of divisive localism and a lukewarm commitment to pan-Maya struggles, threatening the success of shared political goals. Some called for the expulsion of foreign linguists who expressed strong views on the subject (Narciso Cojtí, personal communication, 2005).

Technical arguments obscured the profound cultural association between regional speech markers and local ethnic identification in K'ichee', as we saw in Chapter 1. It is well known that in societies in which dialectal differences are emblematic, mutual intelligibility does not guarantee the smooth construction of a standard form that transcends local identities (Silverstein 2000). In K'ichee' the theatrical performance of ethnicity is grounded on a semiotic ideology

that turns emblematic cultural artifacts such as local dialects, traditional dress, ritual calendars, and artisanal specializations into iconic indices of ethnic affiliation (Tedlock and Tedlock 1985). The iconic construal of dialect stereotypes shapes K'ichee' representations of language, explaining also the important indexical role of Spanish loanwords and K'ichee'-Spanish code switching. Identification with local varieties is not only a factum of dialect geography or local politics but also an active structural principle of interaction. It is the point of articulation of political economy, ethnicity, and linguistic practice, bringing together not only the performance of boundary work but also pragmatic tropes in which dialectal emblems act as stance markers, stylistic cues, and discourse register repertoires.[39]

To understand the contentious nature of K'ichee' orthographic conventions requires a consideration of K'ichee' semiotic ideologies.[40] K'ichee' language ideology posits an iconic relationship between local varieties, ethnic identification, and interaction frames. The scholarly literature on the K'ichee', however, tends to identify language boundaries with unspecified "ethnolinguistic groups" without any elaboration of the social meaning of such a category within K'ichee' communities themselves. Benedict Anderson's teleological presupposition that language boundaries defined in terms of mutual intelligibility must necessarily coincide with national or ethnic boundaries is widespread in Maya studies (Anderson 2006; Gabbert 2006). Furthermore, discussions of ethnicity among Mayanist scholars and Maya activists have concentrated on the historical and socio-political implications of the ethnic dichotomy *indio/ ladino*,[41] or in more contemporary guise *maya/ mestizo*, in the modern Guatemalan nation-state (Nelson 1999; Fischer 2001; Cojtí 1995; González Ponciano 2004; Hale 2004; Casáus-Arzú 1998; Guzmán-Boeckler 1970; Martínez-Peláez 1970; Maxwell 1986; Morales 2002; Velásquez 2000; Warren 1978, 1997). This emphasis has certainly furthered our understanding of the Guatemalan body politic and the historical roots of the marginalization of the Maya since the Spanish invasion, but it also has minimized the socio-political role of local constructions of identity and the long history of interaction and conflict among indigenous communities, not always mediated by Spanish officials or *ladinos*. Such views have also overlooked the communicative grounds of ethnicity in the Maya highlands. Local identities and the *indígena/ladino* dichotomy coexist and structure linguistic interactions as alternative ethnic frames that the Maya strategically inhabit in different social spaces and speech events (see Chapter 1). They are not simply ideological constructs but concrete regimentations of discourse and indexical practice, the precipitate of more than five hundred years of colonial history. The perspectives on ethnicity in Guatemala dominant in the literature privilege the *indígena/ladino* frame at the expense of other local identities, patterns of interaction, and interethnic conflict, all of which are as crucial as the former for interpreting the social history and communicative performance of the Maya today.

The precise demarcation of ethnic boundaries has been a controversial subject in Guatemala. First of all, the spatial distribution of ethnic groups does not always overlap with the boundaries of the *municipio* "township," the smallest geographic circumscription in the Guatemalan nation-state. It has been argued in the anthropological literature that the *municipio* is the fundamental sociopolitical unit for the Maya,

as the historical and cultural continuity between prehispanic polities and many highland *municipios* is well documented (Tax 1956; Wolf 1958; Colby 1969; Brintnall 1979; Bunzel 1981; Hill and Monaghan 1987; Piel 1989; Carmack 1995; Becker Richards 1998; Van Akkeren 2000; González 2002; Fischer 2001; Gabbert 2004).

The model of the "peasant closed corporate community" was dominant in the 1960s among Mayanists. It posited an isolated, culturally and linguistically homogeneous community bound by a common history and traditions as the fundamental social unit in Mesoamerica. Spatially, it generally coincided with the *municipio*, direct descendant of the Spanish *reducción*. Ethnicity was conceptualized as the result of sets of more or less permanent diagnostic artifacts, practices, and ideologies rather than the result of boundary work (Wolf 1957, 1958). The model was rightfully criticized for being rigidly ahistorical and for ignoring the internal complexity of indigenous communities (Warren 1978; Wolf 1982; Nelson 1999; Fischer 2001; Carmack et al. 2006). It made inconsistencies and idiosyncrasies in locality and ethnic boundary making invisible. Furthermore, migrations and changes in the political status of submunicipal circumscriptions such as villages and hamlets have modified township boundaries, rendering the overlap between *municipio* and ethnic group an imperfect approximation.

In multiethnic *municipios* such as Zacualpa, east of the Department of El Quiché, at least two different K'ichee'-speaking groups with distinct ethnic identities coexist.[42] They speak different regional varieties; women wear distinct emblematic outfits; and each group follows a different ritual calendar. Migrants from Chichicastenango, called Maxeños or Maxes [maʃes], settled in two haciendas west of the township seat, which they had purchased from a wealthy local *ladino* family (McCreery 1994). Maxeños congregated in two separate villages on the former hacienda grounds, San Antonio Sinaché and Chixacol, where they held individual family plots. Current residents claim descent from the first Maxeño settlers. The descendants of the *ladino* landowning family that sold the property are regularly invited to participate in village patron saint feasts and school graduations in the two Maxeño villages. These ritual visits recapitulate the foundational event in the history of the community: the acquisition of the hacienda from a local family that granted the Maxeños a legitimate claim to Zacualpa lands. Ethnic Zacualpeños,[43] who regard themselves as the only true descendants of the original inhabitants, are excluded from ownership of Maxeño lands unless they marry in.

Linguistic variation and ethnic representation are therefore intertwined in K'ichee' language ideologies. The iconization of language and ethnicity is embodied in phonological and lexical alternations independently of denotation of linguistic expressions.[44] The K'ichee' selectively recruit this variation to index ethnic affiliation, interaction frames, and derived indexical effects. This is crucial in three sociolinguistic fields: dialectal variation (Chapter 3), code switching (Chapter 4), and reverential speech (Chapter 5), which are explored in the following chapters.

2.7. Bill Gates Speaks K'ichee': Globalization and K'ichee' Writers

We have explored in this chapter the complex history of writing in K'ichee' since the Spanish arrived in 1523. Contrary to the circular claims of scholars presupposing that native writing possesses the intrinsic capacity to subvert colonial structures (Rabasa 2011; Pizzigoni 2013), writing in K'ichee' has played a changing but crucial role as vehicle for indoctrination, administration, and ideological co-optation. The K'ichee' maintained a dynamic and tense, if ever subordinate, interaction with external religious and political entities mediated by oral and written discourses in both their own language and Spanish. From the exquisite homilies of Fray Domingo de Vico, through the uncouth, rambling exhortations of Celso Teletor, to the glib biblical translation of William Cameron Townsend's cohorts, Christianity and colonialism have spoken and written in K'ichee'. Nevertheless, responding to relentless native resistance, on the one hand, and changing Spanish and *ladino* elite needs, on the other, such discourses have shifted in form from the sixteenth century, when Dominicans and Fran-

ciscans spearheaded linguistic *reducción*, to the present. To understand the complex history of writing in K'ichee' and other Mayan languages, we must therefore acknowledge the capacity of non-Maya institutions to engage and subtly modify K'ichee' language practices, including writing, often in unforeseen ways (Bryce Heath 1972; Burkhart 1989; Durston 2007; Hanks 2010).

The Foucaultian archive, briefly introduced earlier, helps us understand the constraining role of church and state discourse in K'ichee' discourse history. Colonial doctrinal registers, state *indigenismo*, Protestant translation, and Mayanization mark successive stages in the history of the K'ichee' archive, creating the conditions for intelligible indexical orders and intertextual relations. Each of these stages involved subtle and not-so-subtle adjustments, innovations, and recalibrations—both lexical and discursive—of K'ichee' linguistic practices. Writing, in particular, has undergone substantial transformations in form and content since 1523, as we have seen in this chapter.

The K'ichee', for their part, have contributed to the archive, appropriating colonial innovations to carve for themselves spaces for autonomous creation and creative resistance. From the *cholq'ij* composed in the Latin script and surreptitiously shared among *ajq'ijab'* "calendar specialists" in the sixteenth and seventeenth centuries, to the cadences of Humberto Akabal's poetry and the gritty words of political graffiti on the walls of government buildings in Guatemala City in the twenty-first century, the K'ichee' have successfully used alphabetic writing in the task of self re-creation and boundary work, affirming their unique histories and distinct cultural identities in the midst of an ever-changing, globalized society (see Figure 2.10). Through the linguistic construction of culturally different, and at times structurally hybrid, ethnic frames the K'ichee' have themselves co-opted the rhetorical weapons of colonialism. This dialectic between co-optation and resistance continues to leave its imprint in the Maya movement today.

The success of the Maya movement in enhancing the public role of writing in Mayan languages has brought new dilemmas with it,

FIGURE 2.10. K'ichee' graffiti in Guatemala City: *Ronojel chujkastajok* "Let's all awaken!" (photograph by Lilian Márquez).

however. The social capital wielded by indigenous movements in the global market is being co-opted by corporate forces previously indifferent to indigenous cultures (Comaroff and Comaroff 2009). In 2012, for example, Microsoft became interested in translating its Office software to K'ichee' and hired a Spanish consultant to organize a team of translators in Guatemala. After contacting a few well-known native K'ichee' professionals who showed no interest in doing the translation on Microsoft's meager terms, the Spanish consultant subcontracted the services of a *ladino* anthropologist from Guatemala City who had recently developed some fluency in K'ichee' by attending courses offered by the Academy of Mayan Languages of Guatemala (ALMG). He proceeded to hire a group of young K'ichee' speakers from Nahualá, paying them a fixed rate per number of words translated (Diego Alburez, personal communication 2012). Microsoft prohibited the team members from sharing any of their translations before the 2015 release of the new Office version, thus appropriating their work, which may well have been the first systematic attempt to develop the lexicon of "computerese" in K'ichee' (Elena Tambriz, personal communication 2013). Furthermore, the lack of consultation with township authorities led to the ostracization in Nahualá of some of the translators, who were seen as usurping collective knowledge and violating traditional consensus practices for a profit (Juan Manuel Tahay,

personal communication 2013). To add insult to injury, the Nahualá-based translators offered to translate the entire Facebook lexicon for free, via a corporate proxy based in the United States.

As with other forms of indigenous cultural capital, as documented by Comaroff and Comaroff (2009) and Little (2004), corporations have started to appropriate the K'ichee' language, turning it for the first time into a commodity useful in casting themselves as progressive, politically correct institutions. The standardization efforts of the K'iche' Mayab' Cholchi' are undermined by such initiatives, however, given the already contentious relations between local communities and academy officials. These initiatives bypass the fragile pan-K'ichee' consensus and raise questions about the viability of a centralized institution to regulate standard usage in today's globalized world. Microsoft's inexhaustible coffers seem to be gaining the upper hand over the interethnic consensus strategy that K'ichee' language activists had agreed on in the early 1980s (England 2003; Maxwell 1996; French 2010).

In a globalized world, corporations have joined churches and the state as institutional powers co-opting writing in K'ichee'. We cannot predict how Maya institutions will react to such neocolonial appropriations of indigenous knowledge, although if past history is a clue, such challenges will probably be met in ever more creative ways by activists.

Notes

1. The *policía* consisted of Spanish political institutions as well as ritual and moral norms regulating the life of the ideal Christian, well-ordered polity.
2. *Lenguas*—from the Spanish "tongues"—were Spanish clergy fluent in indigenous languages.
3. There is some evidence of continuity in elite social class background between prehispanic and colonial K'ichee' scribes. Not long after the Spanish took control, however, the power and privileges of Maya nobles waned and control of the office of town scribe was no longer their exclusive privilege.
4. *Criollos* were ethnic Spaniards born in the Americas. *Lienzos* were paintings combining pictographic and logosyllabic images executed on cloth or animal skins.
5. The form *popol* is a nominal derivation of *pop* "mat." The suffix /–Vl/ is known as the "abstract" marker and indexes an intimate relationship between the referent of the free morpheme and the referent of the derived "abstract" form. The mat was the symbol of the K'ichee' ruler, who was known as *aj pop* "He of the Mat." The derived noun *popol* referenced the signs and practice of kingly rule in prehispanic polities.
6. There is indirect evidence that K'ichee' writing was similar in structure to Aztec writing. For many years, the consensus among Mesoamericanists was that the latter was "pictographic," lacking systematic correspondences between graphemes and linguistic structures. However, recent work by Alfonso Lacadena argues persuasively that Aztec writing was logosyllabic, like other documented Mesoamerican writing systems (lowland Maya, Epi-Olmec, and Zapotec) (Lacadena 2008). This opens the tantalizing possibility of a structural convergence between Maya lowland and highland writing.
7. Alphabetic writing systems are based on correspondences between phonemes and graphemes whereas logosyllabic systems establish correspondences between syllables and graphemes.
8. Other Maya languages were used in *reducción* in the highlands of Guatemala, but Kaqchikel and K'ichee' were the first. K'ichee', however, played a crucial role as poetic and lexical template (see Chapter 6).
9. The Spanish colonial legal edifice was built on different bodies of laws, rights, and obligations for Spanish and indigenous subjects. They are referenced respectively with the terms *república*

de españoles and *república de indios*. The latter guaranteed indigenous communities a measure of political autonomy and government protection of communal lands (Cortez y Larraz 1958; Cambranes 1985; Taracena 1997; Woodward 1993).
10. From the Spanish for "talk," *pláticas* were models for homilies and other forms of public doctrinal discourse written in indigenous languages for the benefit of Spanish priests lacking the proficiency to write their own.
11. Clerical attitudes toward indigenous languages show some regional variation. The production of original pastoral texts in K'ichee' lessened, but in Q'eqchi' they continued to be written and copied, as attested by various pastoral manuscripts scattered in libraries in North America. A comparative study of colonial pastoral writing in K'iche'an languages remains to be done (see Romero [2011] for more detail).
12. The most notable linguistic work of this period is Francisco Ximénez's *Arte de las tres lenguas*, originally published in 1772, which inaugurated the genre of comparative grammar in Mayan languages, describing in adjacent, parallel columns the phonology and morphology of Kaqchikel, K'ichee', and Tz'utujil (Ximénez 1993). A Dominican priest, Ximénez also discovered the original manuscript of the Popol Vuh, which he transcribed and translated into Spanish.
13. Interest in indigenous languages, especially K'ichee' and Kaqchikel, was revived among Guatemalan intellectuals as well. José Villacorta and Adrián Recinos, for example, produced their famous historical works and translations of the *Memorial de Tecpán-Atitlán*, the Popol Vuh, and other indigenous chronicles in the 1930s and 1940s.
14. *Indigenismo* refers loosely to Latin American ideologies articulating representations of indigenous peoples and their present social conditions, on the one hand, and the state and national projects, on the other.
15. This law forced subsistence farmers owning small plots to spend one week per year working in road construction. It was used to recruit laborers for Ubico's grand public works.
16. Topics of Teletor's *pláticas* include public health, national feasts, denunciations of thievery and witchcraft, planting techniques, the three official branches of government, the civic value of work and education, and the prevention of disease.

17. This orthographic idiosyncrasy was probably meant to represent the variable allophonic assibilation of /tʃ/ in fast speech.

18. A more accurate spelling would have been—in the colonial script—*quinghaw chiwe*.

19. *Kitaq iwal pa taq tijob'aal. Man ta kixib'ij ta iwib'!*

20. This could simply be a mistake or hesitation on the part of Teletor regarding audience design.

21. *Kimolob'ej, kikuyub'ej ri kuutaq chiwe. Je la na itzel taj kuub'an chiwe.*

22. *Utz ruk'u'x y saq chi rujoloom ri qatata (qa) mama q'atal tziij.*

23. *I ub'anom k'iy chomab'aal q'atal tziij [leyes] pa ri achijab' eral uleew.*

24. *Xrelesaj ri moso'ib' abilitadores kakik'ayij winaq pa taq pinka.* Due to Teletor's phonetic spelling, there was no past tense marking on the main verb in this sentence. Past tense markers are often elided in fast speech.

25. David Vela, editor of *El Imparcial*, was an enthusiastic *indigenista* and a member of the executive committee of the Instituto Indigenista Latinoamericano despite Ubico's opposition (Castillo Taracena 2013).

26. My translation.

27. Nevertheless, the *Cartilla* ignored native language ideologies in which K'ichee' and Achi are construed as different languages. The fact that Teletor's text—redacted in Achi—passed as K'ichee' for the publishers is further evidence that the colonial standard, based on western K'ichee', had been abandoned.

28. *Ri K'ak' Testament re ri Qanimajawal Jesukriist.*

29. The translators used some loanwords, however. In Figure 2.7 *denar* "denary" and *uv* "grape" were not replaced with neologisms.

30. *E tak'atoj kesaq'oorinik.*

31. *Ronojel ri jun q'ij ix saq'oorininaq.*

32. The war started in 1960, six years after the overthrow of the democratically elected government of President Jacobo Arbenz during a CIA-sponsored coup in 1954. It lasted until 1996, when peace accords were signed between state and guerrilla representatives. During most of those thirty-six years military strong men governed Guatemala.

33. Not all state institutions have embraced the discourse of Mayanization. In fact, other than in the realms of education, culture, and language policy, Mayanization has led to few substantial changes in state policy.

34. In the 1990s the K'iche' Mayab' Cholchi' (Academy of the K'ichee' Language) published several volumes of neologisms that have slowly been trickling into official translations and educational materials.

35. My translation.

36. *Konojeel ri uwinaqiil xaq e junam kiliik xuquje' xa junam ri yatalik ya'om chike.*

37. This picture is complicated by the fact that not all K'ichee' varieties phonetically realize vowel-length distinctions in the same manner. Several dialects realize long/short vowel contrasts as tense/lax articulations.

38. Some believed that long vowels should be spelled as geminates, that is, long /a/ should be spelled with the digraph "aa" and short /a/ as a simplex "a." Others contended that long vowels should be adopted as orthographic default with short vowels taking a diacritic mark. Thus, long /a/ should be represented as "a" and short /a/ as "ä" with a dieresis. Finally, a third group argued that it was not necessary to mark vowel-length distinctions at all as native speakers would be able to read the difference from context. Furthermore, ignoring vowel length had the advantage of making spelling easier for learners.

39. A register of discourse is a "performable model of action linking speech repertoires to stereotypic indexical values, which is recognized as such by a particular population" (Agha 2007:81)

40. Semiotic ideologies are cultural conceptions about the relations between signs and the objects they represent.

41. The term *indio* refers to an ethnically indigenous person, while *ladino* refers to someone who refuses or is denied an indigenous identification. Both categories are heterogeneous in membership and problematic in explanatory accuracy, but they are crucial to understanding Guatemalans' representations of themselves as well as power relations in the republic.

42. By multiethnic *municipios* I mean those with ethnically diverse indigenous populations, not only those having *ladino* as well as indigenous inhabitants.

43. Spanish gentilic for Zacualpa.

44. "Iconization involves a transformation of the sign relationship between linguistic features (or varieties) and the social images with which they are linked. Linguistic features that index social groups or activities appear to be iconic representations of them, as if a linguistic feature somehow depicted or displayed a social group's inherent nature or essence" (Irvine and Gal 2000:37).

CHAPTER 3

"Each Town Speaks Its Own Language"

The Social Value of Dialectal Variation in K'ichee'

3.1. How to Ask Questions in "Pure" K'ichee'

When I first met Guayo, an energetic thirty-two-year-old but also a living encyclopedia of Santa María Chiquimula's traditional lore despite his relatively young age, he was taken aback by this foreign-looking Guatemalan addressing him in K'ichee'. The K'ichee' are not used to hearing foreigners—especially non-indigenous Guatemalans—speak their language fluently, and when they do, they provoke admiration, merriment, curiosity, and/or mistrust.[1] K'ichee' speakers feel compelled sometimes to test the foreigner's knowledge or to show off their own skills performing marked or archaic registers and deliberately avoiding Spanish loanwords and code switching. I had witnessed such ethnolinguistic validations, focusing on archaic lexicon and numbers, for example.[2] However, that afternoon Guayo made me aware that the way in which you ask questions matters as well. He quickly overcame his initial surprise after my polite [Uc watʃ lah, ta:t?][3] "How are you, sir?" and asked:

(3.1)
Jas ab'iʔ
xas a-6iʔ
what 2sE-name
What is your name?

(Guayo, 32 years old,
Santa María Chiquimula)

I was surprised to hear that he introduced the question in text (3.1) with the interrogative pronoun [xas] rather than [su], the form normally used in Santa María Chiquimula.[4] The alternation [xas]/[su] defines a dialectal isogloss between western and central K'ichee' dialects. I was aware that in K'ichee' townships southwest of Santa María Chiquimula [xas] was the unmarked interrogative pronoun, but I was not expecting a Chiquimula, especially one of Guayo's identification with local traditions, to choose a lexical stereotype of another township to index his *best* K'ichee'. The pronoun [xas] is construed in Santa María as a stereotype of the neighboring township of Totonicapán, where it is the form most commonly used in wh-questions (see Figure 2.2). I later learned, however, that Chiquimulas use it also to mark a stylistic shift to *puro K'ichee'*, a discourse register iconic of essentialist representations of traditional culture indexed by archaic lexicon and the avoidance of Spanish loanwords. Chiquimulas consider Totonicapán more "traditional" and successful in preserving the ancestors' ways, and construe the Totonicapán dialect as purer than Santa María Chiquimula's (Romero 2006). Synchronically, the stylistic shift entailed by [xas] is laminated on its status as Totonicapán stereotype. Indexical oppositions such as [su]/[xas] presuppose Santa María Chiquimula's regional ethnoscape as indexical background. K'ichee' "folk" dialectologies flow from a linguistic ideology in which

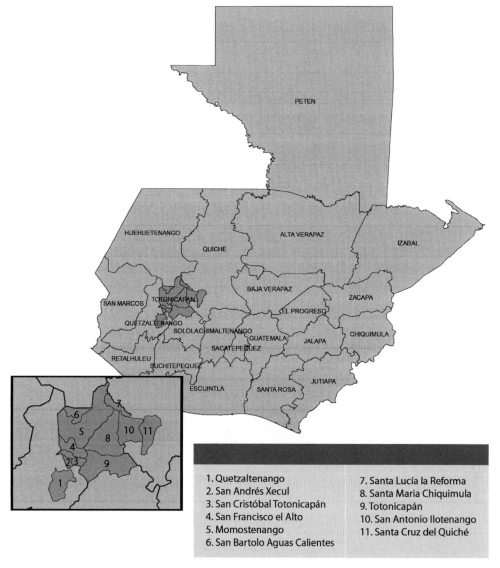

1. Quetzaltenango
2. San Andrés Xecul
3. San Cristóbal Totonicapán
4. San Francisco el Alto
5. Momostenango
6. San Bartolo Aguas Calientes
7. Santa Lucía la Reforma
8. Santa Maria Chiquimula
9. Totonicapán
10. San Antonio Ilotenango
11. Santa Cruz del Quiché

FIGURE 3.1. Santa María Chiquimula and neighboring townships (map by Luís Velásquez).

different ethnic groups entail distinct linguistic codes. Pragmatically, the latter act as indexical tropes cuing speaker stance, stylistic shifts, and ethnic frames.

3.2. Linguistic Stereotypes and Language Ideologies in Santa María Chiquimula

Santa María Chiquimula is a township of about forty-five thousand inhabitants spread over an irregular geography of high mountains and deep ravines (see Figure 3.1). Only five thousand

people live in the town, which is also the township seat. The rest live in sixteen rural circumscriptions subdivided into fairly dispersed villages associated with patrilineal lineages called *q'alpul* in MAR (Figure 3.2).[5]

Until recently Chiquimula's livelihood depended on subsistence agriculture combined with periodic trips to the cotton, sugarcane, and coffee plantations in the southern piedmont during harvest season. The village was, and to a large extent still is, the center of social life.

FIGURE 3.2. The village of Chuisihuan, Santa María Chiquimula (photograph by Sergio Romero).

Villagers visit the town every Thursday for the weekly market, participating in municipal, religious, and political institutions such as religious sodalities, Pentecostal churches, and various unremunerated but important positions in the *q'atb'al tziij*, or city hall. Until the late nineteenth century, relative isolation and agricultural self-sufficiency allowed nearly all Chiquimulas to spend most of their lives within the township limits, where they depended on local social networks for survival (McCreery 1994).

Today Santa María Chiquimula is often represented as poor and backward by its neighbors. It borders on three sides with wealthy K'ichee' townships, seats of large weekly markets and renowned in Guatemala for their industries: Totonicapán, Momostenango, and San Francisco el Alto (see Figure 3.1). In these towns the Chiquimula "accent" indexes poverty, spatial isolation, and the rejection of "progress." In my visits to Totonicapán and San Francisco el Alto, it was often deplored how poor and until recently how isolated Santa María Chiquimula was. Chiquimulas were thought to be mistrustful, prone to violence, and so wary of strangers as to avoid sending their children to school (Marco Tulio Cutz,

personal communication 2005; Ricardo Falla, personal communication 2005). Chiquimulas themselves, however, seldom had to confront such attitudes, as very few depended on their neighbors for a living. This began to change about one hundred years ago when population growth and reduced agricultural yields forced them to seek alternative sources of income. Many chose to migrate, in some cases founding new villages populated entirely by Chiquimula migrants in the townships of Patzité, Cunén, and Sacapulas (McCreery 1994). Others became traveling merchants (*aj b'iyaj*) or tailors who produced shirts and pants for the large regional markets of San Francisco el Alto, Momostenango, or Totonicapán (see Figure 3.3). Still others worked seasonally as field hands in cotton and sugarcane plantations in the southern piedmont. Today very few depend on agriculture for their livelihood, and most work as itinerant merchants, buying and selling their wares as far away as Guatemala City, southern Mexico, and El Salvador. Furthermore, schools have become more common throughout the township. While few Chiquimulas get university degrees, many graduate with high school and teaching

FIGURE 3.3. Itinerant merchants in Totonicapán (1939) (courtesy of the Colección del Museo Etnográfico de Hamburgo sobre Guatemala, Fototeca Guatemala, CIRMA).

certificates. Numerous high school graduates work in schools, nongovernmental organizations (NGOs), and government offices.

For Chiquimulas today, outside contacts and frequent travel to other K'ichee' townships have become part of their lives. It is not uncommon for men to marry women from other towns. During my fieldwork I had occasional conversations in K'ichee' with in-married women. Those who fricativized intervocalic /l/, a Chiquimula stereotype, were usually from Patzité, whose population descends from Chiquimula settlers. I also met several Q'eqchi' women from Alta Verapaz who learned K'ichee' after moving to Santa María with their Chiquimula husbands. They tended to fricativize intervocalic /l/ in the same way as native speakers of the Santa María variety but somewhat less frequently. Boundary work, however, continued to be performed in other ways. For example, María Elena, a Q'eqchi' woman from Cobán, has been a resident of Santa

María Chiquimula for forty years since marrying a Chiquimula merchant. She speaks K'ichee' with a Chiquimula "accent" but has not given up her traditional pleated Cobán *corte*,[6] which visually marks her as a *cobanera*, or native of Cobán (Figure 3.4). She avoids speaking Q'eqchi' in public and has not taught it to her sons and daughters, who identify as Chiquimulas.

In interactions with speakers of other varieties, Chiquimulas often find themselves in unequal power relations, working as hired tailors in a piecework system of clothes production originating in the town of San Francisco or as small retail vendors in large regional markets outside Santa María Chiquimula. The linguistic implications of this change in life orientation from isolation and self-sufficiency to dependence on external markets and social networks are important. On the one hand, the Chiquimula dialect is cherished as emblematic of ethnic *communitas* and traditional values; on the other, it

FIGURE 3.4. María Elena, a Q'eqchi' woman from Cobán and a resident of Santa María Chiquimula (photograph by Sergio Romero).

TABLE 3.1. Examples of Intervocalic Fricativization of /l/ in Santa María Chiquimula.

Gloss	General K'ichee'[1]	Santa María Chiquimula
Head	[xoló:m]	[xoδó:m]
Boy	[alá]	[aδá]
Thus	[xe na lá]	[xenδá]
Shovel	[palá][2]	[paδá]
Pants	[pantolón][3]	[pantoδón]

[1] International Phonetic Alphabet (IPA). Stress is marked with an acute accent.
[2] From Spanish *pala* "shovel," stressed on the penultimate syllable. K'ichee' stress falls on the last syllable.
[3] From Spanish *pantalón* "pants."

elicits unwelcome jokes and even insults from some of the Chiquimulas' customers, suppliers, and bosses elsewhere.

Phonologically, for example, the variable fricative realization of /l/ in intervocalic position [δ] is construed as an ethnic marker, indexing the speaker as "Chiquimula," a native of Santa María Chiquimula or its satellites (the townships of Patzité, Santa Lucía La Reforma, and a few villages in the Sacapulas and Cunén) (Romero 2006, 2009) (see Table 3.1). The intervocalic fricativization of /l/ is rare across the languages of the world, and MAR is the only documented instance in the Mayan stock to the best of my knowledge (Levy 1979; Romero 2006).[7] On the one hand, fricative /l/ is a MAR stereotype,

indexing a common identity, a Chiquimula frame transcending the divide between village and township seat. On the other, Chiquimula's neighbors construe fricative /l/ as iconic of the stereotypes of sloppiness and backwardness they hold about Chiquimulas. The enregisterment of MAR linguistic stereotypes entailed incongruent pragmatic effects within and across Chiquimula ethnic boundaries. Consistent evaluations of particular linguistic forms are precisely what marks members of a "speech community" despite individual and group differences in repertoire access and linguistic ability (Labov 1994).

Chiquimula linguistic stereotypes are not only phonological but also lexical, involving synonyms, homonyms, and idioms. For example, in most western K'ichee' varieties, [minaʃakopix] is a vetative form meaning "do not push me!" (see Table 3.2). However, in San Francisco el Alto the root [-ʃakopix] is used idiomatically to refer to sexual intercourse. The form [minaʃakopix] is ambiguous in San Francisco between "don't push me" and "don't fuck me!," making it taboo in many situations. Chiquimulas are aware of this ambiguity and bring it up as a lexical stereotype of San Francisco el Alto.

Lexical stereotypes are embedded in particular contexts, and their construal as ethnic markers is the pragmatic effect of mutually congruent indexical variables, not exclusively linguistic. Often it is not phonological form or semantic denotation per se but idiosyncratic pragmatic

TABLE 3.2. Some Lexical and Idiomatic Stereotypes Held in Santa María Chiquimula.

Idiom/Lexical Stereotype	Indexed Township	Santa María Chiquimula Equivalent	Gloss
noya	San Antonio Ilotenango	ali	girl
ʃinna wiɓ	Momostenango	ʃinʃeʔx wiɓ	I got scared
yeʔ	San Francisco el Alto	xeʔ	yes
Minaweqleʔex	San Francisco el Alto	Minaʃakopix	Don't push me!
mamaʔ ak'	Patzite	amaʔ ak'	rooster
tʃin	Chichicastenango	nic'	little
baxtʃiʔ[1]	Chichicastenango	atam	early

Note: Glosses are by the author.
[1] From libaxtʃiʔ, a form attested in colonial sources.

or indexical effects that reveal contrasts between townships. In the following fragment Talin answers a question about a particular stereotype of San Antonio Ilotenango mentioned in metalinguistic discourse in Santa María: the vocative use of the noun [noya] to address young women:

(3.2)
Talin: Rə ax San Antonyo kəkiɓi:x "Xeʔ no:ya," ketʃa, "xeʔe no:ya." Xeʔ ketʃʼaw le aʔre. "Xeʔ noya" kətʃa le ax… "Xeʔ no:ya."
Sergio: Waral man kiɓi:ʃ tax…
Talin: Tixo kəqaɓi:x noya pero i: son kasualidades.[8]
Talin: In San Antonio they say: "Yes, *noya!* They say: "Yes, *noya!*" This is how they speak. They say: "Yes, *noya!*"… "Yes, *noya!*"
Sergio: Here [in Santa María Chiquimula] you don't say it…
Talin: We say it occasionally but it is just a rare occurrence.

The use of [xeʔ no:ya] "Yes, *noya!*" as conversational backchannel with a mitigating lengthening of [o] is construed in Santa María Chiquimula as a stereotype of the neighboring township of San Antonio Ilotenango. It is not the noun [noya] "young woman" per se but this particular usage that is recognized as ethnic stereotype. In fact, although Talin is not specific, she claims that Chiquimulas themselves use it, though only as a "rare occurrence." This includes, of course, parodies of the San Antonio accent, of which Chiquimulas are very fond.

Syntactic features are less frequent as ethnic stereotypes because metapragmatic attention tends to focus on content words rather than on function words and agreement morphology (Silverstein 1981; Cheshire 2005). For example, negative concord is a unique syntactic feature of MAR used to mark intense negative force. It has not been documented in any other K'ichee' dialect (Romero 2006).[9] However, even though it is such an idiosyncratic innovation, it fails to elicit the intense reaction evoked by fricative /l/ or by any of the lexical stereotypes discussed above (Romero 2006). Negative concord consists of the spread of one or more additional copies of

the negation marker [ta(x)] over the predicate, as in texts (3.3) and (3.4):

(3.3)
ʃwetaʔmax ta u:waʃ tax.
ʃ-o-w-etaʔmax   ta   u:-watʃ tax.
COM-3sA-1sE-learn NEG 3sE-face NC
I didn't meet him at all.

(María, 51 years old, Santa María Chiquimula)

(3.4)
Man koxkun   ta tʃi qacuqi:k ta qiɓ.
man k-ox-kun   ta tʃi(k) qa-cuqik ta qiɓ.
NPI INC-1pA-able NEG anymore 1pE-feed
    NC   ourselves
We couldn't feed ourselves anymore.

(Treʼx, 48 years old, Santa María Chiquimula)

In text (3.3) a second copy (NC) of the postverbal negator [ta(x)] follows the direct object [u:-watʃ]. Similarly, in text (3.4) a second copy (NC) follows the complement of the auxiliary verb [koxkun], marking a strong negative force, somewhat captured in English with the gloss "at all" or "anymore." Negative concord in MAR is accompanied with sound cues such as faster speech and appropriate head or hand gestures. It is heard in almost every conversation in Santa María Chiquimula. I played recorded fragments of MAR to K'ichee' speakers from the highlands of Nahualá, and their reactions to negative concord were surprise and amusement. They understood the MAR speakers but were unable to identify their provenience, as negative concord is not a stereotype of MAR in Nahualá. Chiquimulas themselves seem not to have been made the butt of jokes on account of negative concord. When I pointed it out to my Chiquimula friends, they seemed amused after realizing that there were two or more negation markers in each sentence. Negative concord is not a subject of metalinguistic discourse in Santa María Chiquimula itself or in neighboring townships. Of course, it is likely that it contributes to the metric structure of MAR as a register in spite of the fact that it is not overtly discussed. As mentioned earlier, syntax seems to play a secondary metapragmatic role in the performance of ethnic differences in K'ichee'.

Metalinguistic discourse lingers on in referential categories such as nouns and address pronouns, explaining dialectal and stylistic differences in terms of phonological form or denotation of emblematic lexicon. In contrast, metric effects due to intonational contours or syntactic variation are peripheral in discussions about language use in K'ichee'. This is an important but paradoxical feature of K'ichee' linguistic ideology because the metrics of speech production play a crucial role in cuing ceremonial styles. The unique history of each regional variety determines not only what lexical categories act as stereotypes but also their degree of salience in metalinguistic discourse. The isoglosses drafted by dialect geographers and diagnosed on the categorical presence of diagnostic forms do not always overlap with "folk" dialectologies of K'ichee'. Many of the dialectal features discussed by Campbell (1977) and Par Sapón and Can (2000), for example, are neither the subject of metalinguistic commentary nor triggers of consistent metapragmatic reactions.

3.3. The Region as Social Space of Dialectal Recognition

The relationship between dialect classifications and regional ethnoscapes is embodied in "folk" dialect nomenclatures. Regional varieties are named after townships, even when the geographic distribution of the diagnostic features does not necessarily overlap with the township's geographic boundaries. Township names consist of a Spanish saint's name followed by a native toponym, of either Mayan or Nahuatl origin. For example, Santa María Chiquimula consists of the Spanish *Santa María* "Holy Mary," patron saint of the township, and *Chiquimula*, a Nahuatl name adopted by the Spanish after they invaded central Guatemala with the crucial support of Nahuatl-speaking troops and other auxiliaries from Central Mexico (Asselbergs 2008; Matthew 2000) (see Figure 3.5).[10] The original K'ichee' toponym [c'olox ʧe] "elder tree" is rarely used today and is construed as a marker of traditional speech styles.

K'ichee' townships are socially diverse spaces, and some are indeed multiethnic, having substantial contingents of ethnically distinct groups of K'ichee' speakers. Ethnic boundaries are visually displayed in place of residence, women's clothing, saints' cults, ritual calendar, and speech. Since the middle of the nineteenth century, Chiquimulas, for example, have been migrating in pursuit of agricultural lands, and a substantial population resides in townships such as Patzité, Santa Lucía la Reforma, Sacapulas, and Cunén (see Figure 3.6). Like the *amaq'* of the Postclassic, today's Chiquimulas are not confined to the limits of their ancestral territory (Van Akkeren 2000).[11]

In K'ichee' metalinguistic discourse the place where an emblematic variety is spoken best acts as a primordial ethnic *origo*, the precise geographic location representing the social and cultural center of ethnic *communitas*. In some cases it is the township seat, or *tinamit* [tinamit]; in others, distant rural communities where a traditional lifestyle is considered the norm or even villages located near the site of ancient colonial or prehispanic settlements. In Santa María Chiquimula, for example, the purest form of the local dialect is believed to be the one spoken in the vicinity of the site of the old colonial town, or *ojeer tinamit* [oxe:r tinamit] (Victoriano Castillo, personal communication 2005).

Chiquimula language ideologies involve two iconic relationships: one between dialect and ethnic community, and another between ethnic community and local landscape. Certain geographic locations act as ethnic icons, concentrating the township's defining ethnic substance, as it were. These include, in Santa María Chiquimula, the archaeological remains at *ojer tinamit*, as we saw above, and the current township seat itself.[12] There is indeed an inverse relation between linguistic "purity" and distance from the township seat, such that the former is compromised near the township borders:

(3.5)

Por exemplo, ri ax ʃesana? i ri ax ranʧo paʧe ri kiʧ'a:w xuc'it ax momos.... Y ri ax raqana? paʧe ri kiʧ'a:w juc'it ax santalusiya.... Ri ax taq ʃekokoʧ y ʧwi kaqa? paʧe ta na keʧ'a:w

FIGURE 3.5. Santa María, patron saint of Santa María Chiquimula (photograph by Sergio Romero).

FIGURE 3.6. Town of Cunén in the Department of Quiché (photograph by Lilian Márquez).

taq ax pac'itze o ax k'ictʃe:ʔ. Y ri ax tʃwakoral xuc'it ax tʃwakoral, patʃe ta na ri kitʃʼa:w taq ax sanantoniyo ilotenango. Osea kʼo xuc'it porke… komo kik'ul kʼa tʃik, kikik'am ri kici:x.… Axa!

For example, people from Xesaná and El Rancho, it's like they speak a bit like folks from Momostenango. And people from Racaná, it's like they speak a bit like people from Santa Lucía. And people from Xecococh and Chuicacá, it's like they speak a bit like folks from Patzite or Quiché. And people from Chwacorral, it's a little bit like they speak like folks from San Antonio Ilotenango. This is because they meet and borrow from their speech. Yes!

(Tilin, 32 years old, Santa
María Chiquimula, June 2005)

Text (3.5) is a fragment of an interview with Tilin, a political activist from Santa María Chiquimula, in which she reflected on her run for township mayor in the 2004 elections, an office usually held by men. Discussing the different degrees of support she found in rural areas, she spelled out the cultural notion that distance from the township seat, the township's ritual and political center, iconically relates to perceived speech differences and cultural authenticity. Villages located near the borders of the *municipio* are believed to have more intense contact with speakers of other dialects; residents of these border villages shop in the others' markets, visit their towns on feast days, and sometimes intermarry with them. Not surprisingly, their lifestyle and speech are construed as less pure, more contaminated by the speech of other townships. Language is imagined as a sensitive, corruptible artifact, not equally distributed across the municipal landscape. Loanwords, bilingualism, and contact with outsiders inevitably lead to mixing and loss. The farther one moves from the town center into surrounding townships and beyond, the more compromised the purity of the emblematic ethnic variety becomes, and once one breaches the township's boundaries, the more imprecise and vague the social construal of dialectal differences becomes.

In the township of Nahualá, about one hundred kilometers east of Santa María Chiquimula (see Figure 1.3), K'ichee' speakers hold generally consistent lexical stereotypes of the varieties spoken in neighboring townships, such as Santa Lucía Utatlán, Sololá, and Argueta, with which they have long-standing commercial and political connections. Nahualatecos (natives of Nahualá) buy and sell in the other townships' weekly markets, and many have worked as teachers or NGO staff in villages under their jurisdiction. However, in contrast with the detailed map of linguistic diversity in their vicinity, Nahualatecos' ideas of varieties spoken at more distant places are rather imprecise. For example, they label all K'ichee' speakers from the western townships of San Andrés Xecul, San Miguel Totonicapán, San Francisco el Alto, Momostenango, and Santa María Chiquimula [axtʃwimiqʼinaiɓ].[13] Few Nahualatecos can specify linguistic differences among the latter, even though dialect geographers claim they are structurally substantial (Campbell 1977; Kaufman n.d.; Par Sapón and Can 2000).

Dialects become registers indexing local ethnic frames when interaction between different townships becomes culturally relevant. Explicit representations of ethnicity, geography, and a common regional history undergird the reactions elicited by dialect stereotypes. Market circuits, land conflicts, and ritual cycles are the social fields binding different townships into regional communities of practice where dialects are recognized as emblematic. Weekly regional markets, for example, are a privileged stage for the theatrical performance of ethnicity. Differences in clothing, food habits, and language display ethnic identities and reproduce the ideologies that support them. In Figure 3.7 the two women in the foreground are wearing distinctive *cortes* on market day in Nahualá. The one on the left is wearing the *morga*, emblematic of Nahualá; the one on the right is wearing the ikat pattern emblematic of Santa Lucía Utatlán, Argueta, and other townships to the east and west of Nahualá. K'ichee' women often wear other townships' *huipiles*, as noted earlier; however, the *corte* plays a central role in boundary work. It is

FIGURE 3.7. Market-day scene in Nahualá, Department of Sololá (photograph by Lilian Márquez).

the crucial emblem marking the young woman on the right as a non-native of Nahualá.

Boundary work in the western highlands involves a sort of intertextual indexicality across different semiotic media, including food. For example, in addition to language and clothing, traditional food is used in boundary work in Nahualá, where *chuchitos*—tamales wrapped in corn husks—are considered a specialty of the neighboring township of Santa Lucía Utatlán. Nahualatecos seldom make them, and the numerous *chuchito* vendors seen on market day in Nahualá are usually *aj Santa Lu's*—Santa Lucía

Utatlán women—as can be seen in their avoidance of the Nahualá *traje*, or traditional clothing (Manuela Tahay, personal communication 2013). Ethnic frames interleave speech and other semiotic media such as dress code and even food in the performance of boundary work.

Long-standing land conflicts are narratives—memory work—defining township cultural representations as well. Conflicts over the proper location of municipal or private land boundaries seldom fail to mobilize the population, provoking strong emotional responses as threats to the co-substantial unity of land and ethnic group

(Abac 1980; González 2002; Camacho Nassar 2003). Even townships as closely related historically, linguistically, and culturally as Nahualá and Santa Catarina Ixtahuacán, for example, characterize each other as threatening and morally flawed as a result of simmering boundary conflicts (Abac 1980; Hostig et al. 1995).

3.4. Ethnicity and Interaction Frames

K'ichee' boundary work involves at least three different but overlapping interaction frames: local, K'ichee', and indigenous/Maya (see Chapter 1).

3.4.1. Local Frame(s)

Local frames are embedded in ethnically diverse regional spaces in which linguistic exchanges occur in the same or related Mayan languages. This frame is the precipitate of a long history of local collective experiences, rituals, conflicts, longterm exchange networks, and semiotic practices. The local frame is the linguistic embodiment of various small-scale corporate identities, not all of which are present in every K'ichee'-speaking area: the village (*komon*), the lineage (*nim ja* in Momostenango, *q'alpul* in Santa María Chiquimula),[14] and the township (*municipio*).

Boundary work does not involve the same type of local frames in every K'ichee'-speaking area. Whether the lineage, the village, the township itself, or a combination thereof is the precise social space embodied in local frames depends on idiosyncratic regional histories and local experiences of colonialism and resistance.[15] In Momostenango, for example, the lineage (*nim ja*) continues to play a crucial role in the socialization and life cycles of individuals. Carmack (1995) documented direct historical continuities between prehispanic forms of social organization and today's lineages. The lineage is still, in its more recent incarnation, one of the spaces framing ethnic identification in Momostenango (Mondloch and Carmack 1989; Carmack 1995; Cook 2000). In contrast, in Santa María Chiquimula the lineage, called *q'alpul* there, is an archaic though not yet completely superseded category. Most Chiquimulas I asked did not know what the term meant, though a

few elders remembered an association between Chiquimulan patronymics and the *q'alpul*, but no one was sure what specific rights and obligations were involved (Romero 2006). The *q'alpul* persist today under a different label as kin and village networks indexed by the distinct geographic distribution of last names through the township's territory.[16] For example, in El Rancho, one of the largest villages in population, Chi Ixcoteyac "At the Ixcoteyacs'" is a *caserío* where the patronymic Ixcoteyac predominates.[17] This *caserío* has its own series of hierarchically ordered *prinsipalib'*, development committees, and Catholic and evangelical churches. It constitutes a distinct social and political unit bound by kinship and territory within the larger Santa María Chiquimula.

Most Chiquimulas identify first as natives of the *municipio* of Santa María Chiquimula and second as residents of a particular hamlet or village. In a few villages along the border, however, these identifications are experienced as mutually exclusive. As we see later, highland Maya rural settlements often show centrifugal tendencies, seeking to gain political autonomy from their municipal circumscription. In Santa María Chiquimula the township (*municipio*) acts as a sort of melting pot in which lineages have partly, and at times unwillingly, coalesced.[18] "Chiquimula" and "village" are the two local frames Chiquimulas inhabit in most interactions among themselves and with others in the west-central highlands (see Table 3.3). Distinguishing between the two frames involves not only an "accent" but also other indexical practices that are discussed in this chapter. Furthermore, the "Chiquimula" frame is regularly performed outside the township territorial boundaries in areas that Chiquimulas migrated to in the nineteenth century. In Sacapulas, for example, after more than a century Chiquimula migrants continue to identify as ethnic Chiquimulas vis-à-vis ethnic Sacapultecos, though many have never personally visited the town of Santa María Chiquimula (Romero 2006). Boundary work in Sacapulas involves female clothing as well. The young women shown in Figure 3.8 were graduating high school seniors born and raised in Sacapulas. In this

FIGURE 3.8. Young women from Sacapulas wearing the distinctive *huipiles* emblematic of the K'ichee' and Sacapulteco (photograph by Lilian Márquez).

TABLE 3.3. K'ichee' Deictic Spaces in the Western Highlands.

Location	Townships
West-Central	Santa María Chiquimula,[1] San Miguel Totonicapán, Momostenango, San Francisco el Alto, San Andrés Xecul
South-Central[2]	Nahualá, Santa Catarina Ixtahuacán, Santa Lucía Utatlán, Argueta, Santo Tomás la Unión, San Felipe Retalhuleu
Central	Santa Cruz del Quiché, San Antonio Ilotenango, Chichicastenango, Santa María Chiquimula

Note: Based on conversations with K'ichee' speakers from Santa María Chiquimula, Totonicapán, Santa Cruz del Quiché, Chichicastenango, Nahualá, and Santa Lucía Utatlán.
[1] In my view, Santa María Chiquimula is part of two different deictic spaces. This is due to the mobility of Chiquimulas, many of whom are itinerant merchants.
[2] K'ichee' speakers in this area are in frequent contact with Kaqchikel and/or Tz'utujil speakers, whose languages they can understand and recognize. However, they are usually not able to identify specific dialects.

school function each of them wears a *huipil* with the patterns and decoration emblematic of their ethnic identification as K'ichee' (Chiquimula) or Sacapultec. The modern Sacapultec *huipil* tends to be of a delicate cloth with hanging decorations (second and fourth in the figure from left to right). The Chiquimula women in this pic-ture, in contrast, wear the *blusa*, a colorful, lay-ered *huipil* emblematic of central Quiché towns such as Santa Cruz (first and fifth in the figure). The *blusa* is less expensive than the traditional Chiquimula *huipil*, which is intricately woven on a hand loom and not usually worn by younger Chiquimula women in Sacapulas.

In the multiethnic regional spaces in which terms such as "Chiquimula" and "Momosteco" denote specific "ethnic frames," different ethnic groups recognize each other's emblematic signs in multiple media (dress code, dialect, ritual cycle, food). Boundary work is performed in consistent, mutually intelligible ways. In these deictic spaces "accents" become intelligible social markers. Outside, accent recognition wanes or is replaced with broader, less defined categories, as we saw earlier. Identities as distinct and intelligible sets of semiotic resources are embedded in deictic spaces in geography, and landscapes are associated with particular ethnic groups.[19] The deictic spaces listed in Table 3.3 are a preliminary synthesis of my conversations with K'ichee' speakers together with my own estimations of how sharply "accent" recognition works. The social basis of such widely shared indexical conventions includes market networks, national-level institutions, migrations, and conflicts over boundaries and access to natural resources (Smith 1984).

3.4.2. K'ichee' Frame

The second ethnic frame introduced above is the K'ichee' frame, emblematically indexed by any K'ichee' variety, all of which are construed as performing the same kind of boundary work; other media, such as dress, are recruited as well. The K'ichee' frame is the result of the native appropriation and resignification of the colonial "mutual intelligibility" diagnostic to classify different native populations as incarnations of the same ethnic substance. In Postclassic society, as we saw in Chapter 1, mutual intelligibility was not often used in boundary work between *amaq'*. Recent work by Van Akkeren, for example, shows that lineage identities persisted in the Postclassic even after language shift and/or geographic displacements occurred (Van Akkeren 2005, 2012).

Today the K'ichee' frame emerges in situations in which ethnic boundaries and mutually unintelligible linguistic varieties overlap. In the twentieth century, migrations took large numbers of K'ichee' speakers looking for agricultural land into areas where other languages

were predominant. For example, in high-altitude areas north of the *municipio* of Nebaj in the Department of Quiché, where the population is 84 percent Ixil-speaking, villages such as Xexocom and Chortiz have predominantly K'ichee'-speaking populations. A few others, such as Xexuxcab, have a mixed Ixil-K'ichee' demography. Although relations between the two groups are generally peaceful, boundary work is constant and the two ethnic communities are sharply distinct. First, communication between them is generally in Spanish, although individuals often develop a passive knowledge of the other's language. Language is iconic of ethnic identification, and a positive stance in interaction is indexed by the use of Spanish, which is construed as neutral. During the 2010 municipal elections the Unión Nacional por la Esperanza (UNE)[20] candidate for mayor marked his own ethnic identification in all his campaign propaganda, openly displaying the Ixil personal classifier *Pap* "Mister" before his first name Lu', the hypocoristic form of Spanish Pedro "Peter" (see Figure 3.9).[21] The sign shown in Figure 3.9 was painted outside the Xexuxcab headquarters of the UNE campaign. Xexuxcab has an ethnically mixed population, as we saw earlier, but there were no signs anywhere in the village displaying the K'ichee' equivalent *tat Lu'*. In fact, nowhere in Nebaj did I see any UNE electoral propaganda in K'ichee' in spite of the sizable K'ichee'-speaking population, effectively erasing the K'ichee'-speaking minority in the township. Linguistic accommodation was not visually displayed in Nebaj during this election cycle.

The K'ichee' frame also recruits and resignifies women's *traje* as visual marker in a sort of indexical synesthesia that binds speech and sight. Traditional female dress in the highlands consists of a handwoven blouse (*po't*), called *huipil* in Spanish, and a one-piece garment worn around the waist down to the ankles (*uuq*), called *corte* in Spanish. Patterns and designs are township-specific, though women often wear other hometowns' *huipiles* to suit individual taste or to follow the latest fashion trend (Hendrickson 1996). Nevertheless, *corte* cross-dressing is rare, and K'ichee' women in Xexuxcab do not

FIGURE 3.9. Electoral sign outside the UNE headquarters in Xexuxcab, Nebaj (photograph by Lilian Márquez).

FIGURE 3.10. High school students from Xexuxcab, Nebaj (photograph by Lilian Márquez).

wear *cortes* with the intense red hues emblematic of the Ixil, while Ixil women seldom wear theirs with the striped *jaspeado* ikat patterns popular in Santa Cruz del Quiché and Chichicastenango (see Figure 3.10).

In Figure 3.10 the two young women on the left wear the emblematic *corte* of the Ixil and the K'ichee', respectively. They grew up in Xexuxcab, attend the same secondary school, and understand each other's language. Nevertheless, they converse in Spanish, contributing also to boundary work on behalf of their ethnic community by wearing the traditional *corte*. There is a gender-based semiotic division of labor in Nebaj that makes women "marked" ethnic subjects in the community while men remain "unmarked" unless Ixil men choose to wear the *koton*, the traditional red vest with black patterns emblematic of the Ixil. Accent and female dress act concurrently as alternative visual media for boundary work.

3.4.3. Indigenous/Maya Frame

The indigenous/Maya frame, in contrast, is set in the broader geographic space defined by the Guatemalan nation-state and has its origin in the caste system instituted after the Spanish invasion in which individual rights and obligations hinged on ethnic ascription. It involves a dichotomy between *indígenas* "indigenous," those who identify ethnically as indigenous and share at least some of the emblematic traits of indigenous culture, and *ladinos*, a broad category including all those who do not identify as indigenous or are not identified as such by mainstream institutions (Lutz 1994; González Ponciano 2004:113; Hale 2006).

Scholars of Guatemala have emphasized this frame but until recently have somewhat neglected the complex patterns of regional ethnic identification (the first and second frames above). This may be an overreaction to the weaknesses of the "closed corporate community" model or a response to contemporary pan-Maya activism (see Chapter 1). However, since most domestic and marker interactions at the regional level occur in indigenous languages that few non-native scholars speak, it should not be surprising that these frames have not received the attention they deserve. Basing sociolinguistic inquiry on the regional articulations of language variation, however, is crucial for understanding social roles and the ways in which the K'ichee' experience dialect differences and language choice.

The three frames discussed above perform distinct deictic roles inside the township as well. Speaking like a Chiquimula is not just a "theatrical" performance. It is also a stylistic shift marker and indexes individual stances vis-à-vis traditional community norms in changing highland communities. Ethnic frames are part and parcel

of the discursive performance and re-creation of ethnic boundaries. Boundary work is not just a show for outsiders but also "memory work" to be performed and transmitted to other members of the ethnic community (Gillespie 2010), as discussed in the next section.

3.5. Dialect, Style, and Boundary Work

Dialect stereotypes—accents—are tropes indexing positive alignments vis-à-vis conventional norms of authority and cultural legitimacy. This can be seen in the arena of intra-township conflict. K'ichee' townships are sites of contention of various kinds. Ethnic groups, individuals, families, and villages are sometimes engaged in conflicts over land boundaries, access to water sources, or access to commons. Furthermore, villages often show centrifugal tendencies, seeking to become independent *municipios* to manage their affairs autonomously when spurred by demographic growth, economic development, or ambitious leadership. Township authorities invariably resist, leading to bitter conflicts (sometimes mediated by central government authorities) and even to violence (Camacho Nassar 2003). Individual and collective stances in ongoing intra-municipal conflicts are rhetorically dramatized through dialectal stereotypes. Examples of villages currently pressing for autonomy from their respective municipal seats include Guineales, in the piedmont of the township of Santa Catarina Ixtahuacán southeast of Nahualá, and Chuicacá, in Santa María Chiquimula (see Figure 3.11) (Baronti 2001; Romero 2006).

Chuicacá, with a substantial population, orderly nucleated settlement, spacious church building, and large weekly market, has been agitating for secession from Santa María Chiquimula for more than a decade, leading to intense animosities on both sides. For other Chiquimulas, idiosyncratic features of the speech of Chuicacá have become iconic of subversive, antisocial behavior that challenges the moral values binding the members of the ethnic community. One such stereotype is the existence of broader licensing conditions for honorific addressee forms in Chuicacá than in the rest of

FIGURE 3.11. Urban center of the village of Chuicaca, Santa María Chiquimula (photograph by Sergio Romero).

Santa María Chiquimula. Chuicacá's speech is construed in Santa María as qualitatively different, akin to that of other townships such as San Antonio Ilotenango and Santa Cruz del Quiché, as shown in text (3.6).

(3.6)
Ri axpac'ite kuk' ri ax ʧwikaqaʔ keʧʾaːw
laːl…keʧʾaw laːl…kikiɓiːx…xeʔ laːl naːn…
algo asi…. Kinkwin ta rin ʧi uɓiʃik pero si
[*laughing*]…. Jun wi ri kiʧʾawɓaːl, jun wi ri
kiɓantaxik.

People from Patzité and Chuicacá speak with [laːl][22] …they speak with [laːl]…. They say: "Yes, [laːl] lady." I can't say it [like them] but yes…. We speak different languages, we're different.

(María, 28 years old, Santa María Chiquimula, March 2005)

Text (3.6) was María's reply when I asked during an interview if Chiquimulas noticed anything special in the speech of the rebellious residents of Chuicacá. A schoolteacher from the township seat, she mentioned the use of the second-person honorific form *laal* [laːl], whose restricted use in MAR is iconic of the shared values said to bind all Chiquimulas. Chuicacá's estrangement is iconically indexed by the more extensive use of honorific forms. In this particular context, wider licensing conditions for honorific address is construed by other Chiquimulas as an affected, unnatural way of speaking that emblematizes, furthermore, the dialects of Totonicapán and Santa Cruz del Quiché. As seen in Chapter 5, the restricted use of honorific forms in MAR is construed as iconic of the primordial equality binding all Chiquimulas. An excessive use of *laal* and *alaq* [alaq], the respective singular and plural honorific addressee forms, is an affectation alien to the MAR exchange norms.

The iconic identification of dialect and ethnic *communitas* translates into a hierarchy of emblematicity in multiethnic townships in which the dominant group imposes its own dialect as quintessential linguistic icon, as in Cunén, north of the Department of Quiché. Cunén's population consists of ethnic Cunetecos (natives of Cunén) and a significant number of second- and third-generation migrants from Santa María Chiquimula. The Cunén variety is so divergent structurally that it has been suggested that it should be considered a different language altogether (Kaufman n.d.:35).[23] Cunetecos regard it as the sole linguistic icon of their hometown, and in public events it is the only variety regularly performed. For example, on October 27, 2009, during a referendum on mining rights in Cunén sponsored by the city hall and several NGOs, every call and political speech to rally the population in the town center was made in the Cunén dialect, as shown in text (3.7). MAR was not used at all in spite of the fact that it is the native variety of thousands of township residents.

(3.7)
Ox xunti:r ra:waʃik qaʔan…koxpetek kʼo xunti:r. Ra:waxik qataɓik usilaxtʃik ter.…
Nikpla wel pwes ʃoxtikiyisax qil qi:ɓ waral.
Y poqʼi riʔ pwes kinwilo tʃo toʔoxo kotʃ riʔ y koxqʼaʃ li kipe pa taq komunidad xik alkaldes auksiliares y nikpla kokodes ya xiqalaq y ri ya xqi qi:bʼ komon pa nikpla kʼi komunidad.
ʃoxwlaoj waral pam ri loqʼlax qatinami:t riʔ, wa qiqam qi:bʼ, waqi kʼox qatʃuqʼa:ɓ qaɓan ta xanti:r pa qasiwan qatinamit.

It's necessary that we all…that we all come here where everyone is [gathered]. It is necessary that those of us standing here heed the call. Today I see […] and we pass by village folks, town marshals, many members of development committees. We see also many common people from many villages. We arose here in our beloved/sacred town, we raised each other, and all of us have put our strength together here in our township.

(Town marshal, Cunén, November 2009)

Text (3.7) was spoken from a stage erected outside the city hall minutes after the polls opened. Several phonological, morphological, and lexical features distinguish this variety from

MAR: elision of [xa] in [raxawaʃix] "It is necessary"; vowel centralization in the phrase final marker /-ik/; and diphthongization of [a:], as well as some lexical differences. The referendum itself was a political performance addressed to local residents and neighboring township officials, who were invited to attend as observers, as well as to government envoys and the press. Although some of the speakers on the stage spoke in both Cuneteco and Spanish, the Spanish was not always a translation of Cuneteco speeches. These speeches were not merely meant to communicate a certain referential content to Cunén residents. Speaking Cuneteco on that day was a theatrical performance displaying Cuneteco identity, cultural values, and general consensus about rejecting the granting of mining licenses in the township's sacred territory.[24] It enacted the ethnic tensions between MAR and Cuneteco speakers that exemplify the political life of the township, marking the claims to hegemony of the latter and effectively erasing the former.

3.6. The Semiotic Function of Dialectal Differences in K'ichee'

Mutual intelligibility potentially transforms regional differences into consistent cultural markers cuing ethnic frames in multiethnic deictic spaces. When structural differences impede oral communication, the deictic roles of perceived differences are more restricted. Nevertheless, they continue to play a role in boundary work, as we saw earlier.

Dialect recognition is sharper and more complex when interactions are frequent and specific representations of the groups involved become shared cultural knowledge in multiethnic deictic spaces. Stereotypes of socially and geographically more distant groups are less precise, often grouping distinct ethnic communities under one label, such as the term [axtʃwimiqʼinaiɓ] "from Totonicapán," used in Nahualá, which conjoins at least five different townships, as we have seen.

In addition to their role in boundary work, ethnic stereotypes act as gender markers. For example, the frequency of the emblematic assibilated variant of intervocalic /l/ is significantly higher among women than among men in Santa María Chiquimula (Romero 2009). This difference reflects a gender division of labor in linguistic boundary work: women sound more Chiquimula than men. They are said to be less likely to be code-switchers, and their K'ichee' is believed to be more pure than men's. Women are construed as the quintessential depository of traditional culture, and until recently very few of them spoke Spanish, according to Chiquimulas themselves (Eduardo de León, personal communication, 2005). As we saw earlier, this is also reflected in the use of the traditional *traje*, which is seldom worn by Chiquimula men today.

Dialect geographers prefer phonological and morphological variables as diagnostics, but K'ichee' "folk" dialectologies emphasize lexical shibboleths, discourse, and pragmatic norms. Although nomenclatures are shared in regional deictic spaces, dialectal evaluations are grounded on local frames: speakers of different ethnic affiliations construe the cultural valence of the same forms differently. Hence Chiquimulas value MAR stereotypes as markers of their own egalitarian cultural norms, but some of their neighbors construe them as markers of an uncouth, poor, and not very progressive populace in the rough northern mountains of Totonicapán.

Communicational competence in K'ichee' requires the ability to interpret and successfully use linguistic stereotypes in boundary work. Learning K'ichee' involves the acquisition of at least one set of socio-indexical rules embedded in a specific regional deictic space.[25] Due to the preeminence of stereotypes in boundary work, accommodation is neither a common practice nor a prescriptive norm in interactions with speakers of other varieties. Rather, whether K'ichee' speakers accommodate or not depends on nondetachable effects of interaction context and power relations in particular speech events. This contrasts with the Q'eqchi' of Alta Verapaz, for example, for whom accommodation is a general strategy to signal a positive stance vis-à-vis interlocutors with different ethnic identifications (Romero 2012). Linguistic boundary work strategies vary across the Maya highlands, reflecting different discursive histories and different modalities of enregisterment of regional variation.

Notes

1. Flores-Farfán (2009) discusses similar exchanges in Nahuatl-speaking communities in Mexico.
2. K'ichee' cardinal numbers—a vigesimal system—were replaced with Spanish decimal numerals in the early twentieth century.
3. In this chapter IPA spellings are used in direct quotations due to the emphasis on subphonemic dialectal differences.
4. The unmarked interrogative pronoun in Santa María is [su], a clipping of [xas uwatʃ] "What is it?" Other central dialects such as Santa Cruz del Quiche and Chichicastenango also use [su] as the unmarked form.
5. I use the initials MAR to refer to the variety of K'ichee' emblematic of the township of Santa María Chiquimula and its enclaves elsewhere.
6. The *corte* is the emblematic indigenous women's one-piece garment worn around the waist down to the ankles.
7. Intervocalic /s/ is variably realized as /θ/ in Huastec (Nora England, personal communication 2013).
8. Originally in Spanish. *Casualidad* can be glossed here as "rare occurrence."
9. I have started to notice occasional occurrences of negative concord among speakers from the piedmont of Nahualá. Its frequency in MAR is much higher, however.
10. *Chiquimula* is from the Nahuatl *Chiquimollan* "Place of *Jilgueros*," where *jilguero* is a local bird species (*Dendrocopos scalaris*).
11. Carmack (1981) argues that Chiquimulas descend from the Tamub' lineage, close allies of Q'umarkaaj at the time the Spanish arrived. They formed the citadel's elite units and were famed as fierce and loyal warriors.
12. According to Fox (1978), the old prehispanic settlement of Santa María Chiquimula was not far from Ik'laja, the sacred hill north of the current location of the town. The Chiquimulas were

conquered by the K'ichee' in the mid-fifteenth century.

13. The label [axʧwimiqʼinaiɓ] is the plural form of the K'ichee' ethnonym of the township of Totonicapán.

14. Lineages used to be segmented in intricate but not always consistent ways across different areas. It is not certain whether *nim ja* and *q'alpul* referred to the same level of corporate organization.

15. There is evidence that even in predominantly non-Maya areas of eastern Guatemala the local organization of ethnic frames is as complex as in the K'ichee' highlands. This seems to indicate a lingering indigenous substrate. See Little-Siebold (2008) for more detail.

16. Chiquimula patronymics include Q'aq', Chib'alam, Xo'r, Tum, Pu, Ixkoteyak, Tojin, Us, Tzunux, Q'alel, Joj, Kaxtro, Lux, Chik, B'atz, Imul, Mexia, and Mulul.

17. In Guatemala, *municipios* "townships" are politically subdivided into *aldeas* "villages," which in turn have smaller dependent settlements called *caseríos* "house clusters." *Caseríos* often develop their own independent village institutions in response to population growth, land conflicts, or geographic isolation.

18. The Spanish policy of *reducción* often forced the resettlement of members of distinct lineages into the same Spanish-style towns.

19. Blommaert (2005) provides an excellent discussion of the relationship between identity and spatially bound regimes of indexicality.

20. The Unión Nacional por la Esperanza (National Unity for Hope) was President Alvaro Colom's political party and one of the two with largest following in the highlands.

21. The hypocoristic Lu' "Pedro" indexes the referent as indigenous. *Ladinos* seldom use Maya hypocoristic forms to name themselves.

22. As explained earlier, [laːl] is the honorific singular addressee marker. It alternates with [at], much more extensively used in MAR.

23. Not all specialists agree with Kaufman, however. John Robertson, who has worked for years in Cunén, argues that the differences between Cuneteco and MAR are not greater than those between any other K'ichee' varieties (John Robertson, personal communication 2011).

24. The final result of the referendum was a nearly unanimous rejection of mining operations in Cunén.

25. The enregisterment of standard K'ichee' seeks to modify this sociolinguistic picture. Standard K'ichee' is a sort of "ethnically bleached" register performing a different kind of boundary work, erasing local identities and foregrounding the K'ichee' ethnic frame (see Chapter 1).

CHAPTER 4

A "Hybrid" Language

Loanwords and K'ichee'-Spanish Code Switching

4.1. Visiting a Famous Healer in Santa María Chiquimula

On a warm afternoon in June 2005, María Tikiram, a friend from Santa María Chiquimula, introduced me to her older sister Xper [ʃper], "Isabel." I was excited about the visit because Isabel was a local celebrity for her skills as a healer and for her knowledge of traditional crafts. María led me to Isabel's house on the outskirts of the town, warning me that her sister was a very busy woman, often required at a moment's notice to attend to sudden childbirths and other emergency situations. She also pointedly noted that Isabel neither understood nor spoke Spanish, as she never attended school and, unlike many younger Chiquimulas, had never left the township for more than occasional, short visits to neighboring markets. We entered Isabel's family's compound and sat on sacks full of beans lining the walls in a large, cool, adobe building. Isabel, an energetic but dignified sixty-five-year-old woman, came out to greet us as María introduced me as a friend interested in learning about traditional healing (see Figure 4.1).

After Isabel served us coffee, I thanked her and explained that I was interested in learning about her crafts and the way she had been trained. She said she would be happy to tell us her story. At that point she commenced a beautiful narrative in a style that I later learned to call *puro K'ichee'*. This metalinguistic Spanish label is used in Santa María Chiquimula to refer to traditional K'ichee' ways of speaking associated with traditional authority and ancestor values. Linguistically, they are indexed by the avoidance of Spanish loanwords as well as by the use of archaic lexicon and emblematic metaphors and idioms. *Puro K'ichee'* is sometimes referred to as *qas qatziijobʾaal* "our true, authentic language." I noticed, nevertheless, that Isabel's performance was punctuated by occasional Spanish words. For example, when making a clarification about the manner she met her husband, she said:

(4.1)
Aora ri'n xaqak'am qiib' ruuk' ri nukulaj; xaqak'am qiib', k'o jun ukyeej. Ri'n **nugaan** xinpee ruuk'. Are wa ri' in k'o wi uchaanim, chiri in k'o wi uchaanim. Re kinchomaj in uchaanim xb'antaj **kwarentikwatr** any qakuli'ik ruuk' uchaanim, **kwarentikwatr any** qakuli'ik, **ba**. Are xub'iij nukulaaj kaqatas qiib' awuuk', kojkeejej pa qachoch awuuk' kecha pwes. Je', je nu la' kan chire.[1]

Now, my partner and I got together.... He had a horse when we got together. I am happy that I came with him. This is where I am now. I am over here now. I think it's been forty-four years since we married, forty-four years since our marriage. My partner said to me: "Let's you and I live on our own. Let's ride to our own home." "Yes, absolutely," I said to him.

(Isabel, 65 years old, Santa María Chiquimula, June 2005)

59

FIGURE 4.1. Isabel outside her residence, Santa María Chiquimula (photograph by Sergio Romero).

The Spanish words in bold in text (4.1) include different syntactic classes: discourse markers, such as *aora* from Spanish *ahora* "now"; nouns such as *gan*, from Spanish *gana* "wish," and *any* from Spanish *año* "year"; cardinal numbers such as *kwarentikwatr* from Spanish *cuarenta y cuatro* "forty-four"; and interjections such as *ba* from Spanish *vaya*. Such mixing of K'ichee' and Spanish is common in Santa María Chiquimula and can be heard even in the speech of monolingual K'ichee' speakers like Xper in (4.1). It reveals the intimate imbrication of these languages in the grammatical and cultural regimentation of speech in the township, a hybrid linguistic habitus whose repertoire is unequally shared through the speech community. Such differentiated command of K'ichee' and Spanish repertoires embody differences in social status, gender, and class among K'ichee' speakers. Individuals with few years of formal education, the elderly, and rural women tend to have less command of Spanish and therefore a more restricted ability to perform hybrid K'ichee'-Spanish registers. Spanish indeed has a lively social life and a plethora of indexical roles among the K'ichee'.

So many Spanish words, idioms, interjections, and speech genres are used in K'ichee' in Santa María Chiquimula—though in the process most Spanish words have undergone substantial semantic and phonological modifications—that seldom does one hear an utterance without at least one etymologically Spanish word. Nevertheless, this hybrid linguistic practice coexists with language ideologies that construct the two languages as distinct, incommensurable entities. This apparent paradox is the result of the status of the two languages as linguistic icons of at least two ethnic identities and cultural value systems coexisting in tension in Santa María Chiquimula itself (see Chapter 3).

Technically, two different contact processes are involved in language mixing: linguistic borrowing, both lexical and structural, and code switching (King 2000; Sankoff 2002; Matras 2009).[2] From an anthropological perspective, the boundary between borrowing and code switching is fuzzy at best and is relevant only in its pragmatic and metalinguistic implications (Bunte and Kendall 1981). Linguists have implemented this conceptual difference in different ways. Poplack et al. (1988), for example, understand switches as any stretch of more than one word in the "embedded" language.[3] Nonce borrowings are considered instances of code switching unless phonologically and morphologically nativized in the "matrix" language.[4] In Santa María Chiquimula, language mixing is a discursive counterpoint of contrasting sets of cultural values and their indexical laminations. Underlying this cline of degrees of "mixing," K'ichee' language ideologies represent language as a corruptible object whose purity is inversely correlated with the use of words construed as non-native. *Kastiiy* "Castilian" and *puro K'ichee'* are cultural registers, models of linguistic behavior that speakers intertwine in speech to perform ethnic frames, marking stylistic differences and levels of social and ritual formality.

In the following sections I attempt to elucidate the indexical roles of language mixing in the linguistic economy of Santa María Chiquimula. I begin with a brief diachronic description of language contact in K'ichee', followed by an examination of the relationship between cultural role and syntactic categories of loanwords and switches. Finally, I discuss K'ichee'-Spanish code switching and the language ideologies that underlie its practice in Santa María Chiquimula.

4.2. Language Contact and Maya Social History

Ethnographers and linguists have noted the substantial lexical influence of Spanish on Mayan languages (Furbee 1988; Brody 1995; Buscher-Grotehussman 1999; Choi 2003).[5] As mentioned above, borrowings from Spanish include not only nouns referring to concepts and objects for which no native terms existed before the Spanish invasion (see Table 4.1), but also verbs, interjections, idioms, literary genres, and a broad class of

TABLE 4.1. Examples of K'ichee' Phonemic Substitutions in Loanwords from Spanish.

Phonological adjustment	Spanish	K'ichee'	Gloss
f > p	café	kapé	coffee
f > x	fuérte	xwért	very
d > t	tiénda	tiyentá	store
g > k	trigo	tirkó	wheat
s > ʃ	señora	ʃinúʔl	lady
r > l, x > ʃ	naránja	alanʃáʃ	orange
r > l	artemísa	altemíʃ	sagebrush
l > r	fiscal	piskár	sexton

Note: Stress is marked with an acute accent. IPA used for spelling K'ichee' substitutions. Glosses by the author.

words usually referred to as "discourse markers," for which, however, "structural" native equivalents arguably exist in most Mayan languages (Bunte and Kendal 1981; Brody 1987, 1995; Flores-Farfán 1999; Torres 2006). Discourse markers are a pragmatic class, lexical expressions drawn from the syntactic classes of conjunctions, adverbials, and prepositional phrases. With certain exceptions, they signal a relationship between the segment they introduce, S2, and the prior segment, S1. They have a core meaning that is procedural, not conceptual, and their more specific interpretation is "negotiated" by the context, both linguistic and conceptual. There are two types: those that relate aspects of the explicit message conveyed by S2 with aspects of a message, direct or indirect, associated with S1; and those that relate the topic of S2 to that of S1 (Fraser 1999).

Table 4.1 shows some examples of lexical borrowing from Spanish into K'ichee'. Intense lexical borrowing has been reported for many other Native American languages as well (Silverstein 1972; Hill and Hill 1999; Calvo-Pérez 2000; Campbell 1997). As early as the late seventeenth century, missionary linguists in Central Mexico were noticing the paucity of new word coinages for things the Spaniards were introducing into the Americas, and the multiplication of Spanish loanwords to refer to them. Frances Karttunen and James Lockhart, working with written historical and notarial texts produced by Nahuatl scribes, have proposed a three-stage model to describe the diachronic development of borrowing into Nahuatl (Karttunen and Lockhart 1976):

- Stage 1. From the arrival of the Spaniards to 1540–50
  Few Spanish loanwords documented. Descriptive circumlocutions, extensions, and new word coinages, especially compounds, were used to refer to objects and concepts introduced by the Spanish.
- Stage 2. From 1540–50 to 1640–50
  Spanish nouns were freely borrowed, though the borrowing of verbs is unattested for this period. Spanish plural marking was sometimes used with borrowed nouns.
- Stage 3. From 1640–50 through the present
  Verbs and discourse particles borrowed. Spanish idioms directly translated.

In Karttunen and Lockhart's model, the diachronic transitions described above were the automatic result of the intensification of contact between Spanish and Nahuatl speakers (Karttunen and Lockhart 1976; Lockhart 1992). As a rough approximation of the diachronic stages of Spanish lexical borrowing into Native languages, the model can be applied to many Mayan languages after some adjustments are made in their specific chronologies (Karttunen 1985; Restall 1997). However, the model is based on philological evidence and therefore is limited to words and sound features captured by Spanish-based writing conventions. It unavoidably restricts the range of contact phenomena and leaves out the metalinguistic and metapragmatic levels of organization of hybrid speech. Furthermore, it simplifies the poetic structure of texts and the polyphony running through colonial documents, and ignores the indexical role of loanwords and code switches as cues to register shifts.

In contrast with Nahuatl-speaking areas in Central Mexico, widespread K'ichee'-Spanish bilingualism is a recent phenomenon. In places predominantly bilingual today, such as the valley of Quezaltenango and the southern Pacific piedmont, knowledge of Spanish, with few exceptions, was rare only a few years before the Liberal revolution in 1871. The revolution marked the rise of the modern centralized Guatemalan state and the downfall of the *repúblicas de indios*, the Spanish colonial legal regime that guaranteed indigenous communities a measure of political autonomy and government protection of communal lands (Cortez y Larraz 1958; Cambranes 1985; Woodward 1993; Taracena 1997). Until the 1870s most K'ichee' speakers had very little direct contact with Spanish because very few non-Maya were allowed to settle permanently in Maya communities. Those who did were frequently fluent in the local language. Often the official scribe at the *alcaldía*, or city hall, was ethnically *mestizo* or Spanish (Lutz 1994; Matthew 2000).[6] The few Spanish loanwords were predominantly nouns, corresponding to Karttunen and Lockhart's Stage 1. Spanish-K'ichee' bilingualism, however, became common in the nineteenth century in Quetzaltenango, where an emerging middle class embraced formal education and the Spanish language as tools for social advancement (Grandin 2000; Taracena 1997). Bilingual professionals became cultural brokers between the state and working-class K'ichee' speakers, both rural and urban. Spanish became the language preferred in formal and even in colloquial interactions among members of K'ichee' urban elites. Newspapers and the minutes of the Sociedad el Adelanto, an organization founded by K'ichee' professionals and wealthy merchants to promote the empowerment of the K'ichee' in Quetzaltenango, attest to the use of Spanish as a prestige language by K'ichee'-speaking urban elites (Velásquez 2000; Camey Barrios and Quijivix Yax 2013).

The second half of the twentieth century saw rapid social and economic changes in the western highlands. The green revolution in the 1960s, the expansion of Catholic Action and evangelical denominations starting in the 1950s, the establishment of a ballot system to elect local authorities, and substantial increases in the number of Maya youth attending schools and universities led to higher levels of Spanish proficiency in Maya communities and qualitatively transformed the use of Spanish between K'ichee' speakers. Code switching became a discourse register, and the scope of borrowing from Spanish expanded significantly (Falla 1980; French 2010).

Today, however, K'ichee' communities vary in the degree to which code switching and Spanish loanwords are used in interaction. Hybrid speech requires a certain command of both languages. Insufficient knowledge of either puts limits on the individual's ability to use them as cultural indices. Young, urban, male, and educated speakers tend to be proficient in Spanish, while elderly, rural, female, and unschooled speakers tend to have very limited Spanish skills, as we have seen. This unequal access to the repertoire of code switching creates a linguistic market in which access to valued cultural capital is contingent on one's command of the prestige language (Bourdieu 2001; Sankoff and Laberge 1978).

4.3. Hybrid Cultures, Hybrid Codes: K'ichee'-Spanish Contact in Santa María Chiquimula

The town of Santa María Chiquimula is probably as close as an ethnographer can get to an ethnically homogeneous township in the Maya highlands, if such a thing ever existed. When I lived there in 2005, there were no *ladino* residents other than two Catholic priests. Although many Chiquimulas had married non-Chiquimulas, most of the latter, if not all, were ethnically indigenous and had attained at least some conversational fluency in K'ichee', when not native K'ichee' speakers themselves. Nevertheless, Spanish was deeply implicated in the local linguistic economy. Not only was it the language used in institutional settings such as schools and government agencies, but, more important, it was recruited to enact local representations of language, identity, and power. Spanish performed boundary work and also indexed status differences among Chiquimulas themselves.

Tradition and modernity are fuzzy at the edges in Santa María Chiquimula. On the one hand, Chiquimulas regard their township as having a long history with cultural values and traditions that antecede the arrival of the Spanish in 1523 (the most iconic instantiation of this historical continuity is their language). On the other, they see themselves as citizens of a modern and vibrant *municipio* whose economy, modes of political organization, consumption patterns, and social networks make it an organic member of the Republic of Guatemala. Furthermore, many Chiquimulas attend secondary schools and universities and travel to faraway places.[7] Thousands send monthly remittances from New Jersey, New York, and Rhode Island. Local soccer teams are named after famous teams in the Spanish professional league: "Barcelona—Chiquimula F.C.," "Real Madrid—Chiquimula," among others. Many homes own desktop computers, cell phones, Xbox sets, and DVD players (Romero 2006).

In this context, Spanish is emblematic of modernization and its ambiguous implications, a vehicle of innovation and an icon of the values and changes the latter entails. I do not mean that Spanish is the only language mediating the political and cultural changes brought about by modernization. In fact, Spanish and K'ichee' complement each other, enacting different aspects of it. The linguistic division of labor observed today in Maya communities has deep roots in the colonial period (see Chapter 2). Today K'ichee' iconically represents ancestral values and traditional authority forms, which are, nevertheless, constantly being transformed and recreated. Traditional institutions and rituals are structurally complex, exhibiting different semiotic layers corresponding to successive episodes in the history of Maya communities. What is crucial, however, is the cultural value accrued by specific artifacts and practices rather than actual Spanish or Mesoamerican etymological pedigrees. For instance, several lexemes considered emblematic of *longue durée* K'ichee' values are in fact Nahuatl and Spanish words borrowed during the colonial period (see Table 4.2). Their etymology is seemingly inconsistent with the cultural values they index.

In Santa María Chiquimula, discourse is a hybrid system in which the metacultural polar opposition between modern and traditional, colonial and prehispanic, *ladino* and indigenous is woven into the texture of communicational

TABLE 4.2. Some Words of Spanish Origin Represented Today as Emblematically K'ichee' in Santa María Chiquimula.

IPA Transcription	Source Language	Original Form in Source Language	Gloss
[karsón]	Spanish	[kalsón]	calzones
[wanké?t]	Spanish	[bankéta]	table
[koʃtár]	Spanish	[kostál]	traditional woolen cloth wrapped by men around the waist in Nahualá and Ixtahuacán
[masát]	Nahuatl	[másaλ] or [másat][1]	deer
[me?s]	Nahuatl	[misλi] or [misti][2]	cat

Note: Glosses by the author.
[1] Pipil etymon. Pipil is the Nahuatl variety spoken along the southern coast of Central America before the arrival of the Spanish. See Canger (1989) for more details.
[2] Pipil etymon.

events. For example, one afternoon in October 2005 I was talking with Ska', a seventy-year old widow from the village of Chwa Korral, while we sat outside her home. During a short description of the traditional clothing her father and grandfather used to wear, she said:

(4.2)
Man kakikooj ta **ween pantoδon sinoke puro** saqakarson.[8]
man kə-ki-ko:x ta we:n pantoδon sinoke purə saq-a-karson.
NPI INC-3pE-put NEG good pants rather pure white-e-calzones
They don't put on good pants but only white calzones.

(Ska', 70 years old, Chwa Korral, October 2005)

In text (4.2) Ska' contrasts the traditional dress worn by her father and grandfather with the Western clothes worn by most Chiquimula men today. Sixty years ago most men wore white pants woven of coarse material known as [saqakarson] "white calzones," originally of Spanish origin. The etymon [karson] is a phonologically nativized form of the Spanish *calzón* (see Figure 4.2). Chiquimulas regard the [saqakarson] today as the iconic Chiquimula men's garment. The fact that the *calzones* were originally a Spanish sartorial imposition designed to replace the ancient loincloth is irrelevant to its current cultural

status. Despite her K'ichee' monolingualism, Ska' exhibited a keen metapragmatic sensitivity to the indexical value of Spanish words, marking her referential transition from a modern item of clothing to an iconically traditional garment with a metaphorical switch from Spanish to K'ichee'.[9]

The Spanish etyma in [we:n pantoδon][10] "quality pants" and [saqakarson][11] "white calzones" underwent different degrees of phonological adjustment, iconically mirroring the contrasting cultural resonance of the objects they refer to. The [we:n pantoδon][12] is construed as a Western garment adopted for strictly practical reasons, while the [saqakarson] is construed as a relic emblematic of traditional cultural values. The difference in degree of phonological adjustment indexes the structurally opposed cultural status of the referents. Qualitatively differing modalities of structural incorporation of Spanish loanwords are metapragmatic indices forming an indexical cline, as it were, of the referent's bona fide traditional credentials.

In [we:n] the original bilabial stop [b] in Spanish *buen* assimilated to the following [w]. In the same way, in [pantoδon] the second [a] in the Spanish *pantalón* assimilated to the following [o] and the intervocalic /l/ was fricativized. In contrast, the compound [saqakarson], emblematic of traditional male clothing, underwent a further degree of phonological nativization in addition to the substitution of sounds lacking

FIGURE 4.2. Itinerant merchants wearing the *saqakarson* in Santa María Chiquimula (courtesy of the Colección del Museo Etnográfico de Hamburgo sobre Guatemala, Fototeca Guatemala, CIRMA).

in K'ichee'.[13] The epenthetic vowel [a] between [saq] "white" and [karson] "calzones" rearranged the syllabic segmentation of the nominal phrase, turning it into a lexical compound. Only etymologically K'ichee' nouns and very early Spanish loanwords are licensed as heads of compounds of this kind. Thus, structural constraints reveal classes in the cultural regimentation of the lexicon.[14] The morphophonology of loanwords indexes different modalities of cultural assimilation of Spanish artifacts, practices, and concepts. Metalinguistic awareness of the structural difference between compounding and phonological substitution enables the emergence of at least two lexical classes with contrasting indexical effects, as we saw in text (4.2).

4.4. "Hybrid" Speech and the Cultural Organization of Language in Santa María Chiquimula

K'ichee' and Spanish are performed as registers in dynamic tension, carrying out "boundary work" and alternatively fusing and separating in different styles and discourse genres.[15] The quantitative contrast between Spanish and K'ichee' lexicon is itself a stylistic cue, generating a cline whose gradations depend on the iconic predominance of one or the other. However, the

FIGURE 4.3. Parish church of Santa María Chiquimula (photograph by Lilian Márquez).

effect is not simply the automatic result of the ratio between Spanish and K'ichee' etyma, but a response to the presence or absence of emblematic lexemes such as K'ichee' cardinal numbers and a series of nouns referring to traditional material artifacts such as [saqakarson]. Their presence indexes a linguistic performance as *puro K'ichee'*, while their absence, reinforced by nonce borrowings and code switching, typifies *K'ichee' mezclado* "mixed K'ichee." *Puro K'ichee'* and *K'ichee' mezclado* are metalinguistic labels classifying K'ichee' discourse in terms of its indexical association with different modalities of power and cultural legitimacy.

Non-indigenous Guatemalans stigmatize code switching. They often view indigenous languages as inferior or structurally incapable of expressing complex thoughts. Indigenous languages are presumed to lack grammar, technical vocabulary, and written literature. Code switching is iconically interpreted as evidence

of an "impure," decaying culture. The stress on lexical purism among Maya language planners in Guatemala responds to this prejudice and aims to falsify it, coining etymologically pure K'ichee' words to replace Spanish loanwords (Maxwell 1996; French 2010).

4.5. Spanish, Authority, and Cultural Legitimacy

On a rainy morning in March 2005 a workshop for Catholic youth catechists was held in the parish church of Santa María Chiquimula (see Figure 4.3). About sixty young men and women between the ages of fourteen and twenty met at one of the large halls in the parish building. The meeting was hosted by Tilin, a vivacious nineteen-year-old, one of the most active leaders of the Catholic youth movement in Santa María. She was wearing a beautiful *po't*, the traditional handwoven *huipil* "blouse," sporting the emblematic colors and weaving patterns of Santa

María Chiquimula. She was leading the meeting as elected representative of Catholics in the parish. Only a few decades ago it was rare for young women like Tilin to achieve positions of authority in Catholic congregations. The dominance of male elders and the exclusion of women are increasingly contested but still normal facts of life in K'ichee' communities.

The audience consisted of men and women fifteen to eighteen years old, though I noticed a couple of elders and the *ladino* parish priest milling around in the back. Tilin was addressing the plenary in K'ichee', speaking confidently and with a diffident flair. Spanish loanwords were a crucial element of her performance, which used them to construct an authoritative, culturally sanctioned persona. It was clear that she spoke standard Spanish well, as her Spanish switches did not show any of the stereotypes marking "K'ichee-accented Spanish," such as unstressed vowel reduction or lack of gender agreement. She sounded modern, educated, and cosmopolitan when uttering text (4.3).

(4.3)
Muy biyen, entonses are kub'an **desaroyar algo**. Xiqak'am loq k'ut jun **mes**. Xib'an **partisipar** reech junje k'o **partisipasiyon**, <u>berda</u>?

<u>Very well, then</u>; he is making a <u>public presentation</u>. And you all took it on a month ago. You all <u>took part</u> in it so that we have wide <u>participation, right</u>?[16]

(Tilin, 18 years old, Santa María Chiquimula, March 2005)

In text (4.3) Tilin reminded participants of decisions made during previous group meetings with an utterance that included nonce borrowings from the Spanish jargon used in Catholic organizations. She refers to an oral presentation as [kub'an desaroyar algo] "to develop something," in which the K'ichee' verb [kub'an] "(s)he does" sets up a syntactic frame for the incorporation of Spanish infinitives such as [desaroyar] "to develop,"[17] stressing the importance of [partisipasiyon] "participation," from Spanish *participación*. Although these Spanish etyma

have K'ichee' lexical equivalents, Tilin's switch responds precisely to the additional indexical value of the Spanish terms, marking the specialized knowledge, cultural prestige, and social legitimacy held by powerful non-K'ichee' individuals such as Spanish-speaking priests, nuns, and teachers.

Tilin recruits the rhetorical force and indexical value of Spanish to buttress her leadership role as educated young woman in the Catholic community. Although in Catholic public events and sacramental practice in Santa María Chiquimula, K'ichee' is the preferred language, Tilin opted for nonce borrowings to navigate the demands of tradition and change, appropriating the ambivalent prestige and discursive force associated with Spanish. The process of enregisterment of *K'ichee mezclado* as a hybrid effected, in fact, a semiotic appropriation of the *ladinos'* language.

4.6. Modalities of Code Switching and Linguistic Performance

Lexically, *K'ichee' mezclado* "mixed K'ichee'" consists of sequences of switches between K'ichee' and Spanish. In Santa María Chiquimula it occurs in two distinct modalities cued by the quantitative predominance of one or the other and the presence or absence of the emblematic words and phrases discussed earlier. In the first, Spanish is the matrix language and K'ichee' the embedded language, as in text (4.4); in the second, in contrast, K'ichee' is the matrix language and Spanish the embedded language, as in text (4.5). These two modalities are deployed to craft subtle distinctions in self-presentation and discursive force.

Text (4.4) illustrates the pragmatic force of embedding K'ichee' in a Spanish matrix. One afternoon in December 2004 I was at the bus terminal in Santa María Chiquimula waiting for the next bus for the commute to the city of Quetzaltenango, two hours to the south. Minutes after I took my seat, a young Chiquimula couple in their late teens sat in the row in front of me. The young man was telling the young woman in Spanish about a fortuitous encounter he had with María, a woman from his village that he was courting at the time. He ran into María in Quetzaltenango on a Friday afternoon, when, unknown to each other, they were both running errands in the city. Feeling lucky, he tried to seize the opportunity to take her out to dinner at a local chain restaurant but then realized that he had only a little cash. At that point in his narrative he said:

(4.4)

No tenía pisto para llevarla a Pollo Albamar o Macdonald, entonces xinya jun chuchiit puq'ap.

I had no money to take her to Pollo Albamar or McDonald's, so [instead] I put a *chuchito* in her hand.[18]

(18-year-old man, Santa María Chiquimula, December 2004)

In text (4.4) the young man marks the transition from a reference to fast-food items emblematic of *kaxlan* culture to a reference to a contrasting traditional food icon with a metaphorical switch from Spanish to K'ichee'.[19] This involved not only reference to distinct food items but also acting out contrasting cultural values through distinct languages. Pollo Albamar and McDonald's, the former a local fried chicken chain and the latter the local franchise of its American namesake, are restaurants with a middle-class clientele in Quetzaltenango. For Chiquimulas, they embody Spanish, urban, middle-class culture. The *chuchiit* "chuchito," in contrast, is a kind of tamale wrapped in corn husks, very popular as a snack food in Guatemala and an icon of traditional Guatemalan food culture (see Figure 4.4). For young Chiquimula adults, the *kaxlan*/K'ichee' semiotic opposition involves ambivalent attitudes and tensions mirroring the bicultural nature of their upbringing and the changes the township has undergone in the last thirty years. These young people exploit the indexical emblematicity of both languages, including intertwining stylistic contrasts from Spanish and K'ichee' in the same utterance.

The existence of two code-switching modalities in Santa María Chiquimula shows that

not only paradigmatic but also syntagmatic contrasts produce systematic rhetorical effects in conversation. Chiquimulas react to the indexical effects marked by word choice as well as the quantitative predominance of each language, the metric structure of each turn. Text (4.5) shows the inverse of the code switching we saw in text (4.4). In text (4.5), rather than embed K'ichee' in a Spanish matrix, one of the interlocutors embeds Spanish in a K'ichee' matrix to construct a particular image of self he wished to convey in this interaction:

(4.5)

Sergio: Uchaanim taan katzukuj?
    And you're looking for [a girlfriend] now?

Lu':   Uchaanim tan kin...kintzukuj pe k'o xun **talbes posiblemente kinub'an responder ya estos dias pero no estoy seguro.**
    Nowadays I'm looking, but there's one <u>who maybe will answer these days but I'm not sure.</u>[20]

(Lu', 27 years old, Santa María Chiquimula, February 2005)

Text (4.5) is part of a recorded conversation with Lu', a twenty-seven-year-old Chiquimula teacher and a committed and highly educated Catholic activist. Embedding Spanish in a conversation conducted predominantly in K'ichee' is a response to the unusual sociolinguistic context of the exchange. Not only was I openly recording at the time, but Lu' knew of my interest in K'ichee' and regarded me, rightly or wrongly, as an "expert" in language in general, including Spanish. The switch to Spanish after [*kintzukuj pe k'o jun*] "I'm looking, but there's one (who)..." foregrounds Lu's noncommittal stance with Spanish adverbs like [talbes] "maybe" and [posiblemente] "possibly." The latter mark *español culto*—a literary, academic Spanish—appropriate in formal situations or as a way to index an educated, refined persona. Such sensibility to the nuances of Spanish style and their use in K'ichee' conversation shows the

FIGURE 4.4. Young woman holding a basketful of *chuchitos* (see the unwrapped *chuchito* in the foreground) (photograph by Lilian Márquez).

deep imbrication of both languages and Lu''s metapragmatic sensitivity to complex levels of organization in Spanish discourse. Following [posiblemente] "possibly," the K'ichee' verb form *kinuban* introduces a syntactic frame in which Spanish infinitives such as *responder* "answer" are incorporated. This sequence of Spanish words marked by the auxiliary verb *kinuban* "I do" in Lu's response yields finally to a Spanish phrase finishing the turn. This is not simply a case of "interference" in second language acquisition but a deliberate articulation of the stylistic repertoires of two different languages (Poplack et al. 1988). Structurally, Lu' simply shifts from a K'ichee' to a Spanish matrix; discursively, the shift foregrounds Lu's refined persona by means of a transition from colloquial K'ichee' to formal Spanish.

4.7. Discourse Markers and Hybrid Speech

"Hybrid" speech—Spanish words in a K'ichee' matrix or vice versa—is not a random juxtaposition of words but is constrained structurally and pragmatically. On the one hand, referential categories—content words—such as nouns, adjectives, verbs, and cardinal numbers elicit intense pragmatic effects, emerging also in metalinguistic comment. On the other, negation markers, n-words,[21] and quantifiers are metapragmatically less salient, constituting a class of loanwords with weaker indexical associations (see Romero 2006 for more detail). The difference is one of degree of iconicity: nouns and verbs are more iconic due to their referential role while negators and quantifiers are the least detachable and therefore least likely to be used as indices or tropes (Silverstein 1981).

Discourse markers, in contrast, offer an interesting paradox. They are nondetachable and yet highly iconic of the *kaxlan* "Spanish" cultural field. Due to their ubiquity as links between utterances and illocutionary cues and their collocation at the boundaries of sentences and larger discourse units, they are the most commonly used loanwords (Brody 1987, 1995; Furbee 1988). They literally frame K'ichee' discourse, marking its margins and linking sentences and larger units. Borrowed discourse markers iconically recreate the pragmatic forces associated with Spanish discourse, weaving K'ichee' speech into a Spanish-like pattern. The language of the colonizer is thus appropriated in another discursive transposition that preserves K'ichee' lexicon, syntax, and semantics but incorporates the pragmatic force and ambivalent cultural prestige associated with Spanish. Text (4.6) is an excerpt from an interview with Paulina, a forty-two-year old widow from Santa María Chiquimula, in which she tells a series of anecdotes about her grade school years in Xecachelaj, a village far from the township seat:

(4.6)
Xaq oxib' junab' xink'oji' pa **eskwela deayi** xinelik. **Ba per** nu**papa** karaj ta kin…kinelik **porke** ri karaj ri are **eske** kaqésaj **seksto** pu…. Wene **seksto**…. Utz chiri chik kixka'yik, biyen kixka'yik, kisik'ij ruwa ri wuj. **Pero komo** in ak'al **pwe**, kinchomaj ta, je'l ruwach b'i xwilo **bay**, xinelik **mismo**. Xaq **tersero** keqesaj taq ri **mas**. **Ba, tos** xinel kuuk'…. Xaq jeri…. **Y de ayi pues, despues, deporsi** nugaan pwaq. K'a in ko'l na **komo de** taq…**kreo ke de, de dies anyos** xinel pa **eskwela, kreo yo, dies anyo, dose anyo** waral xinelik. **Deayi**, kinto'on wati't ruch'ajik u**panyal** ruuk' raal kom plaja' ri kich'ajik, pa ri nimaja' kech'aj wi ri ch'ajo'n. **Ba, tos** kub'iij ri wati't chwe xatto' xtaq ri axib'al, kach'aja ri

tz'iyaq. Kuya jun **asinkwenta sentabos**, kacha chwe, jun laj **bulto** atz'iyaq jeri. Kaya chwe jun **sinkwenta len**. **Pero komo** kikiya ta ri nu**mama pero ni sinkwenta len**, **ni** jun **ketsal, nada**. Ya taj b'a re kintzukuj in kinkiya wi **sinkwenta len** nurajiil. **Toes** kinch'aja ri kipanyal ri ak'al. Je'e.[22]

I was in [grade] school for three years only. After that I dropped out, though my father didn't want me to drop out because he wanted me to pass sixth grade at least. Maybe sixth grade.… At that point they [the students] read well, they read books. But since I was still a child, I didn't know and I dropped out when he lost hope. Third grade is the highest grade most people pass. Well, I dropped out then, just like that…. Afterward, well, the truth is that I wanted to have money. I was still a child, like ten years old when I dropped out of grade school here. After that I helped my grandmother with her laundry, washing of her diapers, her child's, because they washed their clothes in the stream; clothes were washed at the river. So my grandmother tells me: "Go and help your brothers! Go and do their laundry!" She says she'll give me fifty cents for a pile of clothes this size. Fifty cents. But my mother would give me neither fifty cents nor one quetzal, nothing. So I had to look for myself and they would give me fifty cents. So I went to wash the child's diapers. Yes!

(Paulina, 42 years old, Santa María Chiquimula, November 2005)

When I spoke with Paulina in 2005, she was an independent widow employed in the administrative office of the Catholic parish. Until her husband's sudden death she used to travel with him as itinerant merchant to markets in Baja Verapaz, Chimaltenango, and Guatemala City. She spoke very good Spanish, which she learned practicing her trade. The fragment illustrates the manner in which Spanish discourse markers frame K'ichee' speech. Linking discourse units and marking sequence ([deayi],[23] [tons]/[tos]/[toes][24]), opposition ([per],[25] [pero komo][26]), presuppositions ([deporsi][27]), hedging ([kreoyo][28]), and consequence ([tons]), they exploit the ambivalent cultural force of Spanish. The roles of Spanish discourse markers in K'ichee' are dual. On the one hand, they act as discourse deictics, linking phrases and sentences and marking discourse relations between them. On the other, they perform as stylistic indices, building the metric structure of K'ichee' *mezclado*, hybrid speech.

Multiple syntactic categories are recruited for *K'ichee' mezclado*. Far from being sloppy speakers, code mixers exhibit a keen linguistic sensitivity to stylistic and lexical nuance in both Spanish and K'ichee'. It is a magnificent iconic embodiment of the bicultural nature of social life for K'ichee' speakers today. The fact that it is so stigmatized, however, points to the disjunction between discourse and behavior, between sociolinguistic norms and linguistic performance that is the hallmark of ideology (Silverstein 1981; Irvine and Gal 2000; Blommaert 2005).

The opposition between K'ichee' and Spanish is isomorphic to the *indígena* and *ladino* frames nationally. In contrast, the indexical contrasts between regional K'ichee' stereotypes discussed in Chapter 3 are much more circumscribed. Furthermore, the former is also staged in Guatemalan migrant communities in the United States, for example, where the K'ichee' ethnic frames discussed earlier continue to structure interactions among *indígenas* and *ladinos* (Foxen 2007).

The contrast *maya/mestizo* constitutes an alternative, contemporary appropriation of the colonial dichotomy *indio/español* and its republican offshoot *indígena/ladino* (see Chapter 6). The Mayanization of the *indígena* category seemingly multiplies the number of ethnic frames performed in Guatemala today but does not fundamentally subvert the dichotomous ethnic organization of interaction dominant since 1523. There is a sort of Lévi-Straussian continuity between the Spanish and the republican periods, a lasting communicational norm that continues to frame boundary work. The persistence of the *indio/español* dichotomy in new guises attests to the endurance of the colonial socioeconomic structures in spite of changing self-representations among Maya and non-Maya. They show the intricate nexus between macrosocial structures and local regimes of indexicality. As argued by Silverstein (1981) and Blommaert (2005), the creative use of linguistic forms in interaction is constrained by patterns of social control and hegemony that cannot be easily shaken off. They are the blood and marrow of the cultural context of language use. Without changes in the material conditions and political structures that constrain linguistic interaction, changes in ideologies of ethnicity would in all likelihood fail to transform the communication patterns and ethnic frames in which they thrive.

Notes

1. Spanish is in bold.
2. "Code switching" refers to phrase- and sentence-internal transitions between two structurally different languages.
3. The "matrix language" (ML) provides the basic syntactic order and phrase structure, while the "embedded language" (EL) provides words and even entire phrases, as long as ML and EL are structurally congruent (Myers-Scotton 2002).
4. A nonce borrowing is an idiosyncratic single-word code switch.
5. Contact phenomena in Mesoamerica precede the Spanish invasion, and scholars have produced substantial historical evidence of lexical and structural influence between genetically unrelated indigenous languages. Mesoamerica has been cogently argued to be a language area, or *Sprachbund*. Campbell et al. (1986) argue that as a result of long-term contact between unrelated languages, several linguistic features such as phrase types and lexical calques, diffused through Mesoamerica and became areal markers shared by languages of typologically distinct and genetically unrelated stocks. K'iche'an languages, for example, have some lexical input from Nahuatl, especially in the fields of war and calendrics. See Campbell (1971).
6. Some areas had more exposure to Spanish from as early as the mid-seventeenth century, such as the Kaqchikel- and Nahuatl-speaking towns around the city of Santiago de Guatemala, capital of the Spanish province of the same name.

However, observers in the late eighteenth century report that even there very few Maya were fluent in Spanish (Cortez y Larraz 1958).

7. Most Chiquimula men work as traveling merchants, selling their wares as far west as Tapachula in Chiapas, Mexico, and as far east as Nicaragua.

8. Spanish is in bold.

9. "An important distinction is made from situational switching, where alternation between varieties redefines a situation, being a change in governing norms, and metaphorical switching, where alternation enriches a situation, allowing for allusion to more than one social relationship within the situation" (Blom and Gumperz 1986:409).

10. The noun phrase [we:n pantoδon] is composed of [pantoδon], from Spa. *pantalón*, and the attribute [we:n], from Spa. *buen*.

11. The term [saqakarson] is syntactically a nominal phrase but phonologically a compound noun from K'ichee' [saq] "white" and Spa. [karson] "calzones."

12. In Guatemalan Spanish the singular form *pantalón* is much more frequently heard than the plural *pantalones* to refer to a pair of pants, unlike in peninsular varieties. The careful reader might object that [we:n pantoδon] in text (4.2) could be analyzed as an intrasentential code switch or a borrowed quasi-idiomatic phrase. However, in K'ichee' the adjective [we:n] is often heard as an attribute of other nouns, as in [we:n xaʔ] "drinkable water" or [we:n ule:w] "fertile land."

13. The substitution of [l] for [r] may be the result of articulatory differences between Spanish and K'ichee' when *calzón* was borrowed in the sixteenth century.

14. Syntactically, however, the structure of both nominal phrases is K'ichee': attributes precede nouns, and nouns lack gender and number agreement.

15. I ignore the important issue of the structural and cultural influence of K'ichee' on the Spanish spoken by Chiquimulas, which would require a volume by itself, and concentrate on the various modalities of nativization of Spanish in K'ichee' speech.

16. Spanish is in bold in the original text but underlined in the translation.

17. K'ichee' auxiliary verb [-ban] "do" + infinitive form of the Spanish verb.

18. Spanish is in bold in the original text but underlined in the translation.

19. From Spa. *Castellano*, [kaʃlan] is used as an attribute of people and objects of Spanish or *ladino* background.

20. Spanish is in bold.

21. Negative forms of indefinites and conjunctions such as *ni...ni* in Spanish and *neither...nor* in English.

22. Spanish is in bold.

23. From Spa. *de allí* "from there."

24. From Spa. *entonces* "then."

25. From Spa. *pero* "but."

26. From Spa. *pero como* "but since."

27. From Spa. *de por si* "already."

28. From Spa. *creo yo* "I think."

CHAPTER 5

"Ancestor Power Is Maya Power"

The Uses and Abuses of Honorific Address in K'ichee'

5.1. A Linguistic Tourist in Santa María Chiquimula

When I first visited the town of Santa María Chiquimula in late 2004, I was a graduate student looking for a suitable dissertation field site. I had previous acquaintance with the K'ichee' language and was able to follow colloquial conversations reasonably well. My experience with K'ichee', however, was restricted to the varieties spoken in Santa Cruz del Quiché and Zacualpa, east of Santa María Chiquimula. Not long after I got off the pickup truck that brought me on narrow dusty roads from San Antonio Ilotenango, I had my first conversation with a native Chiquimula. A smiling middle-aged man sitting outside his house on the outskirts of the town was rather startled when I addressed him in K'ichee'. Very few Guatemalans of European ancestry speak a Mayan language, and my polite request for directions to the parish church was definitely unexpected. I made sure I addressed him with the reverential addressee pronoun *laal* with its concurrent verbal and nominal morphology, which I thought was the norm for addressing senior people based on what I had seen in Santa Cruz del Quiché. He pointed the way to the central square where the church and other official buildings were located and finished with a question:

(5.1)
Katpe wi, aδa?[1]
k-at-pe wi ala
IN-2sA-come TR boy

Where are you from, dude?

Although I understood his question, I was surprised that he did not reciprocate with the reverential form to address me, using instead the default addressee marker *at*. To add insult to injury, he referred to me as [aδa] "boy," a rather informal vocative, which I had never experienced in my few first acquaintance situations elsewhere. In the next few days I learned that Chiquimulas hold different, more restricted rules of honorific address than other K'ichee'-speaking townships. As they put it: "The only person we address with *laal* is Our Lord," where "Our Lord" (*Qajaaw*) refers to the Christian God. My very first interaction with a Chiquimula exposed me to the complex interrelationship between local representations of ethnicity, personhood, and language variation in this township. Addressee-marker choice is one of the ways in which ideologies of hierarchy and ethnicity are indexed in K'ichee'. On the one hand, the alternation between the unmarked *at* and marked *laal* pronominals embodies local

TABLE 5.1. Addressee Forms in K'ichee'.

Register	Unmarked		Honorific	
Paradigm	Pronominal	Possessive Prefix	Pronominal	Possessive Enclitic
Singular	at	a-z	laal	-lah
Plural	ix	i-	alaq	-alaq

ideas of authority, reverential entitlement, and situational pragmatics. On the other, intertownship disjunctions in addressee marking act as linguistic icons in regional political landscapes. The "proper" use of the marked form *laal* iconically effects elder-sanctioned social authority and traditional values of sociability and respect, while deviations index pragmatic tropes or rhetorical challenges to the social regime legitimated by the ancestors.

5.2. The K'ichee' Honorific Repertoire

An honorific register is "a system of linguistic signs linked by their users to stereotypes of honor or respect" (Agha 2002).[2] Honorific registers are inherently indexical in function. Their primary role is to implement norms of reverence, authority, and prestige. Through lexemes typified as honorific, together with nondetachable, textual configurations, honorific registers index the reverence due to individuals in certain interaction roles (Agha 2002:21–22). Among K'iche'an languages, K'ichee' is unique in having honorific address pronominals: *laal* (singular) and *alaq* (plural) with concurrent verbal and nominal agreement marking. The latter deviates from the regular subject agreement paradigm in two ways, the first of which is discussed here and the second of which is treated below, at text (5.4). First, in honorific address, possessed nouns do not take the usual ergative prefixes co-referring to the possessor but instead take postclitic particles: *lah* in the singular and *alaq* in the plural, simultaneously identifying the possessor and indexing the reverence she or he is entitled to (see Table 5.1).

As seen in Table 5.1, pronominals and possession markers vary along two axes: number (singular/plural) and honorific status (unmarked/honorific). Text (5.2) illustrates the paradigms:

(5.2)

Unmarked	**Honorific**
Singular	
At, jas ab'i'?	Laal, jas b'i' lah?
At xas a-ɓi	la:l xas ɓi la:
2sA what 2sE-name	AHs what name HAs
You, what's your name? (Unmarked)	You, what's your name? (HON)
Plural	
Ix, jas ib'i'?	Alaq, jas b'i' alaq?
iʃ xas i-ɓi	alaq xas ɓi alaq
AHp what 2pE-name	AHp what name HAp
You all, what is your name? (Unmarked)	You all, what is your name? (HON)

In text (5.2) the pronominals *at* and *ix* are the unmarked addressee pronouns, singular and plural respectively (absolutive markers), while [a-] and [i-] mark possessor agreement (ergative markers). The latter are bound morphemes prefixed to the possessed noun *b'i'* "name." In the honorific paradigm, however, the addressee pronouns are *laal* in the singular and *alaq* in the plural. The corresponding possessor agreement markers are *lah* and *alaq*, which are postnominal clitics, not bound morphemes like the unmarked nonhonorific forms. Honorific marking is therefore morphologically irregular.

The pronominal forms *at* and *ix* double as subject agreement markers on intransitive verbs as well as patient markers on transitive verbs (absolutive agreement), while [a-] and [i-] act as agent markers on transitive verbs (ergative agreement). In verbal stems, ergative markers precede the verbal root on transitive verbs. In contrast, absolutive markers precede the verbal

TABLE 5.2. Unmarked Verbal Agreement Paradigm in K'ichee'.

Role	Speaker		Addressee		Nonspeaker/Non-addressee	
	Erg	Abs	Erg	Abs	Erg	Abs
Singular	in	in	a	at	u	0
Plural	qa	oj	i	ix	ki	e'

Note: Erg = ergative agreement; Abs = absolutive agreement.

root when marking intransitive subjects but follow the ergative set when marking transitive objects (see Table 5.2).

(5.3)
Unmarked singular addressee
Subject

Intransitive verbs
Katoq'ik
k-at-oq'-ik
IN-2sA-cry-PF

Transitive verbs
Kinato'o
k-in-a-to'-o
IN-1sA-2sE-help-PF

You cry
(unmarked sing.)

You help me
(unmarked sing.)

Object
Katinto'o
k-at-in-to'-o
IN-2sA-1sE-help-PF

I help you (unmarked sing.)

In text (5.3) [a-] marks the addressee in the transitive *kinato'o* "You help me" (ergative agreement). In intransitive verbs, in contrast, singular addressees are marked with *at* (absolutive agreement), as in *katoq'ik* "You cry." The absolutive marker *at* is required also when the addressee plays the role of object of the transitive verb in *katinto'o* "I help you." In honorific address, however, the same postclitic forms double as absolutive and ergative agreement markers, and nominal possession markers as well. Compare the singular forms *ab'i'* "Your name" and *b'i' la* "Your name (HON)" in text (5.2), or *ib'i'* and *b'i' alaq* in the plural.

The second deviation of honorific address from the regular agreement paradigm involves verbs, as in text (5.4):

(5.4)
Honorific singular addressee[3]
Subject

Intransitive verbs
Koq' la:
k-o-oq' la:
IN-3sA-cry HAs

Transitive verbs
Kinto'w lah
k-in-to'-w lah
IN-1sA-help-AP HAs

You cry
(HON sing.)

You help me
(HON sing.)

Object
Kinto' lah
k-o-in-to' lah
IN-3sA-1sE-help HAs

I help you (HON sing.)

In honorific address a zero morpheme instead of the usual subject markers precedes the verbal root. Additionally, the postclitics [lah] in the singular or [alaq] in the plural attach to the verb, as in [koq' lah] "You cry (HON)" or [kinto? lah] "I help you" in text (5.4). Zeros are unmarked forms indexing nonspeaker/non-addressee intransitive subjects or transitive objects.[4] This agreement type is structurally similar to that of honorific address in Spanish and Italian, in which verbs are inflected as if agreeing with a third person, nonspeaker/non-addressee subject. However, in contrast with Italian, for example, where the feminine third-person pronominal *Lei* indexes the addressee, K'ichee' has specific honorific pronominal forms.

K'ichee' honorific agreement is a pragmatic trope: a zero marker co-indexes honorific reverence laminated on its nonspeaker/non-addressee primary status, enacting a sort of oblique reference, as with *Lei* in Italian (as seen above) or *Sie* in German. Structurally, honorific address involves a defective verbal paradigm, lacking active forms for transitive verbs. The gap is filled by the so-called focus agent antipassive construction, normally used to foreground the subject of transitive verbs, as shown in text (5.5):

(5.5)
(5.5.1)   At xinto'wik.
           At x-in-to'-w-ik
           2sA C-1sA-help-AP-PF

           It was you who helped me.
           You (unmarked) helped me*.

(5.5.2)   Kinto'w la:
           k-o-in-to'-w   la:
           IN-3sA-1sE-help-AP HAs

           You help me (HON).
           It is you who is helping me (HON)*.[5]

The focus agent construction in (5.5.1) requires an explicit subject or pronominal to be preposed to the antipassive verb stem, as in the pseudo-cleft construction in English (Davies and Sam Colop 1990). Pragmatically, the focus antipassive presupposes a set of candidates, of which one is picked as final referent. The nonfocus declarative gloss "You (unmarked) helped me" is therefore pragmatically infelicitous. In honorific address, however, as in [kinto?w lah] "You help me (HON)" in text (5.5.2), the set presupposition is canceled, and hence the best gloss is an unmarked declarative.

5.3. Honorific Address and the Linguistic Construction of Authority in K'ichee'

During my fieldwork in Santa María Chiquimula I was struck by the apparent paradox between the sparse use of honorific address and its ubiquity in metalinguistic discourse. In family conversations, market exchanges, and even public speech events such as political rallies and church homilies, it was rarely heard. The contrast with the frequent use of the polite address form *Usted* when Chiquimulas spoke Spanish was striking. Furthermore, I noticed that K'ichee' communi-

ties had different honorific address rules, a common cross-linguistic feature of honorific systems adumbrated above (Agha 2002:25). I found the existence of geographic variation especially unsettling given the tendency of the descriptive literature to think of honorific address as a categorical structural feature of K'ichee' grammar, rather than as a semiotic praxis varying in its motivation and social effects across township boundaries (López Ixcoy 1997; Campbell 1977). I also noted that even in townships where *laal* usage was commonplace, such as Nahualá and Santa Cruz del Quiché, many speakers felt anxious about their ability to perform honorific speech. Elders don't hesitate to disparage the sloppy renditions of the young. The complexities of verbal agreement, in particular, provoked much argument among my consultants. The younger a speaker, the less likely he or she was to feel confident about using honorific speech in public. For example, one evening in 2007, after Xwan, an eighteen-year-old, addressed an elderly visitor to acknowledge an invitation to go on a day trip, Te'k, his father, a fifty-four-year-old teacher from Nahualá, corrected his son's flawed honorifics and volunteered a sarcastic comment about the difficulties of the young with honorific forms:

(5.6)
Xwan: …Xinsik'ij alaq…
Te'k: Xinsik'in alaq! Le alab'om na si ta
         kekowin che le "laal"…
Xwan: I invited you all (HON)…
Te'k: You all invited me (HON)! The boys
         can't really do the "laal"…
                              (Xwan, 18 years old;
                               Te'k, 54 years old,
                               Nahualá, July 2007)

In text (5.6), which I overheard in Te'k's home, Xwan uttered the active *xinsik'ij* rather than the antipassive *xinsik'in* required by honorific address with *alaq* "You all (HON)," unwittingly inverting the agent and beneficiary markers on the verb and provoking Te'k's paternal correction. Inconsistency in speaker performance despite metalinguistic salience captures in a nutshell the pragmatics of honorific address in K'ichee'. This is neither an accident nor the result of retrenchment of honorifics in the face of social or linguistic change, because honorific address continues to be used and learned. Rather, it is a consequence of the social roles it performs. Following Paul Manning's discussion of social deixis, I surmise that honorific forms in K'ichee' foreground permanent social roles rather than "politeness" or other emerging situational variables (Manning 2001). Honorific address is the linguistic embodiment of authority and hierarchy rather than of undefined "politeness" norms. In this it differs from honorification in languages such as Spanish and French, in which honorific forms may index not only authority but also other situational features (age and gender differences, social class, formality, etc.) (Brown and Gilman 1987; Morford 1997; Geyer 2008).

In K'ichee', as in any language with honorific registers, the crucial interface between linguistic repertoire and social function is metapragmatic. Explicit rules do not exhaust the possible effects of performing honorifics, though they constitute a normative baseline that helps identify the forms and textual configurations in which they play a role (Agha 2002, 2007). K'ichee' metalinguistic commentary targets honorific lexicon but usually glosses over syntax, intonation, gesture, and interactional co-texts. In regard to honorific address, it focuses on the social persona entitled to it, and—in a speaker-focal twist—on the challenges of performing honorifics felicitously due to the complexity of agreement rules. Tradition and authority are the focus of prescriptive normativity. Although honorification involves special prosodic features and bodily demeanor, even native K'ichee' scholars of ceremonial language rarely mention them. For example, the late Florentino Ajpacajá, a well-known K'ichee' linguist and lexicographer, does not discuss the cadence and demeanor of ceremonial language in his excellent book on the subject (Ajpacajá 2001). He focuses instead on the texts themselves, especially on the form and content of metaphor. Metalinguistic discourse stresses the textual building blocks rather than the channel of delivery.

Exposure to honorific address increases in adulthood as people start to take *cargos*, unremunerated positions of communal authority, in local committees and churches and to enter into *compadrazgo*, or ritual kin, relationships.[6] The acquisition of honorific competence is concurrent with individual socialization into traditional authority and village institutions. It intensifies when speakers grow older, especially after marriage, a rite of passage marking the onset of adulthood with its accompanying rights and communal obligations (Rosenbaum 1993; Forand 2002).

5.4. The *Prinsipalib'* and Honorific Address

Honorific speech is tightly interwoven with K'ichee' constructions of power and ethnicity. Culturally sanctioned authority derives either from ancestral practices or from modern institutions endowed with social legitimacy. The former are associated with traditional values, village councils, elder authority, the K'ichee' language, and indigenous self-identification; the latter, in contrast, are associated with capitalist modernity, mainstream Guatemalan political and economic institutions, state power, formal education, the Spanish language, *ladinos*, and foreigners.

Traditional authority is staged in collective, consensual village and township decisions in local institutions. It is embodied in the *prinsipalib'* "elders," men and women of prestige who have risen to positions of considerable influence in local affairs after years of uncompensated service in the city hall and in village civil and religious institutions (see Figure 5.1).[7] Elder authority today is a metonym for grassroots power structures involving ad hoc development committees as well as religious congregations of various denominations (Carmack 1995; Cook 2000; González 2002; DeHart 2010; Ordóñez 2012). What sets these apart from "modern" forms of political power is their relative autonomy from mainstream Guatemalan economic and political life. Traditional institutions constitute an autonomous discourse sphere in which every village resident can participate. Formal education, individual wealth, and proficiency in Spanish are not

FIGURE 5.1. *Prinsipalib'* during the ritual washing of the staffs of office in Nahualá, Guatemala (photograph by Sergio Romero).

requisites for leadership, unlike in mainstream Guatemalan institutions. In the traditional discourse sphere the K'ichee' language, respect for elder-sanctioned authority, and service to the community are the cornerstones of a harmonious, moral life.

In contrast, nontraditional forms of cultural legitimacy demand formal education, contacts in government offices or churches, client relationships with NGOs and political parties, and the like. They do not require the collective sanction of the village or the explicit approval of town elders but often coexist in tension with them. Although nontraditional forms of authority are construed as iconic of foreigners and their antivalues, many local K'ichee' fill the social roles they require: teachers, government employees, Catholic priests, Pentecostal pastors, NGO activists, and so on.[8] As linguistic repertoires, *puro K'ichee'* and Spanish are the ends in a continuum of linguistic codes used to index disjoint forms of authority and political values that nevertheless exist side by side in the township (see Chapter 4).

As noted earlier, K'ichee' metalinguistic discourse focuses on persons entitled to honorific address rather than on the dynamics of particular situations. The former include traditional religious and civil authorities, elders, and ritual

specialists and healers (see Table 5.3). Not unexpectedly, K'ichee' metalinguistic discourse emphasizes the marked honorific address forms *laal* and *alaq* rather than their unmarked counterparts *at* and *ix*, as in text (5.7):

(5.7)
"Laal" kab'iix che jun nimalaj achi, che jun nimalaj ixoq. Nim ub'antajiik le "laal"!

One says 'laal' "you (HON)" to a great man, or great woman. 'Laal' is of great consequence.
(To'n, 51 years old, Nahualá, summer 2008)

I heard the utterance in text (5.7) from To'n, a fifty-one-year-old housewife and well-known women's rights activist from Nahualá, during a conversation in the summer of 2008. To'n stated that *laal* was to be used to address people she labeled "great man" *nimalaj achi* or "great woman" *nimalax ixoq*. The attributive use of *nimalaj*[9] "great" with *achi* "man" or *ixoq* "woman" refers to an individual of prestige in the traditional discourse sphere (see Table 5.3). The nominal phrase does not denote an individual whose merits accrue from self-centered individual success. Metalinguistic commentary in Nahualá places honorific forms firmly within the realm of traditional authority. They do not mark prestige earned on account of material wealth or formal education, though elder status may overlap with any or all of them. A wealthy merchant, for example, is not entitled to *laal* address if his only claim to authority is his individual economic success. Although reaching the status of *prinsipalib'* is nearly impossible for the poorest community members due to frequent financial outlays, travel, and labor obligations, wealth or formal education is definitely not a prerequisite.

Schoolteachers or government officials, though usually treated with respect, are seldom addressed in K'ichee', even if born and raised in the township. The preferred language used to address nontraditional authority figures is Spanish. Of course, in colloquial interaction with kin and village co-residents, when official roles are put aside, K'ichee' is the language normally used. However, in such situations, these individuals are addressed with the unmarked form *at* rather than the honorific *laal*, unless they also hold a position of traditional authority.

Honorific address is also normative when one addresses certain in-laws. In Nahualá it is expected that one's father- and mother-in-law be addressed with *laal* from the beginning of the protracted engagement process. Lu', a thirty-seven-year-old carpenter, confessed to me shortly before his father- and mother-in-law came on a family visit in 2007 that he was always uncomfortable when speaking to them because he didn't feel confident about his ability to use *laal* properly:

(5.8)
Kinmayow ma na si ta kinkowin che le *"laal."*

I am worried because I am not really good at using *"laal."*

(Lu', 37 years old,
Nahualá, June 2007)

Addressing one's in-laws with honorific forms simultaneously indexes and compounds the social distance and potential conflict involved in affinal relationships. When used to

TABLE 5.3. Social Roles Entitled to Honorific Address in Nahualá.

Office/Role	English Gloss
alkalte[1]	township mayor
pare'[2]	parish priest
prinsipalib'[3]	village elders
aj patan'[4]	member of religious sodality
aj k'axelom	midwife
aj q'iij	calendar divination specialist
aj kun	medicine man/woman
aj k'amal b'e	marriage broker[5]
ji' tat/ji' nan	father-/mother-in-law

Note: Column 1 presents the K'ichee' names of roles entitled to honorific address; column 2 provides the corresponding glosses. The list is not exhaustive. Glosses by the author.
[1] Includes higher-ranking members of the municipal council.
[2] Catholic priests are usually not addressed in K'ichee'. However, when they are, they are addressed with honorific forms in Nahualá, but not in Santa María Chiquimula. The latter is a somewhat deviant practice in K'ichee' communities, as will be explained later in the text.
[3] Includes former members of civil committees, religious sodalities [pasayiɓ], and church committees, both Catholic and evangelical.
[4] Religious sodalities are organized hierarchically. Honorific address is required from lower-ranking members to higher-ranking ones.
[5] Elders speaking on behalf of the groom's and/or the bride's family during marriage negotiations.

address affine relatives, honorific forms effect a pragmatic trope. Addressing affine relatives with honorific forms is—synchronically—a case of second-order indexicality (Silverstein 1976, 2003a).[10] When used with in-laws, the political order is a trope for the extended family and its entitlements and obligations. Honorific address indexes the status and social prestige emanating from traditional authority, acting as its iconic index.

5.5. New Wine in Old Wineskins: The Maya Movement and Honorific Practice

Seeking to bridge the chasm in institutional status between Spanish and Mayan languages in Guatemala, contemporary Maya activists have produced textual artifacts in cultural fields that used to be the exclusive province of Spanish speakers, both Maya and non-Maya, such as the national press, publishing, radio, and television (see Chapter 2). This subversion of the national *marché linguistique* has been echoed in Maya communities in the blossoming of many textual transpositions of traditional speech genres (Bourdieu 2001; Maxwell 1996; England 1996; Jiménez 1997). This includes the expansion of modern pastoral registers, new word coinages,[11] rehabilitation of archaic words, and the expansion of linguistic iconicity as a rhetorical device (Maxwell 1996; England 1996; Morford 1997; French 2010). Maya activists have started to generalize the use of emblematic linguistic forms, such as honorific address, which previously were constrained by restricted licensing conditions. The generalization of honorific address springs partly from an unconscious transposition of Spanish linguistic ideologies and partly from the high emblematic value of traditional forms. Maximizing the number of iconic indices is a rhetorical strategy to heighten cultural legitimacy and pragmatic force. The expansion of honorific forms to public media is a perfect illustration of this. While honorific address is conventionally licensed in face-to-face interactions with high-status interlocutors, radio broadcasts inspired by the Maya movement have turned *laal* and *alaq* into the default audience address form, as in the following recording heard every morning at 6:30 to introduce the K'ichee' daily news service of Nawal Estereo, a popular radio station broadcasting from Nahualá:

(5.9)
(Male voice)
"*El Mensajero*": Ri q'axel qatziij, q'axel qach'ab'aal. Kitziij, kich'ab'aal ri qasiwaan qatinamiit kaq'axex chi apanoq, ri b'antajnaq, xajtajnaq pa le qawokaaj, qatinamiit, qamaaq'. Kojchoman na b'a chirij ri kaqata uuk' alaq chuq chuxaq ta b'a ub'e'al, ub'antajiik, uk'aslemaal wa qatinamiit.

(Female voice)
"*El Mensajero*": Q'axel qatziij, q'axel qach'ab'aal chech alaq pa taq le b'antajnaq, xajtajnaq, le

b'iim, le tziijom, le k'ulman alaq. Utzilaj ulik alaq pa we jun sin xo'kotaj. Are ta b'a wa le kaqaq'axej apan chwach alaq. Chojtatab'ej alaq![12]

(Male voice)
"The Messenger": Broadcasting in our language. The language of our ravines, our towns is now broadcast [to you]; what has occurred, what has transpired in our villages, in our towns, in our nation. We will discuss with you all (HON) what we have heard so that a road may open for the culture and the life of our township.

(Female voice)
"The Messenger": Broadcasting in our language for you all (HON) about what has happened, what has transpired, what has been said, what has been spoken, what has happened to you all (HON). Welcome (HON) to this humble emission. Let this be what we pass on to you all (HON). We hope you all (HON) listen to us!
(Nawal Estereo broadcast, September 7, 2010)

Text (5.9) shows a number of rhetorical devices drawn from traditional speech genres. First, the audience was addressed with the plural honorific pronominal *alaq*, and all co-referring possessed nouns and verb agreement markers were correspondingly inflected with zero morphemes and the enclitic *alaq*, as in *utzilaj ulik alaq* "Welcome (HON)!" and *Chojtatab'ej alaq!* "May you all listen to us! (HON)".[13] Second, the text displays lexical couplets and triplets, both nominal and verbal, a structural feature of traditional speech genres such as prayer, ceremonial greetings, historical chronicles, and myths, enhancing the cultural iconicity of the broadcast (see Table 5.4) (Tedlock 1983; Hanks 1988; Ajpacajá 2001).

By recourse to lexical repetition, the broadcast cumulatively increased the cultural value of the text, stacking it, as it were, with emblematic textual devices: honorific address forms, lexical couplets, and the deliberate avoidance of Spanish loanwords (with the interesting exception of the

TABLE 5.4. Lexical Couplets Used in the Presentation of Nawal Estereo's Morning News Service.

Couplet	Gloss	Denotation
Qatziix, qach'ab'aal	Our word, our language	The K'ichee' language
Qasiwaan, qatinamiit	Our ravines, our towns	The township of Nahualá
Ri bantajnaq, xajtajnaq	What has occurred, what has transpired	News
Ub'eaal, ub'antjxiik,	Its road, its manner	The culture of the township
Le b'iim, le tziijom	What was said, what was spoken	Opinion

name of the news space itself: *El Mensajero* "The Messenger"). Honorific forms mark not only the social status of elders but also project a positive stance vis-à-vis pan-Mayanism by association with traditional authority.

This practice, paradoxically, is changing the indexical function of honorific address, turning it into a situational speaker-focal ideological marker. Most Maya activists represent themselves as speaking on behalf of ancestral values and traditional authority. Nevertheless, they tend to be young, urban, and highly educated (Nelson 1999; Warren 1997; Fischer 2001; Bastos and Camus 2003a). Rarely do they participate in uncompensated community service or achieve the status of *prinsipalib'* in their communities. Thus, the kind of social capital they wield inevitably leads to tensions with traditional authorities. Performances such as text (5.9) seldom go uncontested, and charges of pretentiousness and lack of authenticity are not uncommon. In contrast, text (5.10) illustrates non-activist deictic practice in discourse. It is a transcription of the introduction to an oral narrative told online and recorded for subsequent broadcast in 2000. The narrator was Diego Tum, a respected elder from Nahualá, well known in the township after years of public service as mayor and in other positions in the city hall. An influential Catholic leader, he was also one of the founders of the first radio station broadcasting in Mayan languages in the department of Sololá and had the reputation of being an excellent storyteller.

(5.10)
Saqarik qataat qanaan! Keqaya jun nimalaj
utzil iwach pub'i' le qanimajwaal *Xesukristo*
rachilaam le *Espíritu Santo.* Kaqayi'ej chi
iwonojeel k'o iutz wachil chi rumal ri Qaqajaaw
Diyos. Kenya nimalaj utzil iwach i keqayi'ej
chi kojitatab'ej jachike ri kaqaj sin kaqab'iij.
Nab'e are kinb'iij ub'i le qatinamiit Nawala'. Le
qatinamiit Nawala' k'o pa we *territoriyo osea*
pa le ruleew *Solola.* Le uleew *Solola* k'o pa le
nimalaj qatinamiit *Watemala.*[14]

Good morning, ladies and gentlemen! We bid good morning to you all in the name of Our Lord Jesus Christ together with that of the Holy Spirit. We hope that you all are doing well by the grace of Our Lord God. I bid greetings to you all, and we hope that you all listen to what we all want to say. The title of what I want to speak about first is "Our Township Nahualá." Our township Nahualá is in the territory of the Department of Sololá. The Department of Sololá is in the Republic of Guatemala.

(Diego Tum, 2000)[15]

Text (5.10) shows fewer traditional stylistic devices than text (5.9). The audience was addressed with the unmarked plural pronominal *ix*; there were no lexical repetitions; and several Spanish loanwords were uttered. The loanwords included nouns and discourse markers: *Jesucristo* "Jesus Christ," *Espíritu Santo* "Holy Spirit," *Dios* "God," *territorio* "territory," and *o sea* "I mean." The two texts were relayed in sound media with comparable illocutionary goals. They set the context and prepared the audience for historical narratives on the township of Nahualá. Nevertheless, they differ in social deixis strategies. Text (5.9) exploits the iconicity of traditional discourse to craft a powerful and "authentic" text

FIGURE 5.2. Monument to Manuel Tzo'k outside the church in Nahualá (photograph by Sergio Romero).

FIGURE 5.3. Manuel Tzo'k's hat and personal Bible displayed before township elders (photograph by Arturo Arias).

foregrounding the stated goal of the segment: to mobilize the audience for a pan-Maya political agenda. In contrast, text (5.10) introduces the Nahualá audience to a historical narrative that most are already familiar with: the separation of Nahualá from Santa Catarina Ixtahuacán in 1863 at the behest of Governor Manuel Tzo'k, an elder who led a group of disgruntled residents from Santa Catarina Ixtahuacán to settle in what became the town of Nahualá, thereby laying the foundations for a new autonomous township (Baronti 2001). For Nahualatecos, Tzo'k is a cultural hero and a tellurian force co-substantial with the local landscape (see Figure 5.2). Scores of stories are told of Tzo'k's miraculous interventions on behalf of Nahualatecos in times of need (Hostig et al. 1995; Abac 1980). His legacy

continues to be celebrated in Nahualá, where Wel (Manuel) and We'l (Manuela) are the most popular first names. His old leather hat and personal Bible are treasured heirlooms; on special occasions they are taken out in solemn procession and placed next to the staffs of office of the mayor and the other members of the municipal council (see Figure 5.3).

The indexical contrast between (5.9) and (5.10) reflects different language ideologies articulating language and ethnicity. Nawal Estereo's editorial line embraces a pan-Maya political agenda, which foregrounds shared cultural values transcending township boundaries. Emblematic forms such as honorific address and lexical repetitions are deployed as indices of pan-Maya cultural values, involving ancestor-sanctioned institutions. This discursive project has an inherent ambiguity due to the contradiction between the Maya movement's pan-Maya political agenda and the highly local linguistic forms used to index them. Not all Mayan languages have honorific registers. In fact, K'iche' is the only K'iche'an language with honorific address forms. They exist in Mamean languages but are lacking in the Yukatekan and Ch'olan branches of the Mayan stock.

Diego Tum's performance, in contrast, embodies a local ethnic frame in which the township is the social space delimited by boundary work. Unmarked address forms index the familiarity of *communitas*, mutual complicities and cultural presuppositions held by the residents of Nahualá. The local boundary work in this ethnic frame coexists in tension with a trans-local pan-Maya project espoused by Maya activists.

5.6. Honorific Address and Ethnicity

One of the most interesting facts about honorific address in K'ichee' is the remarkable degree of regional variation in licensing norms. Belying claims that honorific address is a homogeneous structural feature of all K'ichee' varieties, individual speakers and townships differ in the scope and focus of reverential forms (López Ixcoy 1997; Par Sapón and Can 2000). Deviations in usage are often construed as iconic of morally flawed or socially deviant communities, those that flaunt the proper norms of civility and respect. Regional differences involve, on the one hand, disagreements as to the social personae entitled to honorific address and, on the other, inconsistent accounts to explain such differences.

For example, during my fieldwork in Santa María Chiquimula, Catholic friends often claimed that only God should be addressed with the honorific pronominal *laal*. This stipulation stands well to the evidence. Honorific address is indeed infrequent in comparison with Nahualá or Santa Cruz del Quiché. It is restricted to the field of ritual and prayer, especially since the parish opted to institutionalize K'ichee' as the language of sacramental practice in the late 1980s. In other cultural fields honorific address is rare. Even during solemn official functions in the city hall, in which the mayor and town elders would be addressed with *laal* or *alaq* in other townships, Chiquimula authorities are addressed with the unmarked pronominals *at* and *ix* without any detriment to the solemnity of the occasion.

Limited honorific usage epitomizes the egalitarian nature of *communitas* for Chiquimulas: because every Chiquimula has the same rights and obligations, there is no need to mark status differences with *laal* or *alaq*.[16] However, this idealization glosses over obvious class differences as well as the considerable authority held by the *prinsipalibʼ*, especially in rural areas. Restricted to the ritual/religious field in Santa María Chiquimula, the pragmatics of honorific address has, however, undergone some readjustment in the last century. A palpable downsizing of the rituals in which honorific registers were required since the late 1960s was prompted by the successive expansion of Catholic Action and Pentecostal denominations in the western highlands of Guatemala.

Starting in the 1940s, orthodox forms of Catholicism that disapproved of ritual drinking and Maya-Catholic "syncretism" began to expand through the western highlands. Carried by indigenous catechists who spoke the local languages, Catholic Action rapidly effected a radical transformation of local religion, shaking the ideological foundations of traditional authority (Warren 1978; Brintnall 1979; Cabarrús 1979; Falla 1980; Rojas Lima 1988; Piel 1989; González 2002). Religious affiliation became an individual choice. Massive numbers of conversions led to the abandonment of rituals and saints' cults not sanctioned by the church. Traditional Maya religion, called *kostumbr*,[17] was regarded as archaic, bearing the stigma of "paganism." In text (5.11) Juan Mus—one of the first catechists in his village—attested to the rapid expansion of Catholic Action and the communal divisions it caused:

(5.11)
Ba, ensegidə, xaqabʼan *segir*, xojpetik. Pues ri winaq xokik, xok ri winaq. Xaqabʼan *konbertir alma*. Uuuu! *Kwantas* ekʼolik! Xeepetik *pero* winaq ya…. *Lo mas* xaqabʼan *empesar, kwando* xujach, xubʼan *dibidir* riibʼ, xujach riibʼ taq ri *komunidad*.[18]

So immediately we went on, we came in. And so the people joined in, yes, the people joined in. We converted souls…. So many of them! They came in throngs! As soon as we started, the community divided itself, the communities split apart.

(Juan Mus, 70 years old, Santa María Chiquimula, August 2005)

The allure of conversion attracted entire households and extended families. Rituals and objects emblematic of the *kostumbr* were stigmatized, especially *cofradía* rituals[19] and the *tzʼonooj*,[20] or traditional weddings. These institutions involved elaborate ritual speeches in which honorific address was normative. The required rhetorical skills ceased to be transmitted, becoming an ambiguous form of knowledge still emblematic of traditional authority, a powerful cultural force in the township but iconic also of stigmatized rituals.

The ethnographic work of Eduardo León Chic, a native Chiquimula scholar, shows that honorific address was a regular occurrence in ritual before the spread of Catholic Action in the 1950s (León Chic 2002). Ceremonial speeches were addressed, respecting hierarchical order, to fellow *cofradía* members and attending audiences at elaborate functions during feasts and transitions between incumbent and entering *aj patanib'*.[21] Text (5.12) is a fragment of a public prayer performed by the first *ajkalté* "mayor" of the *cofradía* of Our Lord of Esquipulas on the occasion of the ritual washing of the robes of the saint's image. While lower-ranked *cofradía* members and their wives watched, the *ajkalté* acted as mediator, speaking on their behalf. The ritual stipulated that all should be kneeling as the proceedings were enacted:

(5.12)

Laal qanan qatat, lal rajaaw uwinaqil, rajaw usantil, udiosil we loq'alaj chak patan, we loq'alaj chi'bal wachib'al ri'.

Kaqata ba ri mayij toq'ob chikiwach ri Oxlajuj chi Nan, Oxlajuj chi Tat.

Chikiwach ri etewerinaq chik, chikiwach ri xikina' numik, chaqi'j chi' che uch'akik ri k'in tzuqb'al q'ob'al kib'.

Uchanim b'a lal qanan qatat xopan che we q'iij rech uch'ajo'mik ri Qatat Eskipu'l.

Sib'alaj kink'awomaj, sib'alaj kintyoxij utz kiwach ri ewajch'ab'en; utz kiwach ri ukab' nuxoq'ajaw e ri rajaw rixoqil.

Maltiox nujuyub'al nutaq'ajal utz uwach ri nab'e nuxoq'ajaw e ri rajaw rixoqil.

Maltiox Nan, maltiox Tat utz uwach ri ukab' umortom e ri rajaw rixoqil.

Maltiox tew kaqiq' utz uwach ri ukab' ajkalte e ri rajaw rixoqil.

Sib'alaj maltiox rajaw uwinaqil we loq'alaj chi'b'al wachib'al, we loq'alaj chak patan.

Maltyox ya'om la rutzil qachi', rutzil qawach jun q'iij, jun ik', jun junab'.

Sib'alaj k'amo, sib'alaj maltiox k'o ta qak'ulman;

maltiox rutzil kichi' kiwach ri exu'm kotz'i'j, maltiox ya'om la ri qab'inib'al qawa'katajib'al.

Maltiox oj chajim la pa taq ri qab'e qajok, maltiox k'o ri utzil koq'em kisik'im kanoq pa ri qab'e qajok; k'o ri ki'kotemal kitikom kanoq ri Eqanan Qatat.[22]

You (HON) mother and father, you lord of the people, lord of the holiness of this sacred work, of this sacred *cofradía*.

We ask before the Ladies and before the Gentlemen, before the Thirteen Ladies, before the Thirteen Gentlemen.

Before those who have already gone cold, before those who felt hunger and thirst to win a livelihood.

And now, you (HON) mother and father, the day has come to wash the clothes of Our Lord of Esquipulas.

I give many thanks because my fellow *cofradía* members, my second xoq'ajaw and his wife are doing well.

Thanks my mountain, my valley for the first xoq'ajaw and his wife are doing well.

Thanks Mother, thanks Father for the second mayordomo and his wife are doing well.

Thanks for the first mayordomo and his wife are doing well.

Thanks Mist, thanks Wind for the second ajkalte and his wife are doing well.

Thanks lord of the people of this sacred *cofradía*.

Thank you (HON) for giving us well-being for one day, for one month, for one year.

Many thanks for nothing bad has happened to us, thank you very much for the health of the buds, the flowers; thank you (HON) for you have given where to walk, where to stroll.

Thanks for you (HON) have watched over us on the road, thanks for they have made good calls on our behalf; there's the happiness that our Mothers and Fathers have sown. (León Chic 2002:35–36)[23]

Text (5.12) is a transcription of a *ch'ab'al* "prayer" chanted by one of León's elderly interviewees. Repetitions, especially lexical couplets, as well as honorific address, cue the performance as ritualistic. Note the use of the honorific forms *laal* and *alaq* with concurrent nominal and verbal agreement. With the demise of such ceremonies, honorific address, always more restricted in Santa María Chiquimula than in other townships, became even less frequent.

The emergence of the Maya movement, however, led to a functional resignification of traditional stylistic markers, influencing the Chiquimula church. Catholic activists, inspired by pan-Mayanism and post–Vatican Council critiques of Eurocentric theologies, began to change once again the institutional role of indigenous languages in ritual and proselytism in the 1980s and 1990s (Parra 2004; Wilson 1995).

The Santa María Chiquimula parish is one of the most successful examples of this process: since the late 1980s its entire sacramental practice and its catechetical training, youth workshops, and public events have been conducted in K'ichee'. Inspired by enculturation theology, parish priests and Chiquimula activists encouraged the revival of religious sodalities, traditional ceremonies, and the crafts of ritual specialists such as *ajq'ijab'* (calendar divination specialists), formerly stigmatized by Catholic Action. There has been a deliberate effort to revive archaic discourse registers and to regulate their performance, sometimes keeping the forms but changing the intended meaning. This has led to a relative expansion of the licensing conditions for honorific address. New *cargo* holders are being coached in the intricacies of ceremonial speech (Eduardo León Chic, personal communication 2005).

The reversal of antitraditionalist parish policy in the late 1980s provoked confusion and dismay among some Chiquimula Catholics. Many were unhappy about the resurrection of practices that not long before were deplored as pagan relics. This partly explains the conversions of numerous former Catholics to Pentecostal denominations, whose negative views on traditional religion are even more radical than those of Catholic Action.

In the 1980s and 1990s, teaching K'ichee' literacy became one of the strategic tools of Chiqui-mula activists to promote the newly "enculturated" church. Scores of Catholic publications argued for the revival of discontinued rituals and their incorporation into Catholic practice. These texts were purposefully written in K'ichee', avoiding Spanish loanwords and often presenting long transcriptions of ritual speeches and Catholic prayers, many of them translated for the first time into modern K'ichee' (León Chic 2002; Ricardo Falla, personal communication). The use of couplets, archaic words, and honorific forms resignified traditional speech registers as markers of church membership, separating the modern Chiquimula church from mainstream Catholicism and Pentecostalism.

Table 5.5 compares two K'ichee' versions of the Lord's Prayer: the first appeared in Bartolomé de Anleo's eighteenth-century *Arte de la lengua 4iché*, a descriptive K'ichee' grammar written in Spanish that included an appendix with K'ichee' versions of several common prayers (Anleo 2002). The second version is the one currently recited in Santa María Chiquimula, which was first introduced in the late 1980s. Before this time, Chiquimulas used to say the Lord's Prayer in Spanish, as is still customary in many K'ichee' towns. Catholic catechists in Santa María were not acquainted with colonial translations of Christian prayers and other sacramental texts and developed their own translations in the late 1980s in cooperation with indigenous activists from the diocese of Totonicapán (Eduardo León Chic, personal communication 2005).

Coincidences in form and content between the two versions are substantial. First, both use the honorific pronoun *laal* "You (HON)" to address God. The preference of honorific over colloquial address during prayer is the opposite of both the English and Spanish versions, which prefer the colloquial pronouns: *tu* in Spanish, and *thou* in English. In contrast to the latter, which emphasize intimacy and familiarity, honorific forms index authority and social distance. In K'ichee' households, parents are addressed with *at*, not *laal*.[24] In fact, the earliest version of the Lord's Prayer in Table 5.5 closely follows the original Spanish, translating "kingdom" as *ahauarem* [*ajawarem*], which refers to the

TABLE 5.5. Two K'ichee' Versions of the Lord's Prayer.

Arte de la Lengua Quiché y Otros Textos (1700–50)[1]	Santa María Chiquimula version (Castillo 1998)	Gloss
Kacahau chi ɛafɲ lal 4oui	Qajaw Chikaj Lal k'owi	Our Father who are (HON) in heaven
Utz tafɲ uɛahariçaxíc maihalafɲ bij la	Nim ta b'a rilik utayik ri B'i' La	Hallowed be your (HON) name
Chipe tafɲ ahauarem la	Pet b'a' ri k'aslemal	Your (HON) kingdom come
	Ri no'jib'al La pa qawi'	
Chiban tafɲ ahauam la varale chuach vleufɲ	su ri k'o pa anima' La	Your (HON) will be done
Queheri cabano chiɛafɲ	chaqab'an ta b'a' chuwach ule:w pache ri kb'an chila' chikaj	On earth as it is in heaven
Vacamic ya la chiquech	Ya b'a' La kamik	Give us this day
Kahutaɛihil ua	ri k'in qawa quk'ya' rech ronojel q'ij;	Our daily bread
çacha la kamac	kuyu La, sacha La ri qamak,	And forgive (HON) us our trespasses
Queheri cakaçachbefɲ quimac xemacum chike	pache kaqab'an ri oj kaqakuyu, kaqasacho ri kimak ri ajmakib' chaqe	As we forgive those who trespass against us
ru4 mohoɛotafɲ la pa tak chibal mac	mujtzoqopij b'a La pa taq ri makaj	And lead (HON) us not into temptation
Xa kofɲcolta la pa itzel	chujkolo' La pa ri uq'ab' ri itzel	But deliver (HON) us from evil
Quehe chuxoK	chub'e q'ij, chub'e saq	Amen

Note: The original orthography of each version is preserved. English glosses by the author.

[1] The manuscript is identified as "Garrett-Gates Mesoamerican Manuscripts, no. 164" in the Princeton University Library Americana Collection. The description in the catalog reads: "Contains a grammar of K'ichee', possibly following the format of the grammar of Antonio de Nebrija (pp. 1–53). Together with a catechism (pp. 55–71); a Latin prayer (pp. 72–73); a religious text about Moses (adapted form of a biblical story) (pp. 75–78); two remedies, one of them 'comes from China this year of 1733' (p. 79); a 'formulario,' signed by Fr. Ignacio Rafael Macal in 1733, with notation 'Lo que me ha valido esta conventualidad de Totonicapan desde el dia de 17 de agosto de este año de 1728. Promete ahora 31 partimos a 6 ps. 7 rd.—u o ps. 7 rs.' (pp. 80–82); and miscellaneous verses in Spanish (pp. 85–87)."

political and military power wielded by K'ichee' lords, or *ajawab'*. Instead, the version used in Santa María Chiquimula uses a periphrastic couplet: *ri k'aslemal, ri nojib'al lah* "Your (HON) life and wisdom," avoiding the political metaphor entailed by *ajawarem*.

Honorific forms in the Lord's Prayer embody representations of the Christian deity in which he is construed as figuratively inhabiting the realm of traditional authority, a deity entitled to the same linguistic reverence as an elder. The two versions, however, exhibit a crucial stylistic difference: the contemporary Santa María Chiquimula version shows a more deliberate use of couplets (see Table 5.6). As we saw earlier in the radio broadcasts from Nahualá, couplets are rhetorical devices acting as iconic indices in essentialist constructions of Maya ethnicity. The K'ichee' liturgy in Santa María Chiquimula, including the Lord's Prayer, is indeed an ethnicist performance exploiting the essentialist connotations associated with traditional couplets

TABLE 5.6. Couplets in the K'ichee' Version of the Lord's Prayer.

Couplet	Literal Translation	Gloss
Riliik utayiik ri b'i' La	To see, to hear your (HON) name	Your name (HON)
ri k'aslemal, ri no'jib'al La	Your (HON) life and thought	Your will (HON)
qawa quk'ya'	Our food, our drink	Our sustenance
kuyu La, sacha La ri qamak	Bear, forget (HON) our sins	Forgive our sins (HON)
chub'e q'iij, chub'e saq	In the way of the sun, in the way of light	Forever

and ceremonial speech in the age of the Maya movement.

5.7. The Spanish Language and Situational Uses of K'ichee' Honorific Address

K'ichee' reverential forms are sometimes used as situational indices in polite exchanges. For example, in Antigua Guatemala in early 2009 I spoke with an eight-year-old boy from San Miguel Uspantán who was offering shoeshine services to tourists. He asked me, *Su b'i' lah?* "What is your name (HON)?" with honorific address rather than with the unmarked *Su ab'i'?* "What is your name?" Addressing a stranger with honorific forms apparently contradicts their primary indexical function as social indices. In fact, I seldom heard honorific address in market exchanges or during casual conversations among strangers at bus stops or in markets, cantinas, or *comedores* "diners." Prescriptive injunctions do not stipulate addressing all older adults with honorific forms. Furthermore, when I heard honorific address used on first acquaintance, it was dropped after a few polite questions.

To understand this situational use of honorifics, we have to consider first that K'ichee' coexists with Spanish in the same linguistic markets. Speakers of both languages mutually influence and parody each other. In Guatemalan Spanish the polite *Usted* is the default address pronominal; the colloquial *Vos* is normatively used with close friends, kin, and underlings. It is considered rude or patronizing to address a stranger with it, especially when he or she is older than the speaker. *Vos* is also used in jokes and oral narratives to index uncouth, naive, or

rude characters (Saravia 1983; Nelson 1999). In fact, one of the most salient *indígena* stereotypes among *ladino* urban residents is the inconsistent use of polite address forms and concurrent verb inflection.

Paradoxically, Spanish pragmatic norms seem to be spreading to K'ichee', "piggybacking" on their structural similarities.[25] The use of *laal* and *alaq* to index situational politeness is another transposition of Spanish conventions, a case of incipient borrowing of pragmatic norms.[26]

5.8. Honorification and Everyday Forms of Communication

Honorific address is an eminently political form of indexicality, enacting K'ichee' authority schemes and ethnic ideologies. Honorific pragmatic tropes are grounded on their primary role as traditional authority markers. The dual system of authority discussed above involves two poles of social indexicality that have coexisted for centuries in K'ichee' communities: the K'ichee' and the Spanish. Not surprisingly, leakages have occurred, both politically and discursively. The contradiction between borrowing Spanish address norms, one the one hand, while professing a sort of etymological purism in lexicon, on the other, is a case in point. Borrowing Spanish conventions illustrates the imbrication of "Spanish" and "K'ichee'" cultural schemes in K'ichee' interaction.

This bilingual accommodation and interleaving of discourse patterns has been documented elsewhere in Mesoamerica. Jane Hill and Kenneth Hill have shown how the abandonment of metalinguistic stipulations regarding "levels" of Nahuatl honorific speech reflected the proletarianization of formerly independent peasants and the demise of traditional forms of authority indexed by the use of "high level" honorifics. The simplification of honorifics in Malinche Nahuatl was triggered by the latter's emerging status as solidarity marker among a homogeneous indigenous proletariat, marking the incorporation of Nahuatl into the *marché linguistique* of postrevolutionary capitalism in Mexico (Hill and Hill 1999). In K'ichee' the adoption of Spanish addressee norms does not involve such cataclysmic social changes. However, it attests to yet another form of hybridization of K'ichee' and Spanish discourse, enabling and reflecting concurrent social and economic changes.

Notes

1. Note the fricative articulation of intervocalic /l/, a linguistic stereotype of Santa María Chiquimula K'ichee' (see Chapter 3).
2. Readers not linguistically inclined can skip section 5.2 entirely.
3. For plural honorific addressees, the same arguments account for the facts as long as *laal* and *lah* are replaced with *alaq*.
4. I have labeled it 3sA (third-person singular absolutive marker), following the usual practice in the literature on K'ichee'.
5. An asterisk indicates an ungrammatical sentence.
6. See Nutini (1980) for an extensive discussion of *compadrazgo*.
7. From the mid-1940s to the early 1980s the formal authority of the elders took a series of blows due to the introduction of the ballot and party politics, followed by the rapid decadence of the traditional K'ichee' religion with the expansion of orthodox Catholic associations such as Acción Católica (Catholic Action) and Pentecostal churches (see Warren 1978; Brintnall 1979; Falla 1980). The elders maintain considerable informal influence in local affairs, a de facto veto power, especially in rural areas.
8. In Nahualá in 2010, for example, almost all primary and secondary schoolteachers, the local parish priest, the majority of evangelical pastors, and most lawyers and doctors were native to the township.
9. From [nim] "large, big" + [-lax] (superlative suffix).
10. In colonial K'ichee', honorific address included a second honorific pronominal form in addition to *laal*: the unmarked plural form *ix*, attested in the Popol Vuh, where the Hero Twins addressed their grandmother with it (Tedlock 1996).
11. Many activists are involved in the creation of new words for legal, scientific, and technological jargon. Recent neologisms abide by the rules of K'ichee' morphology and phonotactics. Sometimes they involve deliberate semantic shifts, replacing the denotation of archaisms with modern referents.
12. Words in italics were in Spanish in the original broadcast.
13. | Utzilaj ulik alaq! | Chojtatab'ej alaq! |
    |---|---|
    | utzi-laj ul-ik alaq | ch-oj-o-tatab'ej alaq |
    | good-S arrive-N HAp | H-1pA-2pE-listen HAp |
    | Welcome (HON)! | May you listen to us (HON)! |
14. Spanish words are in italics.
15. My translation.
16. Santa María Chiquimula is not the only township with very restricted *laal* usage. For example, Chichicastenango rarely sees any *laal* except in highly ritualized contexts such as ceremonial speeches at weddings and *cofradía* functions (María Ren, personal communication 2013).
17. From the Spa. *costumbre* "custom."
18. Words in italics were uttered in Spanish in the interview.
19. *Cofradías* are Catholic religious sodalities sponsoring specific saints' cults. Members are organized hierarchically, usually in yearly shifts. For details, see Rojas Lima (1988).
20. Literally, "request."
21. Men holding *cargos* in *cofradías*.
22. This is the standard alphabet used in León Chic (2002).
23. My translation.
24. In the original Greek text of the Lord's Prayer, found in the Gospel according to Matthew, the colloquial Aramaic *Abba* "Dad" was used by Jesus to address the Father. In this regard, the Spanish and English translations of the Lord's Prayer seem to be more in tune with the origi-

nal text. The translators of the Lord's Prayer into K'ichee' metaphorically constructed the Christian God as a lord or elder rather than a parent. Both Aramaic and Greek lack honorific address forms.

25. Addressee forms are tripartite in certain varieties of Guatemalan Spanish, especially in Guatemala City, where the honorific form *Usted*, which is also the default form, is structurally in opposition to two colloquial forms: *Vos* and *Tu*. The normative use of each is complex and inconsistent across social classes and ethnic groups. Due to space limitations, I do not discuss it further here.

26. Structural borrowing is mediated by pragmatic transpositions, not the other way around.

The Changing Voice of the Ancestors

Missionaries, K'ichee' Poets, and Pan-Mayanism

6.1. The Linguistic Dilemmas of Pan-Maya Activism Today

Paradoxically, the majority of conversations among pan-Maya activists in Guatemala occur in Spanish. This is not simply a convenient language choice motivated by the lack of mutual intelligibility of their respective mother tongues. Spanish is the only language used in national government offices, nongovernmental organizations, and the headquarters of international agencies in Guatemala. Although the state is legally bound to provide services in Mayan languages in areas where their speakers constitute the majority of the population, the law is not enforced. Spanish continues to be the sole language of prestige, the vehicle of education, journalism, and literature (Cojtí 1995; Jiménez 1997). In *ladino* society, speaking a Mayan language is often construed as a character flaw, a sign of poverty and lack of sophistication at best, of ignorance and racial inferiority at worst (Saravia 1983; González Ponciano 2004; Hale 2004, 2006). Furthermore, until recently, primary school was taught exclusively in Spanish and students were actively discouraged from speaking Mayan languages. In this hostile social scenario, Maya-Spanish bilingualism became a sine qua non for being taken seriously in national institutions. To become successful professionals, Maya students spend many years studying in schools and universities that demean Mayan languages, leaving them no choice but to speak Spanish. The consequence was the exclusion of Mayan languages from the national economic, political, intellectual, and religious domains. In one's hometown, discussing in one's native Mayan language the merits of candidates for a traditional *cargo*, for example, was not simply easier but the expected norm. However, deconstructing Marxism in a university classroom or solving differential equations was done much more easily in Spanish. Political strategizing and negotiations with national state and civil society representatives were less complicated when done in Spanish, especially if the activists involved spoke mutually unintelligible Mayan languages. With the exception of small groups of motivated and linguistically talented activists such as the members of Oxlajuj Keej Mayab' Aj Tz'iib' (OKMA), a prolific group of professional linguists who succeeded in making Kaqchikel their colloquial vehicular language, the Maya movement has opted to speak to itself in Spanish.

Maya activists have acknowledged this contradiction between their linguistic practices and the essentialist political project inspiring them. Unlike in Mexico, where some native Nahuatl writers have argued that Mexican Spanish should be explicitly appropriated as indigenous language on the grounds that it is the native language of many ethnically indigenous Mexicans, in Guatemala, Mayan languages and Spanish are mutually exclusive but complementary ethnic icons, as we have seen in previous chapters (Jiménez 1997; Hernández 1999). Maya activists do not take well to the idea of "appropriating" Spanish.[1] In fact, several Maya intellectuals have proposed that one Mayan language should be made co-official with Spanish in all of Guatemala, becoming a pan-Maya lingua franca and eventually weaning the Maya from their reliance on Spanish for cross-linguistic communication (Pedro García Matzar, personal communication 2008). Among the candidates for pan-Maya lingua franca, the one most often mentioned is K'ichee'. Its advocates include not only K'ichee' activists but also some speakers of other Mayan languages who acknowledge its prestige and emerging iconic role in Guatemala. This chapter explores the cultural role that K'ichee' speakers and their language have played as mediator between the Maya at large and the forces of colonialism and capitalist modernity. First, I argue that the prestige associated with the K'ichee' language is rooted in its role in the early colonial period as template in the process of elaboration of Catholic pastoral registers in Mayan languages. As a case study, I examine its poetic and lexical influence on the first doctrinal texts in Q'eqchi', effecting a veritable "K'ichee'ization" of Q'eqchi' pastoral language.[2] Second, I discuss the role of K'ichee' intellectuals from Quetzaltenango in the emergence of the Maya movement in the twentieth century. I focus on the philological work of Adrián Inés Chávez and the transformation of the Popol Vuh into a "Maya Bible" in his wake. Third, I examine the work of Humberto Akabal and its literary and political impact in Guatemala. Akabal, a K'ichee' poet from Momostenango, is one of the pioneer poets writing in indigenous languages in Latin America today (Flores 2000; Arias 2007). His work has become emblematic of the possibilities offered by Mayan languages as they expand into prestige channels such as poetry and newspapers. Since 1523 the K'ichee' have been cultural brokers between Western modernity and its diverse linguistic embodiments in Mayan languages. This ambiguous, tense mediation sharply distinguishes K'ichee' from its sister Mayan languages.

6.2. K'ichee' and the Emergence of Maya Christianity: A Q'eqchi' Case Study

After the destruction of Q'umarkaaj (Utatlán)— ancient capital of the K'ichee'—in 1523, Dominican missionaries and K'ichee' collaborators led by Fray Domingo de Vico developed new literary genres, adapting the K'ichee' language for use in Catholic proselytism and sacramental practice (Sparks 2011; García-Ruiz 1992; Mondloch and Carmack 1983). These literary efforts planted the seeds of a new hybrid Maya religion that intertwined rituals and symbols from the Spanish and Maya traditions. Using native genres as poetic models, missionary linguists drafted catechetical texts of ambitious theological scope and literary complexity, such as the *Theologia Indorum* (see Chapter 2). They also authored descriptive grammars and dictionaries to teach the language to incoming missionaries.

The Spanish regarded the K'ichee' as a powerful and sophisticated polity and thought the language spoken at Q'umarkaaj capable of unambiguously expressing the complexities of Christian theology and ritual (Sparks 2011). As late as 1722, the Dominican friar Francisco Ximénez argued in his *Historia de la Provincia de Chiapas y Guatemala* that K'ichee' was the ancestral language from which all other Mayan languages originated. He considered it "as perfect as the Hebrew language" (Ximénez 1965). K'ichee' became a linguistic template for the construction of doctrinal registers. The lexical strategies chosen for the translation of Christian theology into highland Maya languages as well as the poetic structures used for the composition of doctrinal texts were first developed in K'ichee' (Romero 2011). K'ichee' texts were the first linguistic artifacts mediating the spread of Christian thought, the diffusion of Spanish social norms and morals, and the resignification of scores of native ritual practices and cultural categories as elements of Maya Christianity. The rest of this section illustrates this process, examining the emergence of pastoral Q'eqchi' and identifying its roots in older K'ichee' doctrinal genres. A caveat is necessary at this point: although K'ichee' and Q'eqchi' are sister languages of the

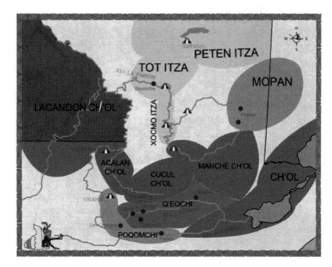

FIGURE 6.1. The Q'eqchi' and neighboring groups in the Verapaz before the Spanish invasion (map by Ruud Van Akkeren).

K'iche'an subgroup of the Mayan stock, they are structurally quite different and are not mutually intelligible (see Figure 1.1) (Campbell 1977; Stewart 1980; López Ixcoy 1997).

During the sixteenth century the Q'eqchi' were a diverse group of *amaq'* inhabiting a small territory deep in the forests of the frontier territories known as the Verapaz in north-central Guatemala (Weeks 1997; Van Akkeren 2012) (see Figure 6.1). The first contacts between the Spanish and the Q'eqchi' were mediated by K'ichee'-speaking lords from Sacapulas, north of Q'umarkaaj. The legendary Dominican friar Bartolomé de las Casas successfully lobbied for a royal decree giving the Order of Preachers exclusive rights to "pacify" the area and prohibiting the settlement of Spaniards except religious and government appointees (Ximénez 1965; Saint-Lu 1968). Years later the Dominicans were finally able to establish a foothold in the Verapaz. In the meantime, the Q'eqchi' turned into Spanish allies during the long and bloody campaigns to subdue the indomitable Acalan and Manché Ch'ol (Van Akkeren 2012; Saint-Lu 1968; Bierman 1960). The Dominicans came to the Verapaz with substantial experience evangelizing K'ichee'-speaking areas under Spanish control. Their attitudes toward the Q'eqchi' were colored by their previous acquaintance with the K'ichee' and their language, and the successful

missionary strategies adopted after the fall of Q'umarkaaj. These included norms for the standardization of doctrinal language, which hinged on the recruitment of native ceremonial poetics, on the one hand, and on a judicious combination of new word coinages, Spanish loanwords, and the active redefinition of the denotation of key native words, on the other.

By the time the *Theologia Indorum* was drafted, the translation controversies had been resolved in favor of translators advocating for Spanish loanwords rather than etymologically native words to denote Christian sacred beings (García-Ruiz 1992). The same rhetorical and lexical strategies were implemented in Q'eqchi'. The *Theologia Indorum* became a cross-linguistic model, an unofficial guide used to draft sermons and other doctrinal texts (Acuña 1985). The *Coplas de Luís de Cáncer*, a collection of Catholic hymns and sermons written in Q'eqchi' sometime in the middle of the sixteenth century and attributed to the Dominican Luís de Cáncer, is a superb example of missionary literature and the strategies used to co-opt Mayan languages as evangelization tools (see Figure 6.2):

(6.1)

V

Cah ah pac yoobom quech
        Our Maker, Our Creator

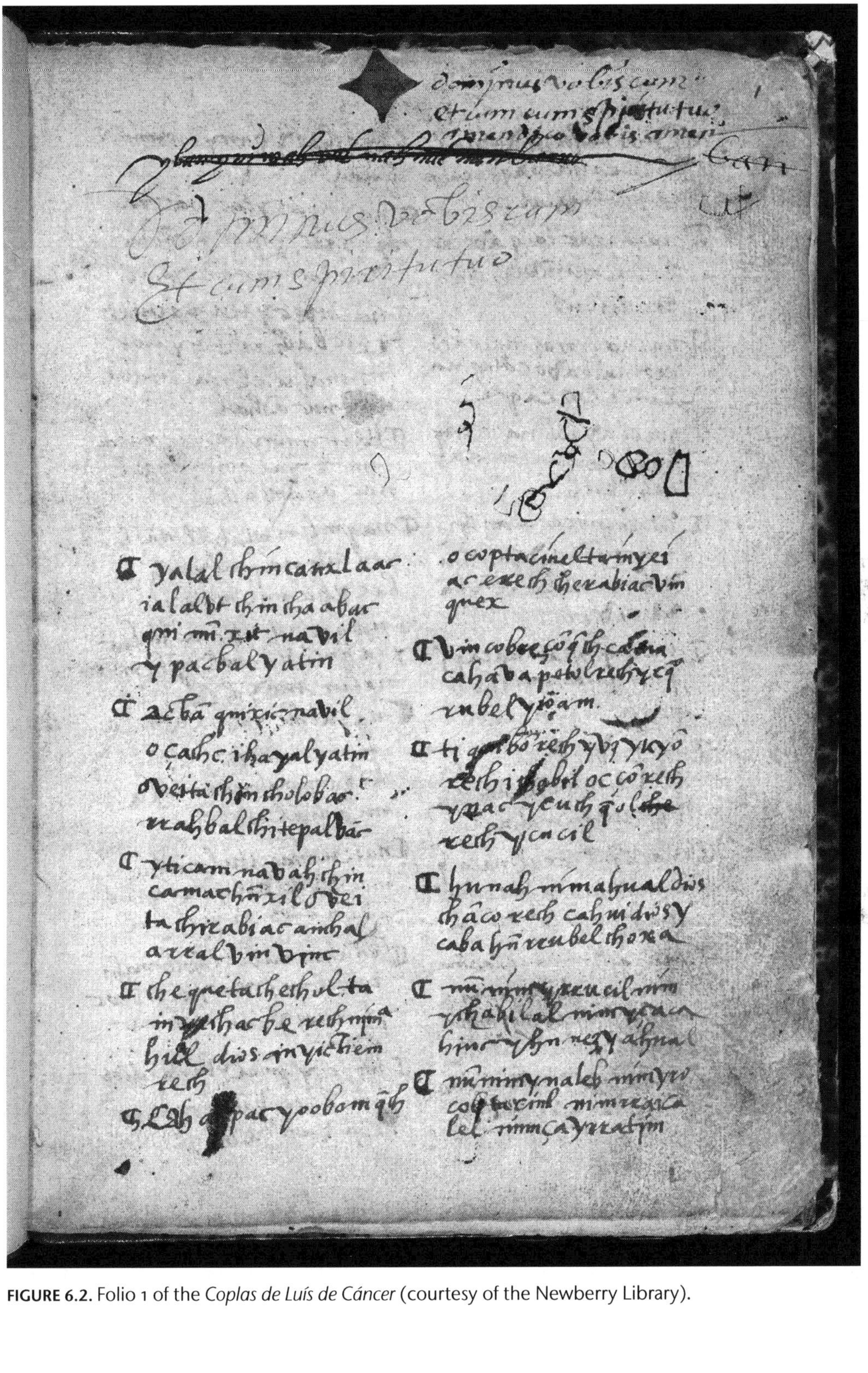

FIGURE 6.2. Folio 1 of the *Coplas de Luís de Cáncer* (courtesy of the Newberry Library).

oçobtacinel ta inyei
    [and] Benefactor. I will tell
ac erech cherabiac cuin
    you all [about] him. Listen up,
quex.
    men!

VI
cuincobresom quech qana
    Our Creator, Our Mother,
qa hacua petol rech y cque
    Our Father, Life Giver
rubel yoam.
    of everything under the sun.

IX
Num nim yrrucil nim
    Great is his goodness,
y chabilal nim y çaca
    great is his grace, his light.
hinc y hunez y ahual.
    He is the only lord.

XI
Dios naqueoc ca cua naque
    Dios is the one who gives (us)
oc cucaha naque e rrabin
    food and drink. He gives you
naque e rralal.
    daughters and sons.

XVIII
Nacacque ca xul, nacacque
    You give us animals,
ca car, nacaque ca tul,
    fish. You give us sapotes.[3]
Nacaque ca çarb.
    You give us water springs.

XX
tamolbec i acach taa
    Turkeys lay their eggs,
lac y cal nayolac y
    their chicks hatch. Water
ha ce choch yban y dios nima
    springs from the ground
hual.
    because of Dios, the great lord.

XXIV
Naquil nimla tzul naquil
    We see great hills, we see
y tacah naquil y bali-
    valleys, we see all things,
bal y banuem anchal.
    all of his works.
        (*Coplas de Luís de Cáncer*, Folio 3)[4]

The fragments in text (6.1), which are stanzas from Chapter 3 of the *Coplas*, show semantic and syntactic parallelism akin to that found in the Popol Vuh and the *Theologia Indorum*. Parallel constructions include lexical couplets and triplets, as well as the juxtaposition of phrases and longer strings with matching syntax, contrasting in noun and verb collocations. Many couplets and triplets were ancient idiomatic expressions attested in other colonial documents that had not been coined by missionary translators. Examples include –*usil/-chaabilal* "goodness/wellness," *-alal/-rabin* "sons of men, daughters of men," *xul/kar* "land animals, fish," *tzul/tacaj* "hills, valleys," and *cua/ucaha* "food and drink." Some of the couplets referring to the Christian God in (6.1) appear also in the Popol Vuh and the *Theologia Indorum*, suggesting that certain parallel constructions had become standard in pastoral registers in Mayan languages. An excellent example is the couplet *ah pac, yoobom* "the Maker, the Creator" in stanza V in (6.1), which is a calque translation of the K'ichee' couplet *tzaqol, bitol* "the Maker, the Shaper."

Regarding Christian concepts and sacred beings, text (6.1) follows the lexical criteria established after the *K'ab'awil* controversy (García-Ruiz 1992; Sparks 2011). The Christian God is directly referenced with the Spanish loanword *Dios*, usually followed by the attribute *nimahual* "great lord," cognate of the K'ichee' *nimaahau*, found in the *Theologia Indorum*. Abstract nouns, such as *chaabilal* and *usilal*,[5] with a semantic overlap between abstract "goodness" and doctrinal "grace," show the semantic adjustment (reduction or expansion) of lexical denotations. Pastoral lexicon and semantic calques borrowed from Spanish via K'ichee' include names referring to the "Devil," such as *Lucifer*, *Diablo*, and *Caxtoc*, all common in pastoral texts in K'ichee'.

In stanza XIV in text (6.2) the Spanish loan-word *Diablo* and the etymologically K'ichee'/Q'eqchi' noun *caxtoc* "Deceiver," a direct translation of the familiar Judeo-Christian epithet, reference the Christian "Devil." *Caxtoc* [k'axtok'] is the most commonly used denominator for "Devil" in Q'eqchi' communities today, bearing witness to the endurance of doctrinal lexical standardizations that originally spread from K'ichee'.

(6.2)
XIV
Diablo y caca oru caxtoc o
    His name is "Diablo" or "Deceiver."
Ru y caba mahi chic rucil
    There is no goodness left in his
y chol humah caxtoquil narah
        heart. All he cares for is deception.
            (*Coplas de Luís de Cáncer*, Folio 5)[6]

The *Theologia Indorum* acted as urtext for doctrinal Q'eqchi', especially in the genre of biblical sermons. Drafted before the Council of Trent reforms started to constrain the pastoral use of vernacular biblical translations, the *Theologia Indorum* includes scores of pages of literary translations, some of which take surprising liberties with the original Vulgate text (Romero 2011; Sparks 2011; Mondloch and Carmack 1983). See, for example, text (6.3):

(6.3)
III
Toha ut nac oyolac y pac:
    In a moment was the great lord's
nimahual limo terre
        creature begotten. "Limo terrae"
y caba y choch ocqueec
    was the name of the earth that
chirixc ca hacua.
        Our Father gave it.

IV
Hunpatah ocuincoc maco
    His creature was created at once.

ohalac yban mamai
    It didn't have to be fixed. Quickly
obiec roc rucm.
    were his hands and feet formed.

V
Orocci yrucm orocci
    He gave them hands.
Y baquel y re orocci y cuxbl
    bones, mouth, voice.
Orocci y quiquel.
    He gave them blood.

VI
Honac ooçoc ypac an
    And so he finished his creation,
chal cui y tçehual: choch
    his entire body. Earth,
ha, i3, xambl, oel cui oquec
    water, wind, fire; this is what
yban y ah pak.
    the Creator used.
        (*Coplas de Luís de Cáncer*, Folio 5)[7]

Q'eqchi' "coplas" inspired by the book of Genesis emphasize the episodic sequence in which humans were created, contrasting it implicitly with Mesoamerican creation myths, exactly as in the corresponding sections in the *Theologia Indorum*. Stanza VI lists the four components of the human body as earth, wind, water, and fire, in contrast to the materials used in Maya creation: three kinds of corn and the blood of mythical creatures.

In summary, Q'eqchi' pastoral texts followed guidelines set during the evangelization of the K'ichee'. Standardized lexical choices and poetic structures first developed in K'ichee' were the core rhetorical strategies use to construct doctrinal registers in Q'eqchi'. K'ichee' was therefore an early vehicle of linguistic innovation in the realm of Q'eqchi' religion and morals. The colonial project co-opted the K'ichee' as key collaborators in the process of evangelization and "pacification" of other language areas. The political influence of the K'ichee' elites around Q'umarkaaj waned soon after the conquest, however. Two centuries later, other K'ichee' speakers, this time in the city of Quetzaltenango, picked up where the former left off, continuing to exert a crucial influence on the history of Guatemala.

6.3. After Independence: The K'ichee' Roots of the Maya Movement

The ancient K'ichee' capital of Q'umarkaaj and the town of Santa Cruz del Quiché, built to settle the former's inhabitants after the Spanish razed it to the ground, soon lost the preeminence it had during the first decades after the Spanish invasion. The area turned into a backwater controlled by local *ladino* families as the economic and political hubs of the Capitanía de Guatemala shifted to the central highlands around Guatemala City and Quetzaltenango (Piel 1989; Carmack 1995). The latter became a crucial intersection of trade routes bridging the southern piedmont and the highlands, and its weekly market became one of the largest in western Guatemala. After independence Quetzaltenango became one of the seats of the coffee boom, stimulating trade and developing a thriving middle class. The latter included not only *ladinos* but also wealthy K'ichee' merchants, doctors, lawyers, and teachers. Despite the prevailing racism, they were a confident, educated, and well-organized group. The high-profile Sociedad el Adelanto was founded in 1898 to represent their corporate interests (Woodward 1993; Taracena 1997; Grandin 2000; Velásquez 2000; Camey Barrios and Quijivix Yax 2013). K'ichee' professionals became important political actors at the regional level. Their national standing was given a boost after they sided with President Rafael Carrera' central government during his campaign to subdue a secessionist attempt led by wealthy *ladino* planters from Quetzaltenango in 1838: the fleeting República de los Altos, or Republic of the Highlands (Woodward 1993; Taracena 1997). K'ichee' elites regarded themselves as progressive citizens of Guatemala and supported the Liberal agenda of the central government while remaining critical of its blatant ideological racism, of the expropriation of communal lands, and of forced labor laws affecting poor indigenous peasants drafted for the benefit of coffee planters.

In the 1940s many K'ichee' from Quet-zaltenango were involved in the civic movement that led to the overthrow of the dictator Jorge Ubico in 1944. Prestigious professionals and intellectuals ran as local candidates of revolutionary parties for the first post-dictatorship elections in 1945 (Grandin 2000; Velásquez 2000). This long tradition of K'ichee' political participation and engagement with the Guatemalan state is an important precursor of the contemporary Maya movement. The latter is both a continuation and a strategic modification of the former, transcending its regionalism and political conservatism and assuming an overtly pan-Maya political agenda. Some of the most influential contemporary K'ichee' activists today cite the political participation of their predecessors as motivation and communal experience guiding their own activism (Velásquez 2000).

In particular, the philological work of Adrián Inés Chávez, native K'ichee' scholar and translator of the Popol Vuh, had a foundational impact on the contemporary Maya construal of colonial history, especially on the way colonial texts in indigenous languages such as the Popol Vuh, the Memorial de Tecpán-Atitlan, and the Books of Chilam Balam are read and interpreted today (Lima Soto 1995; Cabrera 1997). Chávez is without a doubt one of the most important ideological precursors of the Maya movement. He has been called a *k'ab'awil contemporáneo* "contemporary sacred being" as precursor and moving spirit of the current blossoming of Maya-inspired spirituality (Matul 1997). The next section examines this influence.

6.4. The Popol Vuh and the Invention of Linguistic Tradition

Adrián Inés Chávez was born in 1904 in the town of San Francisco el Alto, thirty kilometers from Quetzaltenango. San Francisco el Alto is the seat of one of the largest markets in the western highlands, well known for its thriving apparel industry, a place of encounter between modernity and tradition since the early nineteenth century (Goldin 1987). Trained as a schoolteacher, he worked for many years in urban and rural elementary schools and high schools.[8] After moving to the city of Quetzaltenango, he became involved in the anti-Ubico civil movement that eventually overthrew the dictator after fourteen years of autocratic rule. Chávez was a supporter of Juan José Arévalo, the first democratically elected president after Ubico's downfall, and served as the secretary of culture in Quetzaltenango's labor federation under Arévalo and his successor, Jacobo Arbenz. Early in his career he developed an interest in colonial K'ichee' writings, especially the Popol Vuh. His elegant Spanish prose includes a grammar sketch of K'ichee' and articles on K'ichee' writing, K'ichee' religion, and Maya history (Chávez 1974). In one of his first academic works, a presentation given in 1945 at a conference of indigenous teachers in Cobán, he introduced a new alphabet with seven additional consonants and two accent markers, a script he himself invented, which, he argued, was more accurate than the Spanish-based orthography used in both colonial and contemporary texts. The proposal did not receive much attention but gave its author a reputation for scholarship and deep knowledge of the language.[9] In 1959 he founded the Academia Maya Kí-chè (Maya K'ichee' Academy), and in 1967, with support from friends in Costa Rica and Germany, he acquired a typewriter built with keys modeled on his orthographic script. The typewriter made his work much easier, and in 1979 he published (in Mexico) his translation of the Popol Vuh, which he renamed the *Pop-Wuj*, adumbrating a new and influential interpretation of the text, which I discuss below. Adrián Inés Chávez died in 1987, a celebrated and respected elder scholar (Chávez 1979; Fischer 1996).

Paradoxically, Chávez places the Popol Vuh squarely in the Eurocentric narrative of universal "world history." In seemingly capricious manner, he identifies episodes of the Popol Vuh as significant events in ancient Western history, some of them legendary, such as the mythical destruction of Atlantis (Chávez 2010). Influenced by a literal reading of the first chapter of the *Título de Totonicapán*, a colonial text in which prehispanic K'ichee' and biblical narratives seamlessly intertwine in a solid historical sequence, he locates migration histories in the Popol Vuh in Babylon and Egypt (Chávez 2010:63–65). He believed the K'ichee' to have been descendants of the ancient Israelites, an idea that was popular among Spanish mendicant friars in the colonial period. Chávez approvingly quotes from the relevant paragraphs in Antonio Fuentes y Guzmán's seventeenth-century chronicle *La Recordación Florida* (Chávez 2010:68–72). Fuentes y Guzmán believed that cultural traits shared between the ancient Israelites and the K'ichee' were evidence of a common ancestral origin in Palestine. Chávez, who claimed that Fuentes y Guzmán obtained these ideas from native informants who presumably shared ancient oral traditions with him, did not seem to have been cognizant that claims of a Hebrew-K'ichee' genealogy were used in late-sixteenth-century Spain to forge historical links between official biblical history and the native peoples of the Americas (Cañizares-Esguerra 2006).

To understand Chávez's controversial yet innovative reading of the Popol Vuh, we should approach it as the creative work of a spiritual prophet rather than merely a piece of philological scholarship. Chávez construed the text partly as a pantheistic allegory in which philological precision and historical accuracy were secondary to analogy and prophetic inspiration, and partly as a precise historical chronology, a migration story of a journey that took the K'ichee' ancestors to distant places such as Egypt and Babylon (Chávez 2010). Modern scholars have pointed out numerous philological and linguistic errors as well as serious historical misconceptions underlying some of his claims (Breton 1990). For Chávez, the Popol Vuh was fundamentally a story loosely based on the Old Testament, in which prehispanic deities and historical characters were construed as metaphors of a unitary God, the Ajaw (Chávez 1997:xxxii; López 1999; Cabrera 2007). Historical narratives and myths were construed as moral allegories, helped in this by Chávez's seemingly capricious orthographic and morphological alterations of Francisco Ximénez's text.

Francisco Ximénez was the Dominican friar who found the Popol Vuh in the church archives of Chichicastenango. After retranscribing it, he wrote a Spanish translation, but unfortunately,

TABLE 6.1. Three Transcriptions of a Fragment of the Popol Vuh.

Francisco Ximénez (Popol Vuh, Folio 5 verso)	Adrián Inés Chávez (Chávez 1997:10)	Allen Christenson (Christenson 2004)
Are cut xa hubic zac na tanoh vvachvleu mahabi	Arè Rut, sha juBiQ sT natanoj u wach ulew, m juBiQ Qij. Jun Rut ku nimarisaj riB "WuTuB T Rish" u Bi, Ro naBe kaj, ulew; sha k maymot u wach Qij, iT. Kchà	Are k'ut xa jubiq' saqnatanoj uwach ulew, majab'i q'ij, jun k'ut kunimarisaaj rib' Wuqub' Kaqix ub'i'. K'o nab'e kaj ulew; xa kamaymot uwach q'ij, ik' kacha k'uri. Xawi xere usaq etal winaq ri' xb'utik. Kejeri nawal winaq uk'oje'ik. "In nim kik'oje' chik chuwi winaq tzaq, winaq b'it. In uq'iij, in pu usaq, in nawi pu rik'il. Ta chuxoq! Nim nusaqil, inb'inib'al, in pu chakab'al rumal winaq, rumal pwaq."
quih hun cut cunimarizah rib, vvcub caquix vbi, qo nabe cah vleu, xa ca maymot v vach quih ic caqha curi: xaui xere vza quetal vinac rÿ, xbutic queheri naual vinac vqoheic. in nim quiqohe chic chuvi vinac tzac vinac bit in vquih in pu vzac in naipu riquil ta chuxoc, nim nu zaquil in binibal, in pu chacabal rumal vinac. rumal pu vac	Rurí: sha we sharé u sTetal winaT ri sh Butik je ri u nawal winaT sh Rijik, in nim kin Rji chik chu wi winaT ZaT winaT Bit, in u Qij in pu u sT, in pu r'iTil tz chushoT; nim n sTil in BinBal, in pu XakBal ru-Mal winaT, rumal puaT	

Note: See the respective translations in Table 6.2.

the manuscript he discovered was lost and his K'ichee' transcription became by default the oldest version of the text (Carmack 1973; Van Akkeren 2003). Chávez was critical of Ximénez, arguing not only that the latter lacked sufficient knowledge of the K'ichee' language and cosmology but also that the colonial script itself was inadequate to represent the sounds of the language.[10] These presumed deficiencies are Chávez's first argument to justify his numerous spelling alterations of Ximénez's text. Chávez considered himself an expert on the esoteric theological and historical background of the Popol Vuh, lost soon after the Spanish invasion and—according to Chávez himself—ignored by most contemporary K'ichee' (Chávez 1997:xxv). Some of his more controversial claims were probably borrowed from New Age authors, such as the speculative historical nexus between K'ichee', Babylon, and Egypt. His reading of the pyramid as icon of the universe and its spiritual forces is widespread among contemporary Maya shamans and New Age practitioners (Chávez 1997; Valencia Tolanilla 2001; Mercier 2008).

Chávez's interpretation of the myth of Wuqub' Kaqix and his sons, the mythical bird that pretended to be the sun, illustrates his reading technique. In his 1979 translation of the book, which he renamed *Pop Wuj*,[11] the text is organized in four columns. The first is

Ximénez's transcription; the second is Chávez's own transliteration into the idiosyncratic alphabet he invented; the third shows Chávez's "literal translation," preserving the original syntax of the K'ichee' text; and the fourth is Chávez's "literary translation," which abides by the canons of standard Spanish syntax.

Table 6.1 shows three transcriptions of fragments of the Popol Vuh: Ximénez's seventeenth-century transcription in column 1, followed in column 2 by Chávez's 1973 version. Column 3 presents Allen Christenson's transliteration into the contemporary standard alphabet, which generally agrees with the views of most contemporary Popol Vuh specialists. The spelling conventions used by Ximénez were introduced by Catholic missionaries in the early 1530s.[12] With the exception of vowel length, this system accurately represented the phonemic inventory of K'iche'an languages. However, Ximénez's use of it was erratic: velar, uvular, and alveolar stops were not consistently distinguished, for example. As noted earlier, it is unclear whether this was Ximénez's fault or the result of errors in the document from which he transcribed, possibly an earlier copy of a lost original manuscript. Chávez correctly pointed out these transliteration issues and sought to correct them as initial steps for a new translation. However, he was unacquainted with many of the colonial chron-

FIGURE 6.3. Stone-incised pictograms at the Rossbach Museum, Chichicastenango, Guatemala (photograph by Ruud Van Akkeren).

icles, dictionaries, grammars, and philological techniques used by Popol Vuh specialists today, making his transliteration seem capricious and inconsistent, if not seriously flawed (Breton 1990). His orthographic conventions included graphemes invented by Chávez himself, which were loosely based on the pictograms incised into a prehispanic stone monument kept in the Museo Rossbach in Chicastenango, Guatemala (see Figure 6.3). He believed the pictograms to be examples of an ancient prehispanic K'ichee' writing system (Chávez 1974:25–34). Furthermore, his parsing of K'ichee' words followed Spanish orthographic canons. Possessed nouns were spelled as two separate morphemes: *n wach* "in front of me" instead of *nuwach*, as is currently the norm, according to the Academy of Mayan Languages. Ergative markers were also separated from the verbal root as if they were Spanish pro-

nouns, as in *ku nimarisaj* "he augments it" rather than *kunimarisaj*. Chávez's exegesis of the text in Table 6.1 presupposes that the text allegorizes the social history of the Maya, which is construed as a conflict between moral principles and cosmic forces.

For example, in Table 6.2 Ximénez writes *Vvcub Caquix*, which he glosses as "Siete Guacamayas"—normally rendered in English as "Seven Macaw"—a mythical bird that tried to pass as the sun using the shining reflection of the jewelry he wore around his eyes. In the IPA phonetic script "Seven Macaw" would be rendered [Wuquɓ Kaqiʃ]. As in the latter, Ximénez's transcription identifies the second consonant of each word as [q] while following colonial orthographic conventions in which *k* is written as *qu* when preceding *i* or *e* but as *c* elsewhere. Chávez, however, rewrites Ximénez's *Vvcub*

TABLE 6.2. Three Translations of a Fragment of the Popol Vuh.

Francisco Ximénez (Popol Vuh, Folio 5 verso)	Adrián Inés Chávez (Chávez 1997:10)	Allen Christenson (Christenson 2003)
Y entonzes avía poca claridad sobre la haz de la tíerra, y aun no auía sol. y entonzes vno llamado Vvcub Caquix. (esto es Siete Guacamayas) se ensoberbezía. Auía entonzes cielo y tierra, pero estaba turbia la luz de el sol, y la luna. Y este Vvcub Caquíx, dezía: Solo aquella poca gente q' se anegó fueron como brujos. Yo agora seré grande sobre todas las criaturas, yo soy su sol, yo soy su blancura, yo seré su luna. Es grande mi claridad, y soy por quien han de andar los hombres, y pararse.	En ese entonzes había poca claridad sobre la tierra, no había Sol. Y había uno que se engrandecía, se llamaba "Nuestras Siete Verguenzas." Ya había cielo y tierra, pero todavía era tenue la luz del sol y la luna. Y dijo Nuestras Siete Verguenzas: "Si es señal clara de la gente que se mutiló, es origen de la gente que existe, yo seré grande sobre la gente construída, formada; seré su Sol, su luz, mejor dicho su Luna, así se estableció. Grande es mi iluminación, soy su camino, soy mejor dicho su amuleto para ganar."	While the face of the earth was only a little brightened, before there was a sun, there was one who puffed himself up named Seven Macaw. There was a sky and an earth, but the faces of the sun and moon were dim. He therefore declared himself to be the bright sign for those who were drowned in the flood. He was like an enchanted person in his essence. "I am great. I dwell above the heads of the people who have been framed and shaped. I am their sun. I am also their light. And I am also their moon. Then be it so. Great is my brightness. By the brilliance of my silver and gold I light the walkways and pathways of the people."

Caquix as *WuTuB T Rish*, using his own script. In the latter, T represents a velar occlusive [q] while R represents a velar palatoalveolar ejective [k']. In IPA we would render Chávez's transliteration [Wuquɓ Qak'iʃ] "Our Seven Shames," a substantial departure from Ximénez's translation. In a footnote Chávez lists the "Seven Shames" without explaining how he ascertained them: "Pride engenders: Ambition, Envy, Deception, Crime, Ingratitude and Ignorance" (Chávez 1997:115).[13] The mythical bird is thus construed as an allegory of seven sins purportedly committed by the prehispanic Maya that eventually led to their conquest and current decay (Cristóbal Cojtí, personal communication, 2000). One of them, Deception, was responsible, according to Chávez, for the destruction of the second creation (Chávez 2010:51–52). Thus, in Chávez's reading of the Popol Vuh, a new theology is adumbrated, a pantheistic, puritanical view of the universe in which its structural forces are identified with moral essences.

Shamans and pan-Maya activists today have generally accepted Chávez's interpretations of *Vvcub Caquix*, turning the Popol Vuh into a sacred book in which they find concrete moral guidelines and a unified, mythological account of their history. Note the Christian associations between the concepts of "shame" and "sin," especially when accompanied with a numerical coefficient, familiar to any K'ichee'.[14] In Maya ceremonies the Popol Vuh is often read, cited, and commented on, and K'ichee' and Kaqchikel shamans use its lexicon and poetics as textual elements in chanting and prayer. Chávez was the visionary who transformed the Popol Vuh from a documentary record of K'ichee' myths and chronicles bearing the perspective of the Kaweq lineage of Utatlán to a pan-Maya sacred book (Chávez 2010). The Popol Vuh turned into a powerful spiritual artifact for the emerging Maya movement, a living link between the changing present and the idealized past, legitimizing new ritual practices and political discourses. Chávez snatched it, as it were, from the stagnant domain of philological scholarship and threw it into the ebullient market of ethnicity and political discourses in contemporary Guatemala. Its archaic language and ancient lexicon became indices of occult esoteric knowledge accessible only through the eyes of authorized Maya spiritual leaders. Scholarly interpretations, in contrast,

FIGURE 6.4. Humberto Akabal at his home in Momostenango (photograph by Arturo Arias).

are often dismissed by Maya shamans as superfluous or irrelevant to Maya struggles (Ruud Van Akkeren, personal communication 2008; Judith Maxwell, personal communication 2008). Following Chávez's innovative interpretation, other native colonial texts such as the Books of Chilam Balam are also being construed as allegories of this ongoing cosmic conflict (Matul 2007; Matzir Miculax et al. 2009).

The prestige gained by Chávez's interpretation of the Popol Vuh in the Maya movement extended to the K'ichee' language itself, buttressing the latter's emblematic status in the Maya movement in Guatemala. Although it is not the most complete native account of the prehispanic history of K'iche'an peoples, nor are the myths narrated in its pages originally or exclusively K'ichee', the Popol Vuh has gained an unparalleled status in pan-Maya political and spiritual discourse (Van Akkeren 2012). As the language in which the Maya holy book was penned, K'ichee' is construed as the quintessential K'iche'an language, and Kaqchikel and

Tz'utijil linguists, for example, use it as important source of standardized lexicon (Pak'al B'alam, personal communication 2009). Therefore, it is not surprising that Maya activists have proposed it as the most appropriate candidate for the pan-Maya national language.

The prestige gained by K'ichee', however, is due not only to its role as vehicle for the reinvention of Maya tradition but also to the tremendous creativity of some of its contemporary speakers, who have opened new paths in other channels and literary genres. One of the most successful is the poet Humberto Akabal, whose work I examine in the next section.

6.5. Humberto Akabal and the Re-creation of Maya Poetry

Humberto Akabal was born in 1952 in the township seat of Momostenango, northwest of Quetzaltenango in western Guatemala (see Figure 6.4). He is one of the best-known Guatemalan poets, and his work has been translated into several European languages as well as Japanese

(Akabal 2011). He is probably the most prolific and innovative poet writing in a Mayan language today. Winner of many literary awards, he turned down the Premio Guatemalteco de Novela (Guatemalan Novel Award), established in honor of the Nobel Prize winner Miguel Angel Asturias, in 2004. Akabal argued that Asturias's senior thesis, published as *El problema social del indio* (The Indian Social Problem), was racist and insulting to the Maya people and therefore he could not in good conscience accept a prize honoring Asturias's memory. Akabal's career in Guatemala has been surrounded by controversy. His bilingual poetry has been criticized in Spanish-speaking *ladino* literary circles as "unsophisticated," "politically reactionary," and "self-plagiarizing." His success abroad is sometimes dismissed as simply another instance of the commodification of "exotic" Maya art (Gustavo Adolfo Wyld, personal communication 1994; Mario Roberto Morales, personal communication 2010). However, his work remains popular in Guatemala, and he has become an icon of the revitalization of Mayan languages. For Maya activists, even those who haven't actually read him, Akabal embodies the success of Mayan languages in expanding to channels that before were exclusive domains of Spanish, the national language.

In addition to poetry anthologies, including poetry for children, Akabal has published essays and short stories (Akabal 1996, 1997, 2000, 2001, 2002, 2004, 2006, 2010, 2011). It has been claimed that early in his career he was influenced by Guatemalan poet Luís Alfredo Arango (Flores 2000); however, Akabal sees himself as a self-taught artist whose readings of the colonial K'ichee' and Kaqchikel chronicles as well as contemporary Spanish literature finally led him to find "his own voice" (Akabal 2011). His bilingual writing technique, subject matter, and original refashioning of K'ichee' poetics make him an innovative, subversive writer, one who breaks the canons of both Spanish and K'ichee' literature. If we conceptualize the poetry genre as a textual channel involving certain composition techniques (verses, stanzas), poetic language (met-

aphor, sound symbolism), and entextualization modalities (printed books), Humberto Akabal is definitely the first contemporary K'ichee' poet.

However, unlike other Maya poets such as the Kaqchikel writer Juan Yool, Akabal generally does not exploit the poetic forms of traditional ritual and ceremonial genres such as parallelism (couplets, triplets, etc.), honorific address, and archaic lexicon (see Yool 1994). His poems are brief and colloquial, like haikus. He characterizes his poetry as testimony in plain language of what he has seen, heard, felt, and personally experienced in his life as a Maya-K'ichee' from Momostenango, and describes his language as "nothing special" but simply the colloquial speech of his hometown (Akabal 2011). Many of his poems are pictures, selected scenes capturing the poet's experiences, memory, and nostalgia.

In Akabal's poem "Ashes" (Table 6.3) wind and ashes are metaphors for memory and nostalgia. In K'ichee' homes there is usually a fireplace where cinders, if not a fire, are permanently alight in the kitchen, the social center of the house, the place where the family gathers to eat or spend time together. Such recruitment of the mundane, the traditionally prosaic, in the life of Momostenango as a trope for the author's emotional state is a defining feature of Akabal's poetry. Many of his poems focus on emblematic K'ichee' traditions, beliefs, practices, and artifacts.

In the poem "White Hair" (Table 6.4) Akabal dramatizes the *awas*, taboos that pregnant women are expected to observe. For the Maya, the moon is associated with fertility of both women and earth. Pregnancy is a dangerous, liminal state in which women should protect themselves from potentially harmful interactions with powerful beings, such as the moon. Traditional systems of knowledge have been under siege in Guatemala for many years, but Maya activists have recently made enormous efforts to deconstruct prejudices against them and to promote remembrance of and respect for the wisdom of elders and ancestors.

In contrast to native K'ichee' scholars such as Florentino Ajpacajá, Eduardo León Chic,

TABLE 6.3. "Ashes," by Humberto Akabal (Akabal 2000:45–46).

Akabal's Spanish Text	Akabal's K'ichee' Text	My Translation of Akabal's K'ichee' Text
Ceniza	Chaj	Ashes
Y todo se consumió.	Juntira[1] xuporoj rib'	Everything was consumed.
La ceniza aún quema, el viento llora, busca, sabe que allí hubo una hoguera.	K'a miq'in kak'at na ri chaaj, koq', kab'ixon ri kaqiq', katzukunik, xa reta'm che chila' xk'oji' wi jun q'aq'.	But the ashes, still hot, keep burning. The wind whines, sings, and looks out, knowing that there was a fire there once.

[1] The word *juntira* "everything" is often misrecognized as a loanword. Because of its superficial similarity to Spanish *de un tiro* "in a single shot," some Maya intellectuals avoid it, taking it for a Spanish borrowing. Nevertheless, there is neither historical nor structural evidence that it is indeed a loanword.

TABLE 6.4. "White Hair," by Humberto Akabal (Akabal 2001:254–255).

Akabal's Spanish Text	Akabal's K'ichee' Text	My Translation of Akabal's K'ichee' Text
Canas	Saq wi'aj	White Hair
Luna, candil de la noche,	Are ri ik' ri uchaaj ri aq'ab'.	The moon is the night's kindling.
fuego blanco luz encaladora.	Saq q'aq' q'aq' chunanel	White fire, fire whitener.
La abuela les decía a las mujeres embarazadas:	Ri qati't kub'ij chi ri e ixoqib' e yewab' winaq	Our grandmother tells pregnant women:
Nunca salgan con ocote ardiendo cuando haya claridad en las noches porque encanecerán antes de tiempo.	Man kixel ta uloq ruuk' ri jun t'iqon chaj are jampa k'o ik' we kib'an wa' kub'an saq ri iwi' lib'ajchi'.	"Don't leave the house with lighted kindling when the moon is out. If you do, your hair will become white before its time."

and Diego Adrián Guarchaj, who have studied and promoted traditional calendrical and ritual knowledge and its associated ritual registers, Akabal celebrates K'ichee' traditions as personal recollections and anecdotes in a colloquial, everyday language (see Ajpacajá 2001; Gómez and Guarchaj 2002; León Chic 2002). This is consistent with his belief that poetry should be the transparent expression of the poet's personal experience and sentiment. In fact, Akabal has explicitly rejected some emblematic practices common among Maya activists such as changing one's first name from a Spanish to an ancient K'ichee' name or calendrical epithet (Akabal 2011). He is passionate in defending his right to follow his heart's bidding rather than serve as a mere echo chamber for the Maya movement, with which his art coexists in sympathetic tension. Finally, one of Akabal's most original innovations is his creative use of the abundant sound-symbolic lexicon of K'ichee' in his poetry. Sound-symbolic words are a rich lexical

TABLE 6.5. "Bird Songs," by Humberto Akabal (Akabal 2001:297–298).

Akabal's K'ichee' Text	My Translation of Akabal's K'ichee' Text
Xirixitem Chikop	Bird Songs
Klis, klis, klis… Ch'ok, ch'ok, ch'ok…	Klis, klis, klis… Grackle, grackle, grackle…
Tz'unun, tz'unun, tz'unun.	Hummingbird, hummingbird, hummingbird. Buqpurix, buqpurix, buqpurix.
Buqpurix, buqpurix, buqpurix.	Hawk, hawk, hawk…
Wiswil, wiswil, wiswil… Tukur, tukur, tukur…	Owl, owl, owl…
K'urupup, k'urupup, k'urupup… Ch'owix, ch'owix, ch'owix…	Barn owl, barn owl, barn owl… Canary, canary, canary…
Tuktuk, tuktuk, tuktuk…	Woodpecker, woodpecker, woodpecker… Urraca, urraca, urraca…
Xar, xar, xar…	K'up, k'up, k'up…
K'up, k'up, k'up… Saqk'or, saqk'or, saqk'or…	Quail, quail, quail…
Ch'ik, ch'ik, ch'ik… Tukumux, tukumux, tukumux…	Woodcock, woodcock, woodcock… Dove, dove, dove…
Xperpwaq, xperpwaq, xperpwaq… Tz'ikin, tz'ikin, tz'ikin…	Nightingale, nightingale, nightingale… Bird, bird, bird…
Kukuw, kukuw, kukuw… Chi'wit, chi'wit, chi'wit…	Sparrow, sparrow, sparrow… Chick, chick, chick…
Tli, tli, tli… Ch'er, ch'er, ch'er…	Tli, tli, tli… Chick, chick, chick…
Si-si-si-si-si-si-si-si Ch'ar, ch'ar, ch'ar…	Si-si-si-si-si-si-si-si Chick, chick, chick…

Note: There was no Spanish translation in the original edition.

category, one of the most distinctive and untranslatable poetic features of traditional K'ichee' folk stories. Nevertheless, few Maya contemporary writers, if any, have used them as extensively as Akabal.

"Bird Songs," the poem in Table 6.5, is a script for a sound-symbolic performance. Each verse consists of a triple repetition of the common K'ichee' name of a bird species, each of which is an onomatopoeic root iconically representing the respective bird song. It recapitulates the sensory experience of a forest in the western highlands of Guatemala, in which bird songs rather than tree and animal descriptions are the linguistic building blocks. Although affect roots and onomatopoeias are common in the oral performance of myths and other traditional narratives in Mayan languages, only Akabal has incorporated them so intensively into poetry. This responds to Akabal's preference for sensory individual experience rather than received tradition as subjective foundation for his artistic craft. The result of Akabal's poetic mettle is the universal appeal of a poetry that can be easily detached, entextualized, and reinterpreted in other contexts—texts that can be more easily depoliticized than those of Yool, for example.

Akabal's poetic work has opened new paths for Maya art. With him, K'ichee' is not only the language of elders' solemn wisdom and timeless knowledge; it is also the language of love, children's play, and bird songs. He incarnates the new Maya subject, both modern and traditional, one that does not hesitate to innovate and selectively choose from the ancestors' ways, while also celebrating their wisdom and experience. In contrast to Maya writers such as Gaspar Pedro González, in whose work an archaizing utopia always beckons in the background, Akabal is a postmodern subject, as it were, comfortable in a multicentered world and not averse to celebrating non-Maya societies, as in his poems on Japan, produced during a writing stint in Kyoto. Akabal acts as a cultural mediator, an unwilling cultural ambassador for the Maya movement, as many of his most faithful readers are not Guatemalan and certainly not Maya. His fidelity to intimate experience has earned him disdain from Guatemalan writers whose leftist revolutionary politics have played a large role in their own creation, but also places him squarely in the company of young writers recreating Guatemalan literature away from the civil war's ideological struggles (Flores 2000; Cortez 2010).

Akabal continues the innovative role played by the K'ichee' in fashioning new ways of articulating tradition and social change. Recasting the words of the ancestors in contemporary poetry,

Akabal joins the tradition started by Fray Domingo de Vico's anonymous collaborators in the sixteenth century, wisely crafting a K'ichee' language that both expresses and embodies the Maya people's adaptation and resistance to the colonial project, in both its imperial and republican guises. Like Vico's coauthors, Adrián Inés Chávez and Humberto Akabal succeeded in making a linguistic synthesis of two distinct traditions in conflict that nevertheless coexist in the souls and minds of the Maya.

The complex, contradictory, and colorful intertwining of prehispanic and European traditions that has defined K'ichee' society since the sixteenth century shows that colonialism is not just a political system or a state of mind but also a hybrid semiotic regime, a tense exchange of signs and ideologies that certain individuals, veritable cultural prophets, constantly recreate. I have discussed some of their work and practices, showing how linguistic innovations have enacted social change in K'ichee' society and beyond. In the regime of political subordination that the K'ichee' have endured since the Spanish invasion, linguistic innovation has been the avenue of adaptation and survival, often out of the hearing of Spaniards and *ladinos*. Representing their own language as the unaltered legacy of the ancestors, K'ichee' voices have not hesitated to turn it into a miraculous artifact, powerful and flexible, with which they have defied their oppressors and laid the foundation for a K'ichee' resurrection.

Notes

1. Nevertheless, Luis de Lión, a Kaqchikel from San Juan del Obispo and one of the most important contemporary Guatemalan writers, wrote exclusively in Spanish, though he always identified as "indio."
2. I have found the same kind of K'ichee' lexical influences on Awakatek. María García (personal communication 2013) reports similar borrowings from K'ichee' into Ixil.
3. *Pouteria sapota*, a soft, sweet, edible fruit found in Mexico and Central America.
4. My translation.

5. From *chaabil* "good" and *us* "fine." The suffix –*ilal* turns both adjectives into abstract nouns, denoting the general quality they reference.
6. My translation.
7. My translation.
8. Chávez taught at the Instituto Normal para Varones de Occidente (INVO) in Quetzaltenango, where many indigenous elementary schoolteachers were trained (Guzman Boeckler 1997:xv).
9. Chávez's alphabet was rejected in 1963 in favor of the one developed by linguists of the Summer

Institute of Linguistics as standard for bilingual schools in Guatemala. The Ministry of Education argued that Chávez's orthography "moved away from recent advances in linguistics" (Guzmán-Boeckler 1997).

10. Ximénez's transcription is indeed inconsistent, though we cannot be sure whether this was his fault or the previous copyist's. However, the colonial script adequately captures all phonemic consonantal features of the language except vowel length, as can be seen, for example, in the *Theologia Indorum*.

11. Chávez argued that *popol* was a transcription error on Ximénez's part, as it does not exist in modern K'ichee', and amended it to *pop* "mat," which he mysteriously glossed as "time" (Chávez 1997:xxxi–xxxii). However, the term *popol* is well attested in colonial K'ichee' dictionaries and Kaqchikel chronicles, which Chávez seemingly was unacquainted with (Chávez 1997:xxviii).

12. In addition to the usual Latin script graphemes, the missionary alphabet added the *tresillo*, which looks like a number three, and the *cuatrillo*, which looks somewhat like a number four. These characters were used in fifteenth-century Spain to represent Arabic and Hebrew phonemes absent in Spanish or Latin and were conveniently recruited as conventions for K'ichee' ejective sounds.

13. In the original Spanish the text reads: "Las Siete Vergüenzas son: El Orgullo Engendra: La Ambición, La Envidia, La Mentira, El Crimen, La Ingratitud y La Ignorancia."

14. The "Seven Capital Sins," for example.

References

Abac, V. R.
1980 *Natajsabal rech nutinamit: Algunos datos sobre la historia de Nahualá*. Guatemala City, Junta Nacional de Educación Extra-escolar.

Acuña, R.
1982 *Relaciones geográficas del siglo XVI: Guatemala*. Universidad Nacional Autónoma de México, Mexico City.
1985 La Theologia Indorum de Domingo de Vico. *Tlalocan* 10:281–307.

Adams, A.
2004 The Transformation of the Tzuultaqa: Jorge Ubico, Protestants and Other Verapaz Maya at the Crossroads of Community, State and Transnational Interests. *Journal of Latin American Anthropology* 6(2):198–233.

Agha, A.
2000 Registers. *Journal of Linguistic Anthropology* 9(1–2):216–219.
2002 Honorific Registers. In *Culture, Interaction and Language*, edited by K. Kuniyoshi and S. Ide, pp. 21–63. Kitsuji Shobo, Tokyo.
2007 *Language and Social Relations*. Cambridge University Press, Cambridge.

Ajpacajá, F.
2001 *Tz'onob'al tziij = Discurso ceremonial k'ichee'*. Cholsamaj, Guatemala City.

Akabal, H.
1996 *Lluvia de luna en la cipreselada*. Artemis Edinter, Guatemala City.
1997 *Retoño salvaje*. Editorial Praxis, Mexico City.
2000 *El animalero*. Editorial Cholsamaj, Guatemala City.
2001 *Aqajtzij*. Cholsamaj, Guatemala City.
2002 *Detrás de las golondrinas*. Editorial Praxis, Mexico City.
2004 *Barco de piedra*. Artemis Edinter, Guatemala City.
2006 *K'ojon che nik'aj ik' = Remiendo de media luna*. Artesanales Tz'ukulik, Momostenango.
2010 *Ri tzij kek'iyik = Las palabras crecen*. Maya Wuj, Guatemala City.
2011 Chi uxo'l ri mayab'—K'ichee' xuquje' ri kaxlan tzij. In *La comunidad Maya K'ichee' de Santiago Momostenango*, edited by H. Akabal and R. Carmack, pp. 141–154. Maya' Wuj, Guatemala City.

Anderson, B.
2006 *Imagined Communities: Reflections on the Origin and Spread of Nationalism*. Verso, London.

Anleo, B. de
2002 *Arte de la lengua 4iche*. Universidad Nacional Autónoma de México, Mexico City.

Anonymous
1946 *Ri Gkagk Testament re ri Ka Nim Ajawal Jesucrist*. American Bible Society, New York.

Appadurai, A.
1990 Disjuncture and Difference in the Global Cultural Economy. *Theory, Culture, and Society* 7:295–310.
1996 *Modernity at Large: Cultural Dimensions of Globalization*. University of Minnesota Press, Minneapolis.

Arias, A.
2007 *Taking Their Word: Literature and the Signs of Central America*. University of Minnesota Press, Minneapolis.

Asamblea Nacional Constituyente
1986 *Constitución política de la República de Guatemala en idioma quiché*. Tipografía Nacional, Guatemala City.

Assad, T.
1970 *The Kababish Arabs: Power, Authority and Consent in a Nomadic Tribe*. Hurst, London.

Asselbergs, F.
2008 *Conquered Conquistadors: The Lienzo de Quauhquechollan, a Nahua Vision of the Conquest of Guatemala*. University of Colorado Press, Boulder.

Asturias de Barrios, L., I. Mejía de Rodas, and
R. Miralbés de Polanco
1989 *Santa María de Jesús: Traje y cofradía.*
      Museo Ixchel, Guatemala City.
Austin, J. L.
1975 *How to Do Things with Words.* Harvard University Press, Cambridge, Massachusetts.
Bakhtin, M.
1981 *The Dialogic Imagination: Four Essays.*
      Edited by M. Holquist. University of Texas Press, Austin.
Baronti, D.
2001 Sound Symbolism Use in Affect Verbs in Santa Catarina Ixtahuacán. Unpublished Ph.D. dissertation, University of California, Davis.
Barth, F.
1969 *Ethnic Groups and Boundaries.* Little, Brown, Boston.
Bartolomé, M. A.
1992 Identidad residencial en Mesoamérica: Fronteras étnicas y fronteras comunales. *América Indígena* 52(1–2):251–273.
Basseta, D. de
2005 *Vocabulario de lengua quiché.* Universidad Nacional Autónoma de México, Mexico City.
Bastos, S., and M. Camus
2003a *Entre el mecapal y el cielo: Desarrollo del movimiento maya en Guatemala.* Cholsamaj, Guatemala City.
2003b *El movimiento maya en perspectiva.* FLACSO, Guatemala City.
Beal, J.
2009 Enregisterment, Commodification, and Historical Context: "Geordie" versus "Sheffieldish." *American Speech* 84(2):138–156.
Becker Richards, J.
1985 Vowel Variability in a Linguistic Transition Zone. *International Journal of American Linguistics* 51(4):549–553.
1998 Case Study One: San Marcos La Laguna. In *The Life of Our Language: Kaqchikel Maya Maintenance, Shift, and Revitalization,* edited by Susan Garzon et al., pp. 62–100. University of Texas Press, Austin.
Becker Richards, J., and M. Richards
1987 Percepciones de inteligibilidad mutua entre las variantes dialectales de la cuenca del lago de Atitlán. *Winak* 2(4):205–222.
Bierman, B.
1960 Fray Bartolome de las Casas und die Grundung der Mission in der Verapaz.

Neue Zeitschrift fur Missiionswissenschaft 16:110–123, 161–177.
Blom, J. P., and J. Gumperz
1986 Social Meaning in Linguistic Structures: Code-Switching in Norway. In *Directions in Sociolinguistics,* edited by J. Gumperz and D. Hymes. Blackwell, New York.
Blommaert, J.
2005 *Discourse.* Cambridge University Press, Cambridge.
Bocek, B.
2009 Everyday Politics in a K'ichee' Village of Totonicapán, Guatemala. In *Mayas in Postwar Guatemala,* edited by W. Little and T. Smith, pp. 124–137. University of Alabama Press, Tuscaloosa.
Boremanse, D.
1986 *Contes et mythologie des indiens lacandons.* Hachette, Paris.
Bossu, E. M.
1990 *Un manuscrito k'ekchi' del siglo XVI: Transcripción, paleografía, traducción y estudio de las coplas atribuidas a Fray Luis de Cáncer.* Ediciones Comisión Interuniversitaria Guatemalteca, Guatemala City.
Bourbourg, C. B. de
1961 *Grammaire de la langue.* Editorial José de Pineda Ibarra, Guatemala City.
Bourdieu, P.
2000 *Esquisse d'une théorie de la pratique.* Seuil, Paris.
2001 *Langage et pouvoir symbolique.* Seuil, Paris.
Breton, A.
1989 El "complejo ajaw" y el "complejo mam." In *Memorias del Segundo Coloquio Internacional de Mayistas,* pp. 17–27. Universidad Nacional Autónoma de México, Mexico City.
1990 Chávez, Adrián I.—Pop Wuh, le livre des événements. *Journal de la Société des Américanistes* 76(1):251–254.
1994 *Rabinal Achi: Un drame dynastique maya du XVème siècle; Edition établie d'après le Manuscrit Pérez.* Société d'Ethnologie/Société des Américanistes, Nanterre, France.
Bricker, V.
2009 *The Indian Christ, the Indian King.* University of Texas, Austin.
Brintnall, D.
1979 *Revolt against the Dead: The Modernization of a Mayan Community in the Highlands of Guatemala.* Gordon and Breach, New York.

Brody, J.
1987 Particles Borrowed from Spanish as Discourse Markers in Mayan Languages. *Anthropological Linguistics* 29(4):507–521.
1995 Lending the Unborrowable: Spanish Discourse Markers in Indigenous Languages. In *Spanish in Four Continents: Studies of Language Contact and Bilingualism*, edited by C. Silva-Corvalán, pp. 132–147. Georgetown University Press, Washington, D.C.

Brown, R., and A. Gilman
1987 The Pronouns of Power and Solidarity. In *Language and Social Context*, edited by P. P. Giglioli, pp. 252–281. Penguin Books, Harmondsworth, U.K.

Bryce Heath, S.
1972 *Telling Tongues: Language Policy in Mexico, Colony to Nation.* Teachers College Press, New York.

Bunte, P., and M. Kendal
1981 When Is an Error Not an Error? Notes on Language Contact and the Question of Interference. *Anthropological Linguistics* 23(1):1–7.

Bunzel, R.
1981 *Chichicastenango.* Editorial José de Pineda Ibarra, Guatemala City.

Burkhart, L.
1989 *The Slippery Earth: Nahua-Christian Moral Dialogue in Sixteenth-Century Mexico.* University of Arizona Press, Tucson.

Buscher-Grotehussman, M.
1999 *Maya-K'ichee' und Spanish: Sprachkontakt und Sprachkonflikt.* Peter Lang, Berlin.

Cabarrús, C.
1979 *La cosmovisión K'ekchi' en proceso de cambio.* UCA Editores, San Salvador, El Salvador.
1998 *En la conquista del ser: Un estudios de identidad étnica.* CEDIM, Guatemala City.

Cabezas, H.
2010 *Independencia centroamericana: Gestión y ocaso del Plan Pacífico.* Editorial Universitaria, Guatemala City.

Cabrera, E.
1997 The Pop Vuh: The Sacred History of the Mayas. In *Crosscurrents in Indigenous Spirituality*, edited by G. Cook. E. J. Brill, Leiden.
2007 *Cosmogénesis maya.* Editorial Kakol Kiej, Alajuela, Costa Rica.

Calvo-Pérez, J.
2000 Partículas en castellano andino. In *Teoría y práctica del contacto: El español de América en el candelero*, edited by J. Calvo-Pérez, pp. 73–112. Velvuert, Frankfurt; Iberoamericana, Madrid.

Camacho Nassar, C.
2003 La lucha por la tierra en las aldeas de María Tecún. In *Tierra, identidad y conflicto en Guatemala*, edited by C. Camacho Nassar, B. Durocher, J. A. Fernandez, and J. V. Letona, pp. 143–200. FLACSO, MINUGUA, CONTIERRA, Guatemala City.

Cambranes, J.
1985 *Coffee and Peasants: The Origins of the Modern Plantation Economy in Guatemala, 1853–1897.* Institute of Latin American Studies, Stockholm.

Camey Barrios, J. I., and U. U. Quijivix Yax
2013 *Memoria histórica de la centenaria sociedad maya k'iche' "El Adelanto."* ADESCA/Cholsamaj, Guatemala City.

Campbell, L.
1971 Nahua Loan Words in Quichean Languages. *Chicago Linguistic Society* 6:3–13.
1977 *Quichean Linguistic Prehistory.* University of California Press, Berkeley.
1997 *American Indian Languages: The Historical Linguistics of Native America.* Oxford University Press, Oxford.

Campbell, L., and T. Kaufman
1976 A Linguistic Look at the Olmecs. *American Antiquity* 41:80–89.

Campbell, L., T. Kaufman, and T. Smith-Stark
1986 Meso-America as a Linguistic Area. *Language* 62(3):530–570.

Canger, U.
1989 Dialectology: A Survey and Some Suggestions. *International Journal of American Linguistics* 54(1):28–72.

Cañizares-Esguerra, J.
2006 *Puritan Conquistadors: Iberianizing the Atlantic, 1500–1700.* Stanford University Press, Stanford, California.

Carey, D.
2001 *Our Elders Teach Us: Maya-Kaqchikel Historical Perspectives.* University of Alabama Press, Tuscaloosa.

Carmack, R.
1973 *Quichean Civilization: The Ethnohistoric, Ethnographic, and Archaeological Sources.* University of California Press, Berkeley.
1981 *The Quiche Maya of Utatlán: The Evolution of a Highland Maya Kingdom.* University of Oklahoma Press, Norman.

1988 *Harvest of Violence: Maya Indians and the Guatemala Crisis.* University of Oklahoma Press, Norman.

1995 *Rebels of Highland Guatemala: The Quiche-Mayas of Momostenango.* University of Oklahoma Press, Norman.

Carmack, R., J. Gasco, and G. Gossen

2006 *The Legacy of Mesoamerica: History and Culture of a Native American Civilization.* Prentice-Hall, New York.

Carmack, R., and J. Mondloch

1983 *Título de Totonicapán: Texto, traducción y comentario.* Universidad Nacional Autónoma de México, Mexico City.

Casáus-Arzú, M.

1998 *La metamorfosis del racismo en Guatemala.* Cholsamaj, Guatemala City.

Casey, D.

1979 Indigenismo: The Guatemalan Experience. Unpublished Ph.D. dissertation, University of Kansas, Lawrence.

Castillo, V.

1998 *Ri loq'alaj k'utb'al rech ri relb'al uk'u'x ri qajaw.* Ediciones Ik'laja, Santa María Chiquimula, Guatemala.

Castillo Taracena, C.

2013 *Iximche': Un lugar de memorias en Guatemala.* FLACSO, Guatemala City.

Chambers, J. K., and P. Trudgill

1980 *Dialectology.* Cambridge University Press, Cambridge.

Chávez, A. I.

1974 *Ki-che Zib: Escritura ki-che y otros temas.* Guatemala City.

1979 *Pop-Wuj: Libro de acontecimientos.* Publicaciones de la Casa Chata, Mexico City.

1997 *Pop-Wuj: Poema mito-histórico K'ichee'.* TIMACH, Quetzaltenango, Guatemala.

2010 *El origen del hombre hebreoamericano.* AMISRAEL, Guatemala City.

Cheshire, J.

2005 Syntactic Variation and Beyond: Gender and Social Class Variation in the Use of Discourse-New Markers. *Journal of Sociolinguistics* 9(4):479–508.

Choi, J.

2003 Language Choice and Language Ideology in a Bilingual Mayan Community: The Politics of Identity in Guatemala. Unpublished Ph.D. dissertation, State University of New York, Albany.

Christenson, A.

2001 *Art and Society in a Highland Maya Community.* University of Texas Press, Austin.

2003 *Popol Vuh: The Sacred Book of the Maya.* University of Oklahoma Press, Norman.

2004 *Popol Vuh, Volume 2: Literal Poetic Version.* O Books, New York.

Cojtí, D.

1995 *Ub'aniik ri una'ooj uchomab'aal ri Maya' tinamit: Configuración del pensamiento político del Pueblo Maya (2da. parte).* Cholsamaj, Guatemala City.

1997 *Ri Maya' moloj pa Iximulew.* Cholsamaj, Guatemala City.

2006 *Runa'oj ri Maya' Amaq': Configuración del pensamiento político del Pueblo Maya.* Cholsamaj, Guatemala City.

Colby, B., and P. Van der Bergue

1969 *Ixil Country: A Plural Society in Highland Guatemala.* University of California Press, Berkeley.

Colson, E.

1968 Contemporary Tribes and the Development of Nationalism. In *Essays on the Problem of the Tribe: Proceedings of the 1967 Meeting of the American Ethnological Society,* edited by J. Helm. University of Washington Press, Seattle.

Comaroff, J., and J. Comaroff

2009 *Ethnicity Inc.* University of Chicago Press, Chicago.

Cook, G.

2000 *Renewing the Maya World: Expressive Culture in a Highland Town.* University of Texas Press, Austin.

Cortez, B.

2010 *Estética del cinismo: Pasión y desencanto en la literatura centroamericana de postguerra.* F&G Editores, Guatemala City.

Cortez y Larraz, P.

1958 *Descripción geográfico-moral de la diócesis de Goathemala.* Sociedad de Geografía e Historia de Guatemala, Guatemala City.

Dakin, K., and C. Lutz

1996 *Nuestro pesar, nuestra aflicción.* UNAM-CIRMA, Mexico City.

Davies, W., and L. Sam Colop

1990 K'ichee' and the Structure of the Antipassive. *Language* 66(3):522–549.

DeHart, M.

2010 *Ethnic Entrepreneurs: Identity and Devel-*

opment Politics in Latin America. Stanford University Press, Stanford, California.

de León, Juan

1945 *Mundo quiché: Miscelánea.* Taller Tipográfico San Antonio, Guatemala City.

Dieseldorf, Erwin P.

1929 Religión y arte de los mayas. *Anales de la Sociedad de Geografía e Historia de Guatemala* 5(2–3). Sociedad de Geografía e Historia de Guatemala, Guatemala City.

Durocher, B.

2002 *Los dos derechos de la tierra: La cuestión agraria en el país ixil.* FLACSO, MINUGUA, CONTIERRA, Guatemala City.

Dürr, M.

2006 *Einführung in das kolonialzeitliche Quiché (K'iche').* FU Berlin, Lateinamerika-Institut, Berlin.

Durston, A.

2007 *Pastoral Quechua: The History of Christian Translation in Colonial Peru, 1550–1650.* Notre Dame University Press, Notre Dame, Indiana.

Edmonson, M.

1997 *Quiché Dramas and Divinatory Calendars.* Middle American Research Institute, Tulane University, New Orleans.

England, N.

1996 The Mayan Language Loyalty Movement in Guatemala. In *Maya Cultural Activism in Guatemala,* edited by E. F. Fischer and R. McKenna Brown. University of Texas Press, Austin.

2003 Mayan Language Revival and Revitalization Politics: Linguists and Linguistic Ideologies. *American Anthropologist* 105(4):733–743.

Errington, J.

2008 *Linguistics in a Colonial World: A Study of Language, Meaning, and Power.* Blackwell, Malden, Massachusetts.

Fabian, J.

1986 *Language and Colonial Power.* University of California Press, Berkeley.

Falla, R.

1978 El movimiento indígena. *Estudios Centroamericanos* 33:356–357, 437–461.

1980 *Quiché rebelde: Estudio de un movimiento de conversión religiosa, rebelde a las creencias tradicionales, en San Antonio Ilotenango, Quiché (1948–1970).* Editorial Universitaria, Guatemala City.

1992 *Masacres de la selva: Ixcán, Guatemala, 1975–1982.* Editorial Universitaria, Guatemala City.

2011 *Negreaba de zopilotes: Masacre y sobrevivencia; Finca San Francisco, Nentón.* AVANCSO, Guatemala City.

Ferguson, C.

1994 Dialect, Register and Genre: Working Assumptions about Conventionalization. In *Sociolinguistic Perspectives on Register,* edited by D. Biber and E. Finegan, pp. 15–30. Oxford University Press, Oxford.

Fischer, E. F.

1996 Induced Culture Change as a Strategy for Socioeconomic Development: The Pan-Maya Movement in Guatemala. In *Maya Cultural Activism in Guatemala,* edited by E. F. Fischer and R. McKenna Brown. University of Texas Press, Austin.

2001 *Cultural Logics and Global Economics: Maya Identity in Thought and Practice.* University of Texas Press, Austin.

Flores, M. A.

2000 *Poetas guatemaltecos del siglo XX.* Calendarios Centroamerica, Guatemala City.

Flores-Farfán, J. A.

1999 *Cuatreros somos y toindioma hablamos: Contactos y conflictos entre el náhuatl y el español en el sur de México.* CIESAS, Mexico City.

2009 *Variación, ideologías y purismo lingüístico: El caso del Mexicano o Náhuatl.* CIESAS, Mexico City.

Forand, N.

2002 The Language Ideologies of Courtship Ritual. *Journal of American Folklore* 115(457/458):332–377.

Foster, G.

1994 Nahualism in Mexico and Guatemala. *Acta Americana* 2(1–2):805–1030.

Foucault, M.

1969 *L'archéologie du savoir.* Gallimard, Paris.

Fox, J.

1978 *Quiche Conquest: Centralism and Regionalism in Highland Guatemalan State Development.* University of New Mexico Press, Albuquerque.

Fox, J., and E. Brumfield

1994 Political Cosmology among the Quiche Maya. In *Factional Competition and Political Development in the New World,* edited by E. Brumfield and J. Fox, pp. 158–170. Cambridge University Press, New York.

Foxen, P.
2007 *In Search of Providence: Transnational Maya Identities.* Vanderbilt University Press, Nashville, Tennessee.

Fraser, B.
1999 What Are Discourse Markers? *Journal of Pragmatics* 31:931–952.

French, B.
2010 *Maya Ethnolinguistic Identity: Violence, Modernity, and Cultural Rights in Highland Guatemala.* University of Arizona Press, Tucson.

Fuentes y Guzmán, F. A.
1932–33 *La Recordación Florida (Vol. 1–III).* Tipografía Nacional, Guatemala City.

Furbee, L.
1988 To Ask One Holy Thing: Petition as a Tojolabal Maya Speech Genre. In *Tojolabal Maya: Ethnographic and Linguistic Approaches,* pp. 39–53. Geoscience Publications, Louisiana State University, Baton Rouge.

Gabbert, W.
2004 *Becoming Maya: Ethnicity and Social Inequality in Yucatan since 1500.* University of Arizona Press, Tucson.
2006 Concepts of Ethnicity. *Latin American and Caribbean Ethnic Studies* 1(1):85–103.

García-Ruiz, J.
1992 El misionero, las lenguas mayas y la traducción. *Archives des Sciences Sociales des Religions* 77:83–110.

Geyer, N.
2008 *Discourse and Politeness: Ambivalent Face in Japanese.* Continuum, New York.

Gillespie, Susan
2010 Maya Memory Work. *Ancient Mesoamerica* 21:401–414.

Goffman, E.
1974 *Frame Analysis: An Essay on the Organization of Experience.* Harper and Row, New York.

Goldin, L.
1987 De plaza a mercado: La expresión de dos sistemas conceptuales en la organización de los mercados del occidente de Guatemala. *Anales de Antropología* 24:243–261.

Gómez, F., and D. A. Guarchaj
2002 *Jupaj kapaj uq'alajisaxik uk'u'xal uxe'al Mayab' kojob'al.* Academia de Lenguas Mayas de Guatemala, Guatemala City.

González, M.
2002 *Se cambió el tiempo: Conflicto y poder en territorio K'iché, 1880–1996.* AVANCSO, Guatemala City.

González Ponciano, J.
2004 La visible invisibilidad de la blancura y el ladino como no blanco en Guatemala. In *Memorias del mestizaje,* edited by D. Euraque, J. Gould, and C. Hale, pp. 111–133. CIRMA, Antigua Guatemala.

Gosner, K.
1992 *Soldiers of the Virgin: The Moral Economy of a Colonial Maya Rebellion.* University of Arizona Press, Tucson.

Grandia, L.
2009 *Tz'aptz'ooqeb: El despojo recurrente del pueblo Q'eqchi'.* AVANCSO, Guatemala City.

Grandin, G.
2000 *The Blood of Guatemala: A History of Race and Nation.* Duke University Press, Durham, North Carolina.
2004 *The Last Colonial Massacre: Latin America in the Cold War.* University of Chicago Press, Chicago.

Grice, H.
1989 *Studies in the Way of Words.* Harvard University Press, Cambridge, Massachusetts.

Grieb, K.
1979 *Guatemalan Caudillo: The Regime of Jorge Ubico, Guatemala, 1931–1944.* Ohio University Press, Athens.

Gumperz, J., and D. Hymes
1986 *Directions in Sociolinguistics: The Ethnography of Communication.* Blackwell, Oxford.

Guzmán Boeckler, C.
1997 Introducción. In *Pop-Wuj: Poema mito-histórico K'ichee'.* TIMACH, Quetzaltenango, Guatemala.

Guzmán Boeckler, C., and J.-L. Herbert
1970 *Guatemala: Una interpretación histórico-social.* Editorial Universitaria, Guatemala City.

Hale, C.
2004 Mistados, cholos y la negación de la identidad en el altiplano guatemalteco. In *Memorias del mestizaje,* edited by D. Euraque, J. Gould, and C. Hale, pp. 133–166. CIRMA, Antigua Guatemala.
2006 *Más Que un Indio (More Than an Indian): Racial Ambivalence and the Paradox of Neoliberal Multiculturalism in Guatemala.*

School of American Research Press, Santa Fe, New Mexico.

Handy, J.

1994   *Revolution in the Countryside: Rural Conflict and Agrarian Reform in Guatemala, 1944–1954.* University of North Carolina Press, Chapel Hill.

Hanks, W.

1988   Grammar, Style, and Meaning in a Maya Manuscript. *International Journal of American Linguistics* 54(3):331–365.

1992   *Referential Practice: Language and Lived Space among the Maya.* University of Chicago Press, Chicago.

2010   *Converting Words: Maya in the Age of the Cross.* University of California Press, Berkeley.

Hendrickson, C.

1996   *Weaving Identities: Construction of Dress and Self in a Highland Guatemala Town.* University of Texas Press, Austin.

Hernández, N.

1999   Noihqui toaxca caxtilan tlahtolli: El español tambien es nuestro. *Estudios de Cultura Náhuatl* 30:256–258.

Hill, J., and K. Hill

1999   *Hablando mexicano: La dinámica de una lengua sincrética en el centro de México.* Instituto Nacional Indigenista and CIESAS, Mexico City.

Hill, R., and J. Monaghan

1987   *Continuities in Highland Maya Social Organization: Ethnohistory in Sacapulas, Guatemala.* University of Pennsylvania Press, Philadelphia.

Holksbeke, M., and J. Montoya

2008   *Los tejidos mayas: Espejos de una cosmovisión.* Cholsamaj, Guatemala City.

Hostig, R., Weisshaar, E., and L. Guarchaj

1995   *Ojer tzij: Cuentos y leyendas del pueblo quiché (version en quiché).* Cooperación para el Desarrollo Rural del Occidente, Quetzaltenango, Guatemala.

Irvine, J., and S. Gal

2000   Language Ideology and Linguistic Differentiation. In *Regimes of Language: Ideologies, Polities, and Identities*, edited by P. Kroskrity, pp. 35–83. School of American Research Press, Santa Fe, New Mexico.

Jiménez, O.

1997   Tensión entre idiomas: Situación actual de los idiomas mayas y el español en Guatemala. Paper presented at the annual meeting of the Latin American Studies Association, Guadalajara, Mexico.

Jonas, S.

2000   *Of Centaurs and Doves: Guatemala's Peace Process.* Westview Press, Boulder, Colorado.

Justeson, J., W. Norman, T. Kaufman, and L. Campbell

1985   *The Foreign Impact on Lowland Mayan Language and Script.* Middle American Research Institute, New Orleans.

Karttunen, F.

1985   *Nahuatl and Maya in Contact with Spanish.* Department of Linguistics, University of Texas, Austin.

Karttunen, F., and J. Lockhart

1976   *Language in the Middle Years: Language Contact Phenomena in Texts of the Colonial Period.* University of California Press, Berkeley.

Kaufman, T.

1976   Proyecto de alfabetos y ortografías para escribir las lenguas mayances. *Guatemala Indígena* 11(1–2):131–166.

n.d.   Some Structural Traits of the Mayan Languages with Special Reference to K'iche'. In *Terence Kaufman's Unpublished Papers.* AILLA, University of Texas, Austin.

King, R.

2000   *The Lexical Basis of Grammatical Borrowing: A Prince Edward Island French Case Study.* J. Benjamins, Amsterdam.

Kirchoff, P.

1960   Mesoamérica, sus límites geográficos, composición étnica y caracteres culturales. *Tlatoani (Suplemento Especial)* 3:1–12.

Kockelman, P.

2003   The Meanings of Interjections in Q'eqchi' Maya: From Emotive Reaction to Social and Discursive Action. *Current Anthropology* 44(4):467–490.

2004   Stance and Subjectivity. *Journal of Linguistic Anthropology* 14(2):127–150.

Konefal, B.

2010   *For Every Indio Who Falls.* University of New Mexico Press, Albuquerque.

Labov, W.

1994   *Principles of Language Change, Vol. 1: Internal Factors.* Blackwell, Cambridge, Massachusetts.

Lacadena, A.
2008   Regional Scribal Traditions: Methodolog-
        ical Implications for the Decipherment of
        Nahuatl Writing. *PARI* 8(4):1–22.

León Chic, E.
2002   *Ajpatanom rech Qatat Esquipulas pa
        Tz'olojche'*. Ediciones Ik'laja, Santa María
        Chiquimula, Guatemala.

Levy, R.
1979   The Phonological History of the Bugotu-
        Nggelic Languages and Its Implications
        for Eastern Oceanic. *Oceanic Linguistics*
        18(1):1–31.

Lima Soto, R. E.
1995   *Aproximación a la cosmovisión maya*.
        Universidad Rafael Landivar, Guatemala
        City.

Little, W.
2004   *Mayas in the Marketplace: Tourism, Global-
        ization, and Cultural Identity*. University of
        Texas Press, Austin.
2009   Language Choice among Maya Handicraft
        Vendors in an International Tourism Mar-
        ketplace. In *Imagining Globalization*, edited
        by H. H. Leung and M. Hendley. Palgrave
        Macmillan, New York.

Little-Siebold, C.
2008   En la Tierra de San Francisco El Conquis-
        tador: Identity, Faith, and Livelihood in
        Quezaltepeque, Chiquimula. Unpublished
        Ph.D. dissertation, Tulane University, New
        Orleans.

Lockhart, J.
1992   *The Nahuas after the Conquest: A Social and
        Cultural History of the Indians of Central
        Mexico, Sixteenth through Eighteenth Cen-
        turies*. Stanford University Press, Stanford,
        California.

López, C. M.
1999   *Los "Popol Wuj" y sus epistemologías*. Edi-
        ciones Abya Yala, Quito, Ecuador.

López-Austin, A.
1994   *Tamoanchan y Tlalocan*. Fondo de Cultura
        Económica, Mexico City.
1996   *Los mitos del tlacuache*. Fondo de Cultura
        Económica, Mexico City.

López Ixcoy, C.
1997   *Gramática K'ichee'*. Cholsamaj, Guatemala
        City.

Lutz, C.
1994   *Santiago de Guatemala, 1541–1773: City,
        Caste, and the Colonial Experience*. Univer-
        sity of Oklahoma Press, Norman.

Manning, P.
2001   On Social Deixis. *Anthropological Linguis-
        tics* 43(1):54–100.

Manz, B.
2004   *Paradise in Ashes: A Guatemalan Journey
        of Courage, Terror, and Hope*. University of
        California Press, Berkeley.

Martínez-Peláez, S.
1970   *La patria del criollo: Ensayo de interpretación
        de la realidad colonial guatemalteca*. Edito-
        rial Universitaria, Guatemala City.

Matras, Y.
2009   *Language Contact*. Cambridge University
        Press, Cambridge.

Matthew, L.
2000   El náhuatl y la identidad mexicana en la
        Guatemala colonial. *Mesoamerica* 21:41–68.
2012   *Memories of Conquest: Becoming Mexicano
        in Colonial Guatemala*. University of North
        Carolina Press, Chapel Hill.

Matul, D.
1997   Don Adrián Inés Chávez: Mensaje de maiz y
        de poesía. In *Pop-Wuj: Poema mito-histórico
        K'i-che'*. TIMACH. Liga Maya Internacio-
        nal, San José, Costa Rica.

Matul, D., and E. Cabrera
2007   *La cosmovisión Maya*. Editorial Amanuense,
        Guatemala City.

Matzir Miculax, M. L., E. M. Valey Sis, L. Méndez
Martínez, D. Hernández Ixcoy, and H. Ch'ok
2009   *Cosmovisión Mayab': Dos tres palabras sobre
        sus principios*. Asociación Maya Uk'ux B'e,
        Chimaltenango.

Maxwell, J.
1996   Prescriptive Grammar and Kaqchikel
        Revitalization. In *Maya Cultural Activism
        in Guatemala*, edited by E. F. Fischer and R.
        McKenna Brown. University of Texas Press,
        Austin.

Maxwell, J., and R. Hill
2006   *Kaqchikel Chronicles*. University of Texas
        Press, Austin.

Mayén, G., I. Mejía de Rodas, and L. Asturias de
Barrios
1986   *Tzute y jerarquía en Solola*. Museo Ixchel,
        Guatemala City.

McCreery, D.
1994   *Rural Guatemala, 1760–1940*. Stanford Uni-
        versity Press, Stanford, California.
1995   El café y sus efectos en la sociedad indígena.
        In *Historia general de Guatemala, Volumen
        IV*, edited by A. Herrarte, pp. 503–531. Asoci-
        ación de Amigos del País, Guatemala City.

Mendelson, E. M.
1965 *Los escándalos de Maximón*. Seminario de Integración Social, Guatemala City.

Mercier, A. P.
2008 *Los secretos de los chamanes mayas*. Ediciones Luciérnaga, Barcelona.

Miller, H.
1996 Las relaciones entre la iglesia católica y el estado de Guatemala, 1927–1944: La disminución del anticlericalismo. *Anales de la Academia de Geografía e Historia de Guatemala* 71:121–152.

Mondloch, J.
1971 *El comerciante y su compañero que se convirtió en cabro*. http://laii.unm.edu/kiche /126_el-comerciante-y-su-companero-que -se-convirtio-en-cabro.php.

Mondloch, J., and R. Carmack (editors)
1983 *El Título de Totonicapán: Texto, traducción y comentario*. Universidad Nacional Autónoma de México, Mexico City.
1989 *El Título de Yax y otros documentos quichés de Totonicapán, Guatemala*. Universidad Nacional Autónoma de México, Mexico City.

Morales, M. R.
2002 *El síndrome de Maximón o la articulación de las diferencias*. Editorial Palo de Hormigo, Guatemala City.

Morford, J.
1997 Social Indexicality in French Pronominal Address. *Journal of Linguistic Anthropology* 7(1):3–37.

Mundy, B.
1996 *The Mapping of New Spain: Indigenous Cartography and the Maps of the Relaciones Geográficas*. University of Chicago Press, Chicago.

Myers-Scotton, C.
2002 *Contact Linguistics: Bilingual Encounters*. Oxford University Press, Oxford.

Nelson, D.
1999 *A Finger in the Wound: Body Politics in Quincentennial Guatemala*. University of California Press, Berkeley.

Nutini, H.
1980 *Ritual Kinship*. Princeton University Press, Princeton, New Jersey.

O'Brien, J.
2012 An Experimental Approach to Debuccalization and Supplementary Gestures. Unpublished Ph.D. dissertation, University of California at Santa Cruz.

Ordóñez, C. S.
2012 *Un pueblo K'iche' de los altos de Guatemala: Entre la espesura de las relaciones interétnicas y de clase en San Miguel Totonicapán*. Ediciones Eón, Mexico City.

Parra, J.
2004 *Persona y comunidad Q'eqchi': Aproximación cultural a la comunidad q'eqchi' de Santa María Cahabón*. Ak' Kutan, Cobán, Guatemala.

Par Sapón, M., and T. Can
2000 *Variación dialectal en K'ichee'*. Cholsamaj, Guatemala City.

Partido Liberal Progresista
1943 *Guatemala en 1943: 1931–1943 administración Jorge Ubico; Album gráfico*. Guatemala Gráfica, Guatemala City.

Patch, R.
2002 *Maya Revolt and Revolution in the Eighteenth Century*. M. E. Sharpe, New York.

Piedrasanta, I.
2011 *Alfabetización y poder en Guatemala: Los años de la Guerra Fría (1944–1984)*. PRODESSA, Guatemala City.

Piel, J.
1989 *Sajcabajá: Muerte y resurrección de un pueblo de Guatemala*. CEMCA, Guatemala City.

Pizzigoni, C.
2013 *The Life Within: Local Indigenous Society in Mexico's Toluca Valley, 1650–1800*. Stanford University Press, Stanford, California.

Pollack, A.
2004 *Levantamiento K'ichee' in Totonicapán, 1820: Los lugares de las políticas subalternas*. AVANCSO, Guatemala City.

Poplack, S., D. Sankoff, and C. Miller
1988 The Social Correlates and Linguistic Processes of Lexical Borrowing and Assimilation. *Linguistics* 26:47–104.

Rabasa, J.
2011 *Tell Me the Story of How I Conquered You: Elsewhere and Ethnosuicide in the Colonial Mesoamerican World*. University of Texas Press, Austin.

Rafael, V.
1988 *Contracting Colonialism: Translation and Christian Conversion in Tagalog Society under Early Spanish Rule*. Cornell University Press, Ithaca, New York.

Restall, M.
1997 *The Maya World*. Stanford University Press, Stanford, California.

Richards, J., and M. Richards
1996   Maya Education: A Historical and Contemporary Analysis of Mayan Language
Education Policy. In *Maya Cultural Activism
in Guatemala*, edited by E. F. Fischer and R.
McKenna Brown, pp. 208–222. University of
Texas Press, Austin.

Richards, M.
2003   *Atlas lingüístico de Guatemala.* Serviprensa,
Guatemala City.

Rojas Lima, F.
1988   *La cofradía: Reducto colonial indígena.* Seminario de Integración Social, Guatemala City.
2004   *Diccionario histórico biográfico de Guatemala.* Asociación de Amigos del País,
Guatemala City.

Romero, S.
2006   Sociolinguistic Variation and Linguistic
History in Mayan: The Case of K'ichee'.
Unpublished Ph.D. dissertation, University
of Pennsylvania, Philadelphia.
2009   Phonological Markedness, Regional Identity,
and Gender in Mayan: The Fricativization
of Intervocalic /l/ in K'ichee'. In *Variation
in Indigenous Minority Languages*, edited
by J. Stanford, pp. 281–298. J. Benjamins,
Amsterdam.
2011   Language, Catechisms, and Mesoamerican
Lords in Highland Guatemala: How to
Address "God" after the Spanish Conquest.
Paper presented at the XVI European Maya
Conference, Copenhagen.
2012   "They Don't Get Speak Our Language Right":
Language Standardization, Power, and
Migration among the Q'eqchi' Maya. *Journal
of Linguistic Anthropology* 22(2):21–41.

Rosenbaum, B.
1993   *With Our Heads Bowed: The Dynamics of
Gender in a Maya Community.* Institute for
Mesoamerican Studies, State University of
New York, Albany.

Sáenz de Santa María, C.
1972   La reducción a poblados en el siglo XVI en
Guatemala. *Anuario de Estudios Americanos*
29:187–228.

Saint-Lu, A.
1968   *La vera paz: Esprit evangélique et colonisa-
tion.* Centre de Recherches Hispaniques,
Institut d'Études Hispaniques, Paris.

Sampeck, K.
In press. Pipil Pictorial Manuscripts. *Ethnohistory.*

Sankoff, G.
2002   Linguistic Outcomes of Language Contact.
In *Handbook of Language Variation and
Change*, edited by J. K. Chambers, P. Trudgill,
and N. Schilling-Estes, pp. 638–668. Blackwell, Malden, Massachusetts.

Sankoff, D., and S. Laberge
1978   The Linguistic Market and the Statistical
Explanation of Variability. In *Linguistic
Variation: Models and Methods*, edited by D.
Sankoff, pp. 239–250. Academic Press, New
York.

Saravia, A.
1983   *El ladino me jodió.* Editorial José de Pineda
Ibarra, Guatemala City.

Saussure, F. de
1968   *Cours de linguistique generale.* Payot, Paris.

Schirmer, J.
1999   *The Guatemalan Military Project: A Violence
Called Democracy.* University of Pennsylvania Press, Philadelphia.

Schultze-Jena, L.
1933   *Indiana I: Leben, Glaube und Sprache der
Quiché von Guatemala.* Gustav Fischer,
Jena, Germany.

Sharer, R.
2005   *The Ancient Maya.* Stanford University
Press, Stanford, California.

Silverstein, M.
1972   Chinook Jargon and the Problem of
Multi-level Generative Systems. *Language*
48(2):378–406.
1976   Meaning in Anthropology. In *Shifters,
Linguistic Categories, and Cultural Descriptions*, pp. 11–55. University of New Mexico
Press, Albuquerque.
1981   *The Limits of Awareness.* Southwest Educational Development Library, Austin, Texas.
2000   Whorfianism and the Linguistic Imagination of Nationalism. In *Regimes of Language:
Ideologies, Politics, and Identities*, edited by
P. Kroskrity, pp. 85–138. School of American
Research Press, Santa Fe, New Mexico.
2003a Indexical Order and the Dialectics of Sociolinguistic Life. *Language and Communication* 23:193–229.
2003b The Whens and Wheres—as Well as Hows—
of Ethnolinguistic Recognition. *Public
Culture* 15(3):531–557.
2005   Axes of Evals: Token vs. Type Interdiscur-
sivity. *Journal of Linguistic Anthropology*
15(1):6–22.

Sis Iboy, M. J.
1997   *Grammatik ubersicht der Achi.* Sauerwein,
Bonn, Germany.

Smith, C.
1984 Local History in Global Context: Social and Economic Transitions in Western Guatemala. *Comparative Studies in Society and History* 26(2):193–228.

Sparks, G.
2011 Xalqat B'e and the Theologia Indorum: Crossroads between Maya Spirituality and the Americas' First Theology. Unpublished Ph.D. dissertation, University of Chicago, Chicago.

Stewart, S.
1980 *Gramática kekchí*. Editorial Académica Centroamericana, Guatemala City.

Stoll, D.
1993 *Between Two Armies in the Ixil Towns of Guatemala*. Columbia University Press, New York.

Svelmoe, W. L.
2008 *A New Vision for Missions: William Cameron Townsend, the Wycliffe Bible Translators, and the Culture of Early Evangelical Faith Missions, 1896–1945*. University of Alabama Press, Tuscaloosa.

Swadesh, M.
1954 Time Depth of American Linguistic Groupings. *American Anthropologist* 3:361–377.

Taracena, A.
1997 *Invención criolla, sueño ladino, pesadilla indígena*. CIRMA, Antigua Guatemala.

Tavarez, D.
2000 Naming the Trinity. *Colonial Latin American Review* 9(1):21–49.

Tax, S.
1956 *Penny Capitalism: A Guatemalan Indian Economy*. Smithsonian Institution, Washington, D.C.

Tecú Osorio, J.
2002 *Memoria de las masacres de Río Negro*. Museo Comunitario, Rabinal, Guatemala.

Tedlock, B., and D. Tedlock
1985 Language and Technology in the Arts of the Quiche Maya. *Journal of Anthropological Research* 41(2):121–146.

Tedlock, D.
1983 *Writing and Reflection among the Maya*. Department of Spanish and Portuguese, University of Maryland, College Park.
1996 *Popol Vuh: The Mayan Book of the Dawn of Life*. Simon and Schuster, New York.

Teletor, C. N.
1942a *Breve manual de conversación*. Tipografía Nacional, Guatemala City.

1942b *Cartilla de civismo en quiché y castellano*. Tipografía Nacional, Guatemala City.
1946 *Memorial de Tecpán-Atitlán*. Tipografía Nacional, Guatemala City.
1951 *Epítome quiché*. Tipografía Nacional, Guatemala City.
1955 *Apuntes para una monografía de Rabinal y algo de nuestro folklore*. Editorial del Ministerio de Educación Pública, Guatemala City.
1959 *Diccionario castellano-quiché y voces castellano-pocomam*. Tipografía Nacional, Guatemala City.
1964 *Compendio de la doctrina cristiana en castellano y lengua quiché para la instrucción de los naturales*. Tipografía Nacional, Guatemala City.
1965 *Síntesis biográfica del clero de Guatemala*. Tipografía Nacional, Guatemala City.

Thomason, S. G., and T. Kaufman
1988 *Language Contact, Creolization, and Genetic Linguistics*. University of California Press, Berkeley.

Todorov, T.
1982 *La conquête de l'Amérique: La question de l'autre*. Seuil, Paris.

Torres, L.
2006 Bilingual Discourse Markers in Indigenous Languages. *International Journal of Bilingual Education and Bilingualism* 9(5):615–625.

Trudgill, P.
1986 *Dialects in Contact*. Blackwell, Oxford.
2004 *New Dialect Formation*. Oxford University Press, Oxford.

Tum Guarchaj, D.
2000 Story of Diego Tum Guarchaj. *Proyecto Rescate Nahualá Cultural, Departamento de Sololá*. http://www.ailla.utexas.org/.

Valencia Tolanilla, C.
2001 El Pop Wuj de Adrián Inés Chávez: Autenticidad, poesía y simbolismo de la cosmogonía maya-quiché. *Ciencias Humanas* 30:1–10.

Van Akkeren, R.
2000 *The Place of the Lord's Daughter: Rab'inal, Its Ethnohistory, Its Dance-Drama*. Center for Non-Western Studies, University of Leiden, Leiden.
2003 Authors of the Popol Vuh. *Ancient Mesoamerica* 14:237–256.
2005 Conociendo a los pipiles de la costa del Pacífico de Guatemala: Un estudio etnohistórico de documentos indígenas y del archivo general de Centroamérica. In *XVIII Simposio de Investigaciones Arqueológicas en Guatemala*

2004, edited by J. P. Laporte, B. Arroyo, and H. Mejía, pp. 1000–1014. Museo Nacional de Arqueología y Etnología, Guatemala City.

2010 Fray Domingo de Vico: Maestro de autores indígenas. *Revista de Estudios Mayas* 2(7):1–61.

2012 *Xibalbá y el nacimiento del nuevo sol.* Editorial Piedrasanta, Guatemala City.

n.d. Achi: Classic Maya Language of the Pacific Coast and Adjacent Highlands. Unpublished manuscript.

Velásquez, I.

2000 *La pequeña burguesía indígena comercial de Guatemala: Desigualdades de clase, raza y género.* AVANCSO, Guatemala City.

Warren, K.

1978 *The Symbolism of Subordination: Indian Identity in a Guatemalan Town.* University of Texas Press, Austin.

1997 *Indigenous Movements and Their Critics: Pan-Maya Activism in Guatemala.* Princeton University Press, Princeton, New Jersey.

Weeks, J.

1997 Sub-regional Organization of the 16th Century Q'eqchi' Maya. *Revista Española de Antropología Americana* 27:59–93.

Weishaar, E., R. Hostnig, and L. Guarchaj

1995 *Ojer tzij: Cuentos y leyendas del pueblo quiché (versión en castellano).* Cooperación para el Desarrollo Rural de Occidente, Quetzaltenango, Guatemala.

Wichman, S.

2003 Contact among Some Mayan Languages: Inferences from Loanwords Source. *Anthropological Linguistics* 45(1):57–93.

Wilson, R.

1995 *Maya Resurgence in Guatemala: Q'eqchi' Experiences.* University of Oklahoma Press, Norman.

Wimmer, A.

2013 *Ethnic Boundary Making.* Oxford University Press, Oxford.

Wolf, E.

1957 Closed Corporate Peasant Communities in Mesoamerica and Central Java. *Southwestern Journal of Anthropology* 13(1):1–18.

1958 *Sons of the Shaking Earth.* University of Chicago Press, Chicago.

1982 *Europe and the People without History.* University of California Press, Berkeley.

Woodward, R. L.

1993 *Rafael Carrera and the Emergence of the Republic of Guatemala, 1821–1871.* University of Georgia Press, Athens.

Ximénez, F.

1965 *Historia de la Provincia de San Vicente de Chiapa y Guatemala, Vol. 1.* Editorial José de Pineda Ibarra, Guatemala City. Originally published 1722.

1993 *Arte de las tres lenguas.* Sociedad de Geografía e Historia, Guatemala City.

Yool, J.

1994 *Rub'is jun Mayab'.* Proyecto Lingüístico Francisco Marroquín, Antigua Guatemala.

Index

colonialism: and appropriation of writing in
K'ichee', 14–15; as hybrid semiotic regime, 105;
imprint of on K'ichee' discourse practices, xiv.
See also neocolonialism; Spanish
Comaroff, J. & J., 36
communitas, and multiethnic townships, 55–56
constitution, translation of into four Mayan languages, 29–32
Coplas de Luís de Cáncer (mid-sixteenth century),
92–95
corporations, as institutional powers co-opting
writing in K'ichee', 36
corte (clothing), 52, 53, 57n6
Cortez y Larraz, Pedro, 18
creation myths, and *Theologia Indorum*, 95
culture: and concept of K'ichee'-Spanish "hybrid"
language in Santa María Chiquimula, 63–66;
Spanish language and issues of authority and
cultural legitimacy in Santa María Chiquimula,
66–67
Cunén (township), 56

dance dramas, and dialectical variation, 8
democracy, and Mayanization of K'ichee' writing,
29–32
dialects, of K'ichee': asking of questions in "pure
K'ichee'," 39–40; boundary works and stereotypes of, 54–56; and definition of dialect emblem,
12n6; ethnicity and interaction frames of, 50–54;
history of Maya highlands and variation in, 7–9;
linguistic stereotypes and language ideologies
in Santa María Chiquimula and, 40–46; and regional variation, 6, 13n17; semiotic function of,
56–57; social space and recognition of, 46–50. *See
also* K'ichee' language
Dieseldorf, Erwin Paul, 20
"discourse markers," and Spanish loanwords, 61,
69–71
doctrinas (indigenous parishes), 17–18
dress: code switching and loan words in Santa
María Chiquimula, 64–65; ethnic boundaries
and social deixis in K'ichee' highlands, 9; and
ethnic identities in Nahualá, 48–49; ethnicity
and interaction frames, 50–51, 52–54

elders. *See prinsipalib'*
El problema social del India (The Indian Social
Problem), 102
embedded language, and code switching, 67, 71n3
ethnic frames: and colonial ethnic categories, 3; as
historical process in Maya highlands, xiii–xiv;
and social identification of highland Maya, 6–7.
See also boundary work

ethnicity: and division of labor during Ubico regime, 24, 25; and gender markers in dialects,
56–57; and geographic variation in K'ichee', 5–7;
and honorific address, 77–79, 83–87; as language
ideology in Maya highlands, xiii, xiv, 34–35; and
social deixis in K'ichee' highlands, 9–10; and
social value of dialectical variation, 46, 50–54.
See also ethnic frames
ethnography, and methodology for study of
K'ichee', xiv–xv
ethnoscape. *See* regional ethnoscapes

Flores-Farfán, J. A., 57n1
food: and boundary work in western Maya highlands, 49; and code switching modalities in
Santa María Chiquimula, 68
Foucault, Michel, 15
Fox, J., 57–58n12
Fuentes y Guzmán, Francisco Antonio, 15, 97

Gal, S., 38n44
García, María, 105n2
gender: and ethnic stereotypes in dialectical variations, 56–57; honorific address in K'ichee' and
politics during Ubico regime, 21; and mixing
of K'ichee' and Spanish terms among K'ichee'
speakers, 60
geographic variation: and boundary work, 5–7; in
honorific address, 76, 83
globalization, and K'ichee' writing, 35–36
Goffman, Erwin, 3
González, Gaspar Pedro, 105
Gosner, Kevin, 17
Guarchaj, Diego Adrián, 103
Guatemala. *See* colonialism; culture; ethnicity;
K'ichee' language; politics; Santa María
Chiquimula; state; townships
Guineales (village), 54
Guzmán-Boeckler, C., 106n9

habilitadores (labor contractors), 18
Hanks, William, 14, 17
healer, and linguistic borrowing, 59–61
Hebrew language, 97
Hill, Jane, 87–88
Hill, Jasper, 21
Hill, Kenneth, 87–88
Historia de la Provincia de Chiapas y Guatemala
(Ximénez 1722), 91
honorific address: and author's first visit to Santa
María Chiquimula, 73–74; ethnic boundaries
and social deixis in K'ichee' highlands, 9–10;
and everyday forms of communication, 87–88;

gender and politics during Ubico regime, 21; K'ichee' repertoire of, 74–76; and linguistic construction of authority, 76–77; and Maya movement, 79–82; *prinsipalib'* and constructions of power and ethnicity, 77–79; regional variation and ethnicity in, 83–87

huipil (clothing), 51, 52

hybrid cultures, concept of in context of Santa María Chiquimula, 63–66

hybrid linguistic practice: and cultural organization of language in Santa María Chiquimula, 65–66; and discourse markers, 69–71; and Spanish loanwords or code switching, 60–61

indígenas (indigenous): discourse markers and hybrid speech, 71; and ethnic frames in study of dialectical variation, 54

indigenismo: definition of, 37n14; influence of on *Cartilla*, 21; and Ubico regime, 25

indigenous. *See indígenas*

indio, use of term, 38n41, 71

Instituto Indigenista Americano (INA), 18

Instituto Nacional Indigenista, 26–27

Instituto Normal para Varones de Occidente (INVO), 105n8

interaction frames, and ethnic implications of dialectical variation, 50–54

International Phonetic Alphabet (IPA), 16

Irvine, J., 38n44

Ixil language, 52, 53, 54

Jehovah's Witnesses, 27, *28*

k'ab'awil contemporáneo (contemporary sacred being), 96

Karttunen, Frances, 61–62

K'ichee' language: accent, ethnic boundaries, and social deixis in, 9–10; cultural construction and history of, 1–4; and emergence of Maya Christianity, 91–96; and ethnic frames of interaction, xiii–xiv; geographic variation in, 5–7; and lexical input of Nahuatl, 71n5; linguistic purism and pan-Maya activism, 11–12, 90–91; loanwords and Spanish code switching in, 59–71; Popol Vuh and linguistic tradition of, 96–101; and recreation of Maya poetry, 101–5; social value of dialectical variation in, 39–57; Spanish in linguistic economy of, 11; uses and abuses of honorific address in, 73–88. *See also* dialects; honorific address; *puro K'ichee'*; writing

K'ichee' mezclado (mixed K'ichee'), 66, 67–69, 71

K'iche' Mayab' Cholchi' (Academy of the K'ichee' Language), xv, 32, 38n34

kristiyan/winaq, as dialectical isogloss, 8–9

laal (honorific address), 73–74, 76, 78, 79, 80, 83, 85, 87, 88n3, 88n16

labor: pan-Mayan activism and traditional division of in state discourses, 32; Ubico regime and ethnic division of, 24, 25

Lacadena, Alfonso, 37n6

ladinos: discourse markers and hybrid speech, 71; and ethnic frames, 54; and use of Mayan languages, 90; use of term, 13n19, 38n41

landscape, and language ideologies in Santa María Chiquimula, 46, 48

language: and classification of native populations by Spanish, 3; conflicting ideologies and standardization of, 32. *See also* Achi language; alphabet(s); Hebrew language; Ixil language; K'ichee' language; Mayan languages; Nahuatl language; Q'eqchi' language; Spanish language

language contact, and Maya social history, 61–63

language ideologies: and ethnicity among highland Maya, xiii, xiv, 7; dialectical variation and linguistic stereotypes in Santa María Chiquimula, 40–46; standardization of language and conflicting, 32

language mixing, and linguistic economy in Santa María Chiquimula, 61. *See also* code switching; loanwords

León, Juan de, 20

León Chic, Eduardo, 84, 88n22, 102

lexical borrowing, from Spanish into K'ichee', 61–62. *See also* loanwords

lexical purism: of *Cartilla*, 25; of *Ri Gkagk Testament*, 29; stress on by Maya language planners in Guatemala, 66. *See also puro K'ichee'*

Ley de Vialidad, 18

lienzos (paintings), 37n4

linguistic borrowing, and code switching, 60–61. *See also* loanwords

linguistic market, and concept of cultural capital, 13n20

linguistic performance, and modalities of code switching, 67–69

linguistic stereotypes, and dialectical variation in Santa María Chiquimula, 40–46

Lión, Luis de, 105n1

Little, Walter, 7, 36

Little-Siebold, C., 58n15

loanwords, use of Spanish by K'ichee' speakers in Santa María Chiquimula, 60–61, 69–71

local frames, and dialectical variation, 50–52

Lockhart, James, 61–62

Lord's Prayer, 85–87, 88–89n24